Owners' Management Company

Law and Best Practice

OWNERS' MANAGEMENT COMPANY

Law and Best Practice

By

AISLING KEENAN

Consultant Editor
DEIRDRE Ní FHLOINN

CLARUS PRESS

Published by
Clarus Press Ltd,
Griffith Campus,
South Circular Road,
Dublin 8.
www.claruspress.ie

Reprinted 2022.

Typeset by
Gough Typesetting Services,
Dublin

Printed by
SprintPrint
Dublin

ISBN
978-1-911611-28-8

A catalogue record for this book is available from the British Library

Preface

This book has come to fruition as a result of a lengthy and inspiring discussion with Dr Padraic Kenna at the Law School in NUI Galway. In discussing the subject with him, he was of the view that this book must be written such was the need to fill the knowledge gap on this subject. Up to this point, the only publication on the owners' management company in Ireland was written by the Office of the Director of Corporate Enforcement in 2008 titled *Company Law Handbook on Residential Property Owners' Management Companies ('Management Companies').* Since 2008 the Multi-Unit Developments Act has been implemented and is currently under review and the Property Services Regulation Act has also been enacted. These new laws have served to facilitate the smooth running of the owners' management company.

There are many problems that abound the sector today and they mainly centre on the fact that the sector is so new to us in Ireland. Some 7.3% of the Irish population live in apartments compared to the EU average of 41.8% or the UK at 14.3%.[1] The locus of sharing our living spaces is new in Ireland where we come from a strong ideation of independently owning our own property and this new model of the owners' management company is counter to that whereby the apartment building or the estate is owned by the collective, represented by the owners' management company and the common areas of the apartment building or the estate are shared spaces.

It is well acknowledged that we need to build more apartments in Ireland to meet population growth into the future; it is estimated that 90,000 extra apartments will be needed in Dublin in the next 20 years.[2] Current Minister for Housing Eoghan Murphy notes that apartment living is essential if we are able to leverage public money and resources properly and if our cities are to continue to work and grow then we need higher density.

This book is an authoritative guide to the law of property management in Ireland in the owners' management company context. It examines in detail, the workings of the owners'

1 Paul Mooney, *Owners' Management Companies, Sustainable Apartment Living for Ireland,* The Housing Agency, Clúid Housing, June 2019, p 12.

2 Paul Mooney, *Owners' Management Companies, Sustainable Apartment Living for Ireland,* The Housing Agency, Clúid Housing, June 2019, p 26.

management company and its implications for all of those who are involved including its members, directors, service providers and residents. The book is designed to be a reference book and deals with all of the legal and practical issues around the ownership and control of the common areas of a Multi-Unit Development which may comprise apartment blocks, housing estates, commercial estates and/or mixed-use developments. The Property Services Regulatory Authority is examined as is some fundamental and relevant provisions of the Companies Act 2014 which apply all owners' management companies in Ireland today. As the subject of the owners' management company traverses land law, housing law and company law, this book will be of great interest to students and anyone wishing to learn more about practicing in the property services sector.

I would firstly like to acknowledge my deep appreciation and gratitude for the encouragement and support that I received from Dr Padraic Kenna at the Law School in NUI Galway. I was fortunate to be one of his students of Land Law while studying for my LLB there. I would also like to thank Cllr Deirdre Ní Fhloinn, Barrister and Phd, for agreeing to act as consultant editor of this book. Her knowledge and work in the area of the owners' management company is of great value to owners who find themselves in apartment buildings with structural defects and her experience of the law in this area was pivotal in the publication of this book. Thanks also to Joe for his continuous love and unwavering support and to Denise at AK Property Services and Sean Cleary. Finally, I would like to thank David McCartney of Clarus Press for awarding this publishing contract to me for this book and also for his guidance and support throughout the journey.

Aisling Keenan
2 September 2019

Table of Contents

Preface v

CHAPTER 1
INTRODUCTION 1

CHAPTER 2
THE DEVELOPMENT OF THE OMC 5
1. The role of the OMC 5
2. The contribution of the Law Reform Commission towards the development of the OMC 7

CHAPTER 3
THE EVOLUTION OF A PROPERLY FUNCTIONING OMC 19
1. The role of the property developer and the Implications of the MUD Act 2011 19
2. Three phases: developer only/developer and owners/ owners only 21
3. Considerations for prospective owners 28

CHAPTER 4
IMPLICATIONS OF BEING A MEMBER OF A MANAGEMENT COMPANY 35
1. Duties and responsibilities of property owners 35
2. The lease agreement 37
3. The company constitution 38
4. The house rules 39
5. Members' register 42
6. Directors 44
7. The culture within an OMC 46

CHAPTER 5
THE BUILDING INVESTMENT FUND AND THE ANNUAL SERVICE CHARGE 51
1. The time-bomb sinking fund 51
2. Calculating the annual service charge 57
3. The debt recovery process 59
4. Excludable debt 68
5. Taxation 69
6. A sinking-fund case study on capital project management 70

CHAPTER 6
THE MULTI-UNIT DEVELOPMENTS ACT 2011 73
1. Introduction 73
2. A summary of sections 75
   Obligation to transfer common areas 75
   The rules on sinking funds, AGM's, calculating Service charges and debt collection 77
3. Areas for reform 83
4. Restoration 85

5. Law Reform Commission recommendations v the Act ... 86

CHAPTER 7
THE PROPERTY SERVICES REGULATORY AUTHORITY ... 89
1. Introduction ... 89
2. Role and responsibilities ... 91
3. The Compensation Fund 2017 Report ... 95
4. Powers of PSRA ... 97
5. The Strategic Plan to 2020 ... 100
Letter of engagement ... 101

CHAPTER 8
COMPANY LAW ... 103
1. Types of companies ... 104
2. Governance ... 109
3. Directors' duties ... 112
4. The company secretary ... 117
5. The CRO ... 119
6. ODCE and penalties for failing to comply with company law ... 121

CHAPTER 9
RECEIVERS AND THE OMC ... 125
1. Introduction ... 125
2. Appointment of receivers ... 125
3. Benefits to OMCs of receiver appointment ... 128

CHAPTER 10
COMPANY STRIKE-OFF AND RESTORATION ... 131
1. What is a company strike-off? ... 131
2. *Heidlestone*: strike-off and restoring an OMC to the Company Register ... 133
The Heidelstone *case summary* ... 135
3. Transfer of common areas where the developer is not trading ... 144
4. Section 30 restoration of a company to the Company Register ... 145

CHAPTER 11
INSURANCE AND THE OMC ... 151
1. Introduction ... 151
2. Insurable perils and uninsurable perils ... 153
3. The claims process ... 156
4. Avoiding insurance pitfalls ... 162
5. Airbnb and insurance ... 163
6. Case studies ... 165

CHAPTER 12
LANDLORD AND TENANT LAW IN THE RESIDENTIAL AND OMC CONTEXT ... 167
1. Introduction ... 167
2. The Residential Tenancies Act 2004 ... 170
3. Landlord obligations ... 171
4. Tenants' obligations ... 174

5. Part 4 tenancy 177
6. Notice periods 180
Required notice periods of termination by landlord 181
7. The Residential Tenancies Board 181
The register 182
8. Dispute resolution 183
The steps in the process for a dispute 184
Third party disputes 185

CHAPTER 13
REGULATION OF THE OMC 189
1. Introduction 189
2. Regulating the OMC 189
3. Funding for regulation 203

APPENDICES

APPENDIX 1
SAMPLE OWNERS' MANAGEMENT CLG 207

APPENDIX 2
SAMPLE ANNUAL SERVICE CHARGE BUDGETS 209

APPENDIX 3
MUD ACT PRE-CONTRACT ENQUIRIES – REQUISITIONS 213

USEFUL RESOURCES 217

INDEX 219

Chapter 1

Introduction

> 'The difference between failure and success is doing a thing nearly right and doing it exactly right.'
>
> *Edward C Simmons*

A general principle in law is that the law must be precise, certain and clear and so when it comes to the law on our property it is important to get it exactly right. Oliver Wendell Holmes, a great source of legal wisdom, suggested that property comprises an umbrella of institutions and contexts: family, community and value.

In the context of our Constitution the right to property is the right to own, acquire, use and dispose of land, chattels and other things that have an economic value. How extensive such a right varies greatly from country to country; there are some societies where private property rights are regarded as extremely important and others where those rights are barely recognised. Next to personal security and liberty, the eighteenth-century jurist, Blackstone, ranked private property as '[t]he third absolute right inherent in every Englishman…'. Whether entitlement to private property should be accorded the status of a fundamental right that cannot be taken away by the legislature, or can be taken only in certain circumstances, is a controversial political and moral question.[1]

Legislation in the area of property management in Ireland is recent; namely the Multi-Unit Developments Act 2011 and the Land and Conveyancing Law Reform Act 2013. For the Owners' Management Company ('OMC'), the former has been enacted following the Law Reform Commission's Report on Multi-Unit Developments in June 2008. This report was commissioned to address the considerable problems with how some apartment complexes were being managed in Ireland given our inexperience of shared living spaces as a nation. These problems included a general widespread lack of transparency and a lack of understanding about the appropriate roles of those involved in apartment developments such as property developers, property

1 Michael Forde and David Leonard, *Constitutional Law in Ireland* (3rd edn, Bloomsbury Professional, 2013), ch 25, 739, [25.01].

owners and property managing agents. Some of the main issues that arose included the fact that the common areas of an apartment complex may not be transferred giving effective control to the property developer after all apartments had been sold. Property managing agents were presiding over considerable service charge funds received from property owners with no regulation and no protection for the property owner. Compliance with the Companies Acts was not being met by officers of the OMC. There was no proper accountability for the calculation and collection of service charges resulting in the running down of some apartment complexes. There was no requirement for a long-term sinking-fund to be set up. Although there have been improvements in the area since 2008, there still remain many OMCs with similar issues today.

The role of the local authority is an ongoing one when it comes to multi-unit developments in Ireland and the level of involvement and interaction they have permeates through each stage of an OMC. Their public role commences at the planning stage and is multi-faceted as they act as a regulator, a planning authority and they hold the bond that the property developer pays before commencing construction. In many cases, the local authority own properties in multi-unit developments and in this regard, they have a private role in the running of the OMC.

Publications in the area of property management are few, most notably in 2008 the Office of the Director of Corporate Enforcement published *The Company Law Handbook on Residential Property Owners' Management Companies ('Management Companies')*.[2] Since then, there have been significant changes in the law and in the property market: the Multi-Unit Developments Act 2011 and the Companies Act 2014 have been enacted. In this publication, Aisling Keenan, the author, brings together all the information concerning the OMC in Ireland with the aim of filling the knowledge gap in bringing legal practitioners and the lay reader up-to-date on the provisions and implications of the law concerning the OMC in Ireland. Having practised in the area as a managing agent for 20 years Aisling gives practical examples of the type of issues arising in practice and the impact of the law in the area. This book will be an essential reference for all practising lawyers who work in the housing and property market including all local authority

---

2 Office of the Director of Corporate Enforcement, *Company Law Handbook on Residential Property Owners' Management Companies ('Management Companies')*, ODCE Decision Notice D/2008/1, 8.

lawyers. This book will also be of interest to law-makers and public officials working in housing and property both at national and local level as well as academics and students. It provides vital information on the organisation of the OMC and will be a useful resource for a variety of persons concerned with management companies, especially owner-occupiers of houses or apartments located within multi-unit developments, persons contemplating the purchase of such properties, persons connected with the central management of management companies, e.g. OMC directors, and persons such as managing agents who are engaged by management companies to deal with day-to-day management tasks. It will also be a useful resource for property developers of multi-unit developments and their solicitors, accountants, estate agents, architects, engineers and other professionals who, from time to time, find themselves called upon to give professional advice to management companies.

This book provides an up-to-date analysis of the law guiding all property owners and legal practitioners through a vital aspect of property ownership in a multi-unit development. The Multi-Unit Developments Act 2011 and the application of the Act is discussed in detail along with the Companies Act 2014 and the Property Services (Regulation) Act 2011 all of which govern the operations of the OMC. The development of the OMC provides the background information that is necessary in gaining an understanding of where the sector has come from and how and where the need for current regulation and legislation arose with explanations of the various stages and the organisation structure of the OMC. The stages that the OMC evolves through are important as it is an understanding of these different stages which will help to further reduce the sector wide massive understanding deficit which abounds the OMC in Ireland. This book provides all of the information that members and directors of OMC's will need to know including their duties and responsibilities in law, dealing with the culture of OMC's in Ireland and the power balance between various parties involved. The building investment fund or sinking fund as it is sometimes known is one of the more challenging issues facing an OMC in Ireland. According to the Society of Chartered Surveyors of Ireland in a recent report they note that more than 75% of apartment developments in Ireland have not set aside adequate funds for maintenance and refurbishment. This situation is what the Apartment Owners' Network have described as the 'time bomb sinking fund'. The effect of OMC's failing in their compliance responsibilities resulting in company strike-off is examined in detail as well as the consequences of the appointment of receivers over properties in an OMC. Other important matters which are covered in this book concerning the OMC are issues such as insurance and landlord and tenant law. Future developments involving the OMC include regulation of the OMC. In 2018 a new bill was introduced in Dáil Eireann for the establishment of an Ombudsman for the OMC. This appointment will help to strengthen corporate governance and quality of life for those living in multi-unit developments. Regulation of the OMC will be a key part of how the Multi-Unit Development sector develops in the years to come.

Chapter 2

The Development of the OMC

1. The role of the OMC 5
2. The contribution of the Law Reform Commission towards the development of the OMC 7

1. The role of the OMC

A relatively new phenomenon in Ireland, the origin and existence of the OMC stems from the necessary requirement to protect the property rights of property owners who share communal spaces. This chapter deals with the development of the owners' management company and charts the early stages right through the legislative stage and the contribution of the Law Reform Commission in this regard. It gives the reader a broad perspective on where the OMC began and how it has developed from the early stages.

The OMC is a company that is set up with the sole purpose of vesting in it, the common areas of a development whether it is an apartment block, shopping centre, housing estate or a mixed-use development. It is also established to manage and maintain these common areas and to be the legal owner of the beneficial or reversionary interest of each unit.

The common element of multi-unit developments is the degree of 'interdependence' they necessarily involve. This has many aspects. One is the purely physical one, which derives from the fact that the owners or occupiers share the same building. Each 'unit', whether apartment, office or shop, is part of a larger building and depends on the other parts for support and shelter. It will also depend on pipes, wires, cables and other 'conduits' running through the building to supply various facilities, such as electricity, gas and water, and services, such as drainage and sewerage. To make full use and enjoyment of a unit, the owner or occupier will need various rights over what are usually referred to as 'common areas', such as entrance halls, stairs, lifts, corridors and other passageways within the building. It is also common for unit owners to enjoy, in common with other unit owners, use of facilities like car parks and gardens. Such rights are usually accompanied by obligations, such as the obligation to contribute to the cost of repair and maintenance of the common areas. The result is that 'interdependence' also involves an important 'legal' dimension. To be fully effective a multi-unit development will require the creation of a wide range of mutual rights and obligations as between the different unit owners.[1]

Prior to 2007 the Stakeholder Forum on Multi-Unit Developments took place publishing their report in 2008. Preceding that was the Law Reform Commission's Consultation Paper on Multi-Unit Developments which was published in 2006 to address the growing awareness that significant difficulties were being encountered in the management and regulation of multi-unit developments including apartments.[2] The National Consumer Agency was established on 1 May 2007 and its chief executive at the time, Ann Fitzgerald, was tasked with providing guidance to property owners who had found themselves to be members of a company that they simply did not understand and so a dedicated website called consumerproperty.ie was established to provide relevant, accurate and up-to-date information to consumers affected by issues relating to their OMC. By that year end, the website had registered over 11,000 visits.[3] That year, the National Consumer Agency published ten separate publications for various consumer markets, the most sought-after publication was called 'Management Companies and You'.[4] It was a loose and laissez-faire approach to the protection of property rights for property owners but it was the beginning of legislative reform for the sector. What followed was The Law Reform Commission's Report on Multi-Unit Developments in Ireland 2008, the enactment of the Multi-Unit Developments Act in 2011 and the establishment of the Property Services Regulatory Authority in 2012 which brought some level of clarity and certainty to the OMC for property owners and everyone involved in OMCs around the country.

In assessing what exactly the OMC is, The National Consumer Agency in 2008 accurately described the OMC as follows:

> 'A multi-unit development may be one of a variety of dwelling types such as a house, apartment or duplex. In a traditional standalone house, the facilities and services

---

1 The Law Reform Commission, *Consultation Paper on Multi-Unit Developments* (LRC CP 42—2006).
2 Law Reform Commission, *Report on Multi-Unit Developments* (2008), 23.
3 National Consumer Agency, *Annual Report 2008*, 28.
4 National Consumer Agency, *Annual Report 2008*, 28.

> or areas such as those referred to above are maintained by the individual Property Owner, or where applicable, the local authority. In a multi-unit development, they are owned and maintained by the unit Owners on a communal basis. This is because all Owners share, use and own the common areas, for example halls, gardens and parking with other units. Unit Owners pay an annual fee known as a service charge to pay for the maintenance of these common areas and other shared services such as cleaning and waste disposal... When you purchase a unit in a multi-unit development, you purchase both your individual property and a share of the Ownership of the common areas. You therefore enjoy two legal interests: one, as the Owner of your individual unit and second, as part Owner of the common areas.'[5]

Although apartment complexes are more dominant in urban cities, there are a significant number of multi-unit developments and apartment complexes in every town in Ireland. Prior to this growth, as a society we had very little experience of owning property in a shared space. A consequence of the great famine of the nineteenth century is our obsession with owning our own property. We were mainly used to purchasing land and property on a freehold basis where the property in its entirety was owned by the purchaser. Historically, apartment buildings had only one owner, typically an investment company. Multi-unit development ownership is based on a long-term leasehold arrangement whereby the OMC owns the building and the common areas, and the lease for the individual units can be sold on to new owners.

2. The contribution of the Law Reform Commission towards the development of the OMC

In their Report on Multi-Unit Developments in 2008, the Law Reform Commission recommended at 8.19, that the title of Owners' Management Company should be a statutorily designated title. Thereafter, the Multi-Unit Developments Act 2011 set out the statutory designated title of the OMC as follows:

> '"Owners' management company" means subject to subsection (3), a company established for the purposes

5 Office of the Director of Corporate Enforcement, *Company Law Handbook on Residential Property Owners' Management Companies ('Management Companies')*, ODCE Decision Notice D/2008/1, 8.

> of becoming the Owner of the common areas of a multi-unit development and the management, maintenance and repair of such areas and which is a company registered under the Companies Acts…'

Normally, the structure of an OMC (a multi-unit development comprising five units or more) is that of an incorporated Company Limited by Guarantee (CLG), with no share capital, as defined by the Companies Act 2014 although some take the form of a Designated Activity Company (DAC). The regulation and reporting requirements for a guarantee company are the same as that for a company that is limited by shares. Both are subject to the requirements of the Companies Act 2014 and are regulated by the Companies Office whose powers extend to striking-off a company for non-compliance. The Office of the Director of Corporate Enforcement is the watchdog over companies in Ireland and exists to enforce and encourage compliance with company law. It has a range of enforcement powers in responding to allegations of company law breaches. One of the conflicting issues of an OMC structure is that on the one hand it takes the form of a body corporate and on the other hand it is a voluntary community organisation which depends on its members volunteering to become directors of their OMC, a not-for-profit organisation. In the vast majority of cases, OMC directors are unpaid volunteers, however in company law they take on the full responsibilities and duties of the office of director.

In its report on multi-unit developments, the Law Reform Commission discussed the benefits of using the company law code for the OMC structure. They identified that the concept of limited liability, for example, is of clear advantage to OMC members. The existence of a regulatory regime which protects members of the company and requires annual meetings, the presentation and transparency of accounts, and rules on corporate governance and compliance generally—and directors' duties specifically—all operate for the benefit of the unit owner. As Keane notes, using the company limited by guarantee has the twin advantages that the members will not be required to provide the company with any cash either on its formation or during the course of its active life and that the management of the company is normally entrusted to a council or committee elected by the members rather than a board of directors.[6] The Law Reform Commission was of the

6 Keane, *Company Law* (4th edn), Tottel Publishing, 2007, para 4.34.

view that once a more widely understood culture of collective management and ownership becomes commonplace in Ireland, as it has in other European states and around the globe, the more the benefits of the company law code would be appreciated. An OMC shares many characteristics with that of a trading company in that it owns and manages assets and it engages in contracts with agents, insurers and other service providers. It works for the benefit of a group of people who have invested financially, and it is ultimately responsible to them.[7]

OMCs are not a requirement of company law and there exist other arrangements and structures for the purposes of discharging similar functions to that of an OMC such as housing co-operative societies and co-ownership agreements. In some developments co-ownership agreements which are similar to residents' associations exist which form the basis for the ownership of common areas and the organisation of shared services. Co-ownership agreements are rooted in the laws of contract and private property, rather than in any particular Act or Acts of the Oireachtas and unlike the OMC and housing co-operatives they do not involve an incorporated structure. Housing co-operative societies are a local self-help movement which dates back to the 1950s in Ireland. The objective is to provide affordable homes for their members. The Law Reform Commission concluded that this informal type of an arrangement was not a suitable structure for the long-term security of property rights for owners.

The main benefits for owners that flow from an OMC being established under the Companies Acts are that each owner in the development has an input into how their property is taken care of in decision making and controlling the costs of common services for the collective benefit. This input is exercised by the power of the members to elect their fellow members onto the board of directors who have the ultimate decision-making powers in the company. In assessing the need for the existence of the OMC, the alternative would be impractical whereby the common areas would be co-owned by all the unit-owners' in their personal capacities, and arrangements in relation to the provision of common services to be dealt with by contracts such as the hiring of fire maintenance contractors and caretakers, lift maintenance agreements, etc., under which each of the owners was jointly and severally liable in their personal capacities for all areas including

---

7 Law Reform Commission, *Report on Multi-Unit Developments* (LRC 90—2008), 60.

contract law and health and safety law. The voting rights of the members of the OMC are normally contained in the articles of association in the company constitution of the company and also the Multi-Unit Developments Act 2011 at s 14(1) contains the following provisions:

> 'the voting rights ... shall be structured in such a manner that in the determination of any matter by the members of the company one vote shall attach to each residential unit in a multi-unit development to which the owners' management company relates, and that no other person has voting rights in respect of such determination.'

It is at the annual general meeting of the company that owners can have the opportunity to be elected as directors of their OMC.

Where it is decided to establish an OMC under the Companies Act 2014 what is brought into existence is what lawyers frequently describe as 'a legal entity separate and distinct from its members'. This means that it is what is sometimes called a vehicle by which a potentially large number of people may combine for the pursuit of a common objective; once they do so, and go through certain formalities associated with the incorporation of the company, they bring into being a new legal person which in its own corporate name can hold land, enter into contracts and embark on legal proceedings. Although the company is owned by its members, they do not personally need to put their names to any contracts or arrangements entered into by the company; in the event of the other parties to any such contracts or arrangements wishing to sue on foot of them it is the company which must be sued: not any or all of the members in their personal capacities.

Where the company is incorporated with limited liability the members typically have at most only an insignificant obligation to contribute to any deficiencies in the assets of the company in the event where it becomes insolvent.

While the OMC structure covers mixed-use developments such as residential and commercial, housing estates and business parks; apartment complexes comprise the greater percentage represented by the OMC. Apartment living involves a high degree of interdependence between unit owners who own and share the common areas. The cornerstone of an OMC is that owners exist in a collective responsibility arrangement where the actions or inactions of one directly affects the other. Where one (or more) property owner fails in their legal obligation to pay the annual service charge, the other property owners will pick up the tab in the short term while the bad debt is being pursued. Equally, where one property owner or resident is in breach of the house rules such as having late-night parties and disturbing the peace of another, this too has a direct effect on the other.

The law around multi-unit developments has followed the new and recent growth of apartment buildings from the 1990s through to today. Fig 1 shows this growth where household net worth had, at the end of 2018, exceeded the pre-crisis peak. This largely reflected increases in housing asset values.[8] As the housing stock continues to grow so too does the multi-unit development sector with increasing need for higher-density homes and urbanisation.

Irish Households Net Worth (Aggregate)

Central Bank 2019

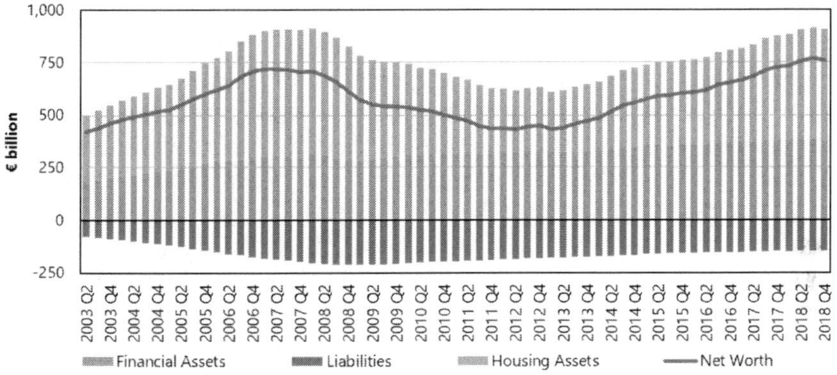

Fig 1

In 2006 the Law Reform Commission issued a consultation paper for the purposes of reviewing the law which up to that point had been developed largely without consideration for the OMC or consumer issues which faced multi-unit developments and their owners. The subsequent *Report on Multi-Unit Developments* by the Law Reform Commission was published in 2008. The objective was to address the difficulties which had arisen as result of a dramatic increase in the construction of apartment complexes

8 Central Bank of Ireland, Statistical Release, **[AQ: please complete the citation"???)** available at https://www.centralbank.ie/statistics/data-and-analysis/financial-accounts/chart-pack.

and multi-unit developments throughout the country and the recent swell of controversy around these developments. One of the more significant problems that owners of units in multi-unit developments had at the time was a lack of understanding of all that is involved in living in such a development. Although there have been improvements in this area since then, there remains an understanding deficit to some degree. These problems also included planning law and its enforcement; the role of the developers; the appropriate ownership legal structure; title and conveyancing issues; the role and regulation of estate agents and property managing agents and connected consumer issues; service charges; sinking-funds and suitable measures to assist OMCs that were already in difficulty (rescue provisions). Due to the large number of difficulties in this area, the commission engaged in an extensive consultation process with numerous bodies and persons including government departments, regulatory bodies, representative groups, the legal profession and individuals involved in multi-unit developments. The commission identified two key factors arising from the difficulties which were: poor governance of OMCs and an understanding deficit of members of OMCs. Up to this point a property developer would apply to the local authority for planning permission to build for example a multi-unit development comprising of either residential only, commercial only or mixed-use development. The provisions set out by the planning authority regarding these types of developments were weak. At that time the Department of the Environment, Heritage and Local Government were just publishing guidelines on the development of multi-unit developments. These guidelines included apartment design guidelines, quality housing for sustainable communities, development management guidelines and taking-in-charge of residential estates guidelines. This showed the lack of provisions which were in place for such developments at the time which was bound to create the difficulties which arose. The result was that such developments were granted planning permission without appropriate conditions around design and sustainable communities. Once the development was under construction, title and conveyancing issues arose which were ultimately dealt with in the Land and Conveyancing Law Reform Act of 2009.

The OMC was established by the developer during the construction phase and in many cases the developer continued to manage the OMC and collect service charges from new property owners' on an ad hoc and informal basis. Property owners who were paying the annual service charge were not getting any account of what their payments covered and for that reason many owners simply did not pay the annual service charge. In many cases property owners found themselves to be a member of an OMC without being informed of this prior to the purchase of their property. It came as a shock to many that they would have to pay an annual service charge each year particularly where there was an OMC in a housing estate such was the massive understanding deficit in the area.

This understanding deficit among owners was further amplified by the inconsistencies of how the local authorities carried out their business. Traditionally, housing estates would have been taken in charge by the local authority upon completion of the development and they would maintain the common areas and cut the grass on the greens, etc. Local authorities were inconsistent in their departure from this practice which was counter to the policy of s 180 of the Planning and Development Act 2000 which required planning authorities, where developments have been completed to their satisfaction, to take in charge new roads, open spaces, car parks, sewers, water mains or drains where requested. One such example is that of a small town where the local authority granted planning permission for the development of 25 houses in a housing estate and as a condition of the planning an OMC was to be established so that the common areas of the development were in the ownership of all property owners. Concurrently, the same local authority granted planning permission to another developer for a similar development in the same town but there was no condition of planning that an OMC was to be established. When both housing estates were completed the residents in one housing estate had to pay service charges and residents in the other housing estate did not have to pay service charges. It is important to mention that both estates were connected to the local authority sewerage system in the town and so an onsite sewage treatment plant was not a factor in this case. Another example of a local authority changing their position on the implementation of an OMC is where a developer was granted planning permission for a large housing estate which was to be constructed on a phased basis. Phase one was completed without the inclusion of an OMC. Afterwards, when the developer was granted planning permission for phase two and three it was on the condition that an OMC was established to take ownership of the common areas. In this case, some houses in the estate were not members of the OMC and some were members of the OMC, equally some parts of the common areas of the estate were owned by the OMC and other common areas of the estate were not. These inconsistencies did little to aid the understanding deficit, they simply added to the confusion among owners.

Given the collective responsibility nature of an OMC, where there are several non-compliant owners, the proper functioning and operation of the OMC can be seriously affected in that there may be insufficient funds to pay the bills such as the annual insurance policy and accountancy fees. Cases of OMCs being struck-off the company register were widespread at the time and apartment buildings were left uninsured because there were insufficient funds to pay the annual premium. The OMC structure was failing due to lack of good governance and legislation in the area was urgently required.

The collapse of the property market and the Banking Crisis in 2008 brought down several property developers who were in the process of developing properties in OMCs. As the property developer no longer had an interest in these developments, the OMCs in these cases were effectively abandoned and struck-off the company register for non-compliance and failing to file the annual return. It was years later when the receivers appointed to these properties sought to sell these assets that the OMCs were restored to the company register and a qualified, licenced and experienced property managing agent was appointed. In the intervening years, owners were forced to subsidise the developer's unsold units and pay much higher service charges. OMCs that failed to operate in a transparent manner led to the refusal of some unit owners to pay their service charges. It was the combination of owners not paying due to lack of good governance and the non-payment of service charges for unsold units that caused the collapse of several OMCs during this period. At the time, the National Consumer Agency was receiving numerous complaints about the operation of OMCs and issues identified included lack of accountability, there was no transparency of financials, no notice of the AGM and no AGM held. These problems mainly occurred in OMCs where there was no managing agent appointed.

The managing agent is distinct from the management company in that the management company is the OMC and the managing agent is the agent employed to carry out the day-to-day business of the OMC. Part of the understanding deficit as mentioned earlier was the inability of owners to make the distinction between the two. The role of the managing agent acting on behalf of all members of the OMC typically includes, *inter alia*, preparation of the annual service charge budget, arranging and attending the annual general meeting, invoicing and receipting of the annual service charge, bookkeeping, liaising with and overseeing service contractors for the development. The potential for abuse from managing agents in this capacity was enormous considering the vast sums of money involved and it was a priority to have the sector licenced and regulated in that regard. The Law Reform Commission concluded that

> '... the best way to counter such abuse is to inject clarification into the system for unit owners. Through the use of licensing and regulation of Managing Agents, standard form contracts, and mechanisms for investigation and dispute resolution, the Commission is convinced that consumers will be in a better position to assert their rights against such abuse in the future.'[9]

The Minister for Justice and Equality, by order under the Property Services (Regulation) Act 2011, established the National Property Services Regulatory Authority on a statutory basis on 3 April 2012. The main function of the Authority is to control and regulate property services providers including auctioneers, letting agents and managing agents. It also includes the licensing of all such service providers, the establishment of a complaints investigation and redress system for consumers and the setting and enforcement of standards in the provision of property services.

In Ireland, the Multi-Unit Developments Act 2011 was a game-changer in how the business was conducted in the OMC. Where there had been no rules or even guidance on managing agents or property developers and their respective roles in the construction and handover of these developments, the legislation now provides this, thus safeguarding the property rights of property owners. Further developments in the law affecting the OMC include the New Companies Act 2014. This is in contrast with the position in England and Wales where there is no statutory requirement that any particular legal framework must be adopted for multi-owned developments.[10] The need for statutory regulation of multi-unit developments was recognised on Continental Europe prior to the 1980s, much earlier than in America. Condominiums legislation of varying kinds was enacted in many European Countries with

---

9 The Law Reform Commission, *Consultation Paper on Multi-Unit Developments* (LRC CP 42—2006), 93.

10 Sarah Blandy, Ann Dupuis, Jennifer Dixon, *Multi-Owned Housing: Law, Power and Practice* (Routledge, 2010), New York, 16.

Ireland and England being the only ones that failed to follow this trend.

Apartment living in Ireland has increased significantly with census data showing that in 2002, 70,500 households lived in flats or apartments in purpose-built blocks, representing 5.5 percent of all households. By 2016 this number had multiplied by a factor of nearly 2.5 to 172,000; and the percentage had very nearly doubled to 10 per cent. While these figures give us some information on apartment living it does nothing to provide accurate data on the number of OMCs in Ireland today and the size of this market. The measurement of the number of OMCs in Ireland is a crucial element to the study in this area. To be able to provide and plan for the sector, it is an inevitable starting point that we must know what the size of the sector is. Up to now, this problem has never been dealt with, not by the Companies Registration Office, the Property Services Regulatory Authority, planning authorities or housing bodies. Clúid Housing in collaboration with the Housing Agency are in the process of conducting a research report on the OMC in Ireland. It is expected that they will, for the first time, provide a directory of OMCs currently operating in Ireland together with research into how these OMCs are performing. The Multi-Unit Development Act was enacted with no real measure of the sector that it sought to govern. All bodies and laws operate around a sector that no-one can categorically confirm the size of the sector. This is referred to in the 2006 report whereby they state that they carried out a 'small survey'.

In researching this further, we set about contacting each of the 31 local authorities in the country to ask them for the data that they had on the number of planning permissions issued which stipulated the incorporation of an OMC. Many local authorities didn't reply and of those that did, the reply from Cork County Council was echoed by almost all other replies from the local authorities.

> 'The information you seek would have to be manually extracted based on text searches. Additionally, we do not hold digitally searchable records going back as far 1995, especially in the former Town Council areas. To highlight how huge a task this would be for us I should point out that Cork Council exceeded 10,000 planning applications per annum during the boom years. I'm afraid I cannot facilitate your request given the huge volume of files and the time-consuming nature of the exercise.'

While the Companies Registration Office ('CRO') keeps a record of all companies in the State, it does not have a record of how many of those companies are OMCs. The Property Services Regulatory Authority is the regulator in this area of service providers to OMCs and they confirmed that the only information that they have in relation to this extends to the number of property service providers that exist in the State. In assessing where we are in relation to the OMC in Ireland the next step is to attain accurate data on the size and operation of the market.

The conclusion reached by the Law Reform Commission in their consultation paper in 2006 was as follows:

> 'The Commission is concerned that the law has not kept pace with the sudden ubiquity of residential multi-unit developments and that as a result, there is scope for mismanagement and abuse. Given the discrete nature of Irish land law; it seems that from a regulatory perspective, it may not be appropriate to follow the schemes of other countries. Moreover, the legislative response to this recent phenomenon in Irish property law seems at best piecemeal. As a result, uncertainty and frustration with regard to the lack of sector-specific regulation and legislation abound. All of this convinces the Commission that a more proactive Government approach is imperative to counter the current problems. Given the numbers of people dependant on multi-unit developments as a source of housing in this country, the current situation requires a planned and structured approach to the issues involved.'[11]

Following on from this, on 1 April 2011 the Multi-Unit Developments Act was enacted and was broadly seen as the legislative response to the problems which had preceded it. Since then there has been no review or reform of the law. Cultural change is required to ensure that apartment living is a sustainable form of housing into the future. There is a compelling case for reform of the law and the regulation applicable to OMCs. Current issues that abound include the volunteer-director model, lack of adequate sinking-funds and financing structures including a suitable remedy for collecting outstanding service charges.

There are more Multi-Unit Developments in the country today

---

[11] Law Reform Commission, *Consultation Paper on Multi-Unit Developments* (LRC CP 42—2006), 21.

than ever before and the sector continues to grow. The fact is that owners are more protected today than they were prior to the enactment of the Multi-Unit Developments Act. However, although the collective management system and operation of the OMC is better understood and more commonplace today there remains a significant knowledge gap among members of OMCs.

Chapter 3

The Evolution of a Properly Functioning OMC

1. The role of the property developer and the implications of the MUD Act 2011 19
2. Three phases: developer only/developer and owners/owners only 21
3. Considerations for prospective owners................... 28

Whilst chapter 2 dealt with the reasons as to how and why the OMC developed, this chapter will deal with the stages that a new development will go through when an OMC is established for the purposes of vesting the common areas of the development in it. The stages include the 'developer only' phase, the 'developer and owners' phase and the 'owners only' phase. The role of the property developer and the implications of the MUD Act 2011 are set out as well as some very important considerations that owners should be aware of before purchasing a property in an OMC.

An OMC will generally evolve through a number of phases with a number of actors involved at the various phases. These actors are individuals and incorporated companies and they include solicitors, accountants, the planning department of the local authority, purchasers, managing agents, property developers, designers and builders.

1. The role of the property developer and the Implications of the MUD Act 2011

A property developer will establish a property development company, normally a company that has limited liability and a share capital. The property developer will operate and promote this company and will be one of the company's directors. This property development company has a separate legal personality as distinct from the property developer. The principle of separate legal personality was established in the case of *Salomon v Salomon*[1] and some of the consequences which flow from that case are that

1 [1897] AC 22.

a company can sue and be sued, a company has the capacity to contract and it can own property. This company will purchase the site which will be developed into a scheme of houses, an apartment complex, or a mixed-use development comprising commercial units, houses and/or apartments all together in the one development and the one OMC.

This property development company normally employs a solicitor to conduct its legal business and an accountant to conduct its financial business. All transactions in relation to the site are now between the property development company and others.

The property development company will then apply for planning permission and in doing this they may employ a firm of architects and engineers to design the buildings and to complete and submit the planning application. The extent, character and nature of the development is a product of commercial imperatives and compliance with local development plans in place which are adjudicated by the normal planning process.

The developer has a legal obligation under planning law to complete the development in accordance with the planning permission granted by the planning authority, including any conditions attached to the permission. Section 35 of the Planning and Development Act 2000 provides that the planning authority can refuse planning permission to a person on the basis of past failures to comply with previous planning permission, or with a condition to which the previous permission is subject. The planning authority may form the opinion that there is a real and substantial risk that the development in respect of which permission is sought would not be completed in accordance with such permission if granted or with a condition to which such permission if granted would be subject. However, the Act also states that where the planning authority forms that opinion, the failure to comply must be of a substantial nature.

In the case where the developer is seeking to build a housing estate in certain circumstances, the local authority will have discretion as to whether or not an OMC must be established to take ownership of the common areas when the estate is completed. They will exercise their discretion in the conditions of planning. In some cases, local authorities are likely to stipulate that an OMCs must be established to take ownership of the common areas of the development upon achieving practical completion at which point the local authority will then take charge of the roads and lighting in the development.

In the case of an apartment block, there is no such discretion as the solicitors acting on behalf of the property development company automatically incorporate an Owners' Management Company. Section 3(1) of the Multi-Unit Development Act 2011 stipulates that this OMC is 'established at the expense of the developer' who has a responsibility in accordance with s 4 of the Act to transfer the common areas of the completed development to the OMC. At this stage, the directors of the OMC are usually the directors of the property development company.

2. Three phases: developer only/developer and owners/owners only

Upon the grant of planning permission, the property development company enters into various contracts with many individuals and companies for the construction phase of the development. For very large developments, the developer may contract a building company to complete the construction works. In other cases, the developer acts as the main building contractor on the site. This is commonly known as the Developer-only phase which is the first stage and begins with the formal incorporation of the OMC. This usually happens sometime after the developer has begun to build the multi-unit development but before any units have yet been offered for sale. During this time the only members of the management company are usually the Developer of the multi-unit development and/or persons nominated by them.[2]

Once the construction stage commences and before the first unit in the development is offered for sale, the developer's solicitor commences the preparation of conveyancing documents which includes the drawing up of lease agreements and deeds for each property in preparation for offering the units for sale. A condition of the lease agreement states that purchasers automatically become members of the respective OMC. At this stage it is recommended that developers define the brief for property management companies and seek competitive proposals from qualified managing agents. Such an agent will prepare a

[2] Even one member will be enough if the management company is incorporated as a private company limited by shares. At least seven members will be required if the management company is incorporated as a company limited by guarantee not having a share capital.

comprehensive property management proposal for consideration by the developer which will include the annual service charge budget with full explanatory notes and a roadmap of the steps in the process from their appointment through to the handover of common areas and the appointment of new property owners to the board of directors of the OMC whilst resigning the developers. When the developer selects and appoints the managing agent, then the managing agent will furnish the developer's solicitor with a copy of the contract between them and the OMC. This contract is a specified form and must be put in place in accordance with the requirements set out by the Property Services Regulatory Authority.[3]

The first service charge and sinking-fund contribution for the units is normally calculated by the newly appointed managing agent in agreement with the property developer. The problem with this is that it is not in the interest of the property developer to have a high service charge, it is in their interest to have as low a service charge as possible in order to attract buyers of the units. Equally, the newly appointed managing agent must act in accordance with the wishes and instructions of the directors of the OMC or risk losing their job. These competing interests are problematic in that very often the true cost of the annual service charge and sinking-fund contribution is much higher than what it is set at when the units are offered for sale. The amount of service charge is dictated by the marketing of the development rather than any scientific costing by the engineers or quantity surveyors associated with the original build. As a result, the service charge may be set at a level that will not prove an impediment to the sale of the units. There is much debate about this issue and its effects on the OMC in the long term; almost fooling property owners at the point of purchase who are very resistant in general to large hikes in service charges and sinking-fund contributions in the subsequent years. If the service charge is always below the true cost of the services then the OMC will continually struggle to pay its bills. Various lobby groups such as the Apartment Owners' Network have recommended that the first service charge and sinking-fund contribution should be calculated by a chartered quantity surveyor because of the difficulties which arise with trying to increase service charges in an OMC given the culture that exists within OMCs.

---

3 The Property Services Regulatory Authority Specified Form, S43 D1 2014, for the Provision of Property Management Services.

Each property in the development will have a different closing date of sale and the annual service charge is then calculated on a floating scale until the first service charge year-end is determined. Fig 2, below, shows that the annual service charge is divided into 365 days to get the per-day rate and each new property owner will pay the service charge only for the number of days that they are in occupation of their property. This is applicable for the first service charge only. Once the date of the first service charge year-end has been determined then the annual service charge is fixed to that property and is payable to the OMC by the property owner. In some cases, a developer may not have all of the properties sold by the time that the first service charge period has been closed, but if this is the case then the developer is obliged to pay service charges for unsold units.[4] The first year expenses from the OMC for which expenditure is required for items in the budget normally returns lower than in subsequent years and this will be due to the overlap of services while the developer is on site. For example, the buildings will be insured by the developers up to a particular stage and when the OMC incepts the buildings insurance policy it is likely that the number of days that the policy will cover in the first OMC year will be less than 365 days.

When it comes to this stage in the process, there exists a lack of understanding by developers and owners about this complicated period in the cycle of a development and this understanding deficit has caused and is still a cause of much confusion for property developers and property owners. There is a real need for clarification around the steps in the process from the early stages to when the developer will arrange for their solicitors to transfer the common areas and resign as directors of the OMC.

4 Multi-Unit Developments Act 2011, s 18(10): '[t]he owner of each unit in a multi-unit development (including a person who is the developer or building contractor of the development) shall be under an obligation to pay all service charges levied under this section.'

Apt. No	1st Ser Chg	Cost per day	Closing Date	Year End	No of Days	Due	Paid	Bal Due	2nd Ser Chg	Total Due to y/e 28/2/18
1	€1,000.00	€2.74	3-Mar-16	28-Feb-17	362	€991.78	€1,000.00	-€8.22	€1,000.00	€991.78
2	€1,000.00	€2.74	24-May-16	28-Feb-17	280	€767.12	€1,000.00	-€232.88	€1,000.00	€767.12
3	€1,000.00	€2.74	26-May-16	28-Feb-17	278	€761.64	€1,000.00	-€238.36	€1,000.00	€761.64
4	€1,000.00	€2.74	7-Oct-16	28-Feb-17	144	€394.52	€1,000.00	-€605.48	€1,000.00	€394.52
5	€1,000.00	€2.74	30-May-16	28-Feb-17	274	€750.68	€1,000.00	-€249.32	€1,000.00	€750.68
6	€1,000.00	€2.74	29-Apr-16	28-Feb-17	305	€835.62	€1,000.00	-€164.38	€1,000.00	€835.62
7	€1,000.00	€2.74	2-Apr-16	28-Feb-17	332	€909.59	€1,000.00	-€90.41	€1,000.00	€909.59
8	€1,000.00	€2.74	24-Jun-16	28-Feb-17	249	€682.19	€1,000.00	-€317.81	€1,000.00	€682.19
9	€1,000.00	€2.74	4-Jul-16	28-Feb-17	239	€654.79	€1,000.00	-€345.21	€1,000.00	€654.79
10	€1,000.00	€2.74	13-Dec-16	28-Feb-17	77	€210.96	€1,000.00	-€789.04	€1,000.00	€210.96
	€10,000.00					**€6,958.90**	**€10,000.00**	**-€3,041.10**	**€10,000.00**	**€6,958.90**

Fig 2

Historically, this issue has caused problems for developers and owners alike and it is important that developers understand how to avoid the pitfalls. Developers who did not appoint a professional Managing Agent at all or in time got caught up in the mix of building works and OMC management. Some developers decided to take on the management of the OMC themselves. In these cases, property owners were to pay the service charge to the developer. While this was lawful prior to the Property Services Regulation Act 2011, it is now not permitted as the regulation states that it is an offence to provide a property service without a licence which is punishable by an unlimited fine and up to five years in prison. Prior to this regulation there were many cases where the developer acted as managing agent but did not have the required skillset to organise the specific administration for the invoicing, collecting and reporting on the annual service charges. This situation continued for many years with the result that most property owners never paid the service charge. For those who did pay, it was nowhere near enough to cover the overheads in the running of the OMC or maintenance costs for the development as a whole. The result of this was that the services provided to the common areas fell short, property owners felt aggrieved that their development was deteriorating, lifts were switched off and the expectations that the owners had of the property that they had purchased were not met. Property owners were suspicious of developers pocketing service charges and providing no services.

On the other hand, the developer felt aggrieved that 'the owners wouldn't pay' and they were left in some cases with having to pay themselves for services and items such as the annual insurance policy. This recurrent circular conflict can be avoided by appointing an independent, competent, professional and qualified managing agent at the outset who can take responsibility for the running of the OMC from the beginning, to properly represent the new owners and the Directors who at this stage are still normally the Developers, in unison. This type of developer/owner conflict is widespread in OMCs in Ireland and has its origins rooted primarily in the property boom and thereafter in the subsequent property crash and the financial crisis of 2008. A solution to this problem is vital as these conflicts have a detrimental effect on the health and wellbeing of the OMC and all property owners involved including the value of their investment.

Where the managing agent is appointed at the initial stages before any unit is sold in the development then this will provide independent representation for the owners and also the developer.

In order to avoid such a developer/owner conflict, one proposal would be to have the annual service charge and sinking-fund contribution accurately calculated by a qualified quantity surveyor and compel all owners to pay the first three years of service charges upon the close of sale. This would provide for a definitive time frame and eliminate all of the problems associated with variables concerning unknown timeframes and contracts. This period of three years of service charges is preferable as it is compatible with the contractual period of the standard managing agents contract in accordance with point 6 of the PSRA, s 43, Form D1, 2014, Provision of Property Management Services. This definitive time period would see the sale through of all of the properties by that date and in the event where not all units are sold, then as with s 18 of the Multi-Unit Developments Act 2011, the developer will be obliged to pay the service charges for unsold units. At the end of the three years, all service charges are closed off at the same date as per Fig 2, and a comprehensive financial report is furnished to each owner. Owners will, at this stage, have the benefit of making contractual decisions based on historical performance of contracts, etc. This will substantially reduce the existence of doubt and suspicion that owners have of the developer and the managing agent, and it will foster a trust and confidence between the managing agent and owners as owners will at this stage 'know what they are getting' for their money. Owners are then better able to assess what needs to be provided for in the budget and the amount of sinking-fund payments to be set aside.

The second stage is commonly known as the Developer-and-Owners' phase and is one which usually begins as soon as the sale of the first unit in the multi-unit development is completed. As each successive sale is completed, the unit purchasers become members of the OMC with the result that the membership now consists of the developer and/or their nominees and each of the purchasers of the units in the associated multi-unit development.

As each sale closes, the new owners should receive all of the following documentation in relation to their purchase of a property in an OMC:

1. Lease agreement;
2. House rules;
3. Property services agreement as between the OMC and the managing agent;

4. Annual service charge budget together with budget explanatory notes.

The managing agent is responsible for arranging the annual general meeting of the OMC and must ensure that the annual return and annual accounts are filed at the Companies Registration Office on time each year.

The period of time from the incorporation of the OMC to the sale of each unit and the subsequent transfer of common areas can be a lengthy one and during this period there are administrative and compliance matters for the OMC to be dealt with. Most importantly, the first annual return of the company must be filed after a certain date regardless of whether all units are sold at that stage or not. The failing of an OMC to file the B1, Annual Return form, at the Companies Registration Office each year is the most common reasons for an OMC to be struck-off the company register. The only remedy available for the developer in this circumstance is to arrange to have the OMC restored to the company register. Where a company has been struck-off for a period exceeding 12 months, an application for restoration must be made to the court. This can be an expensive and arduous process. There are numerous cases each year where the OMC is not struck-off the register but because the annual return was not filed on-time, late filing penalties apply. The initial late filing penalty is €120 plus €3 per day thereafter and this can go up as high as €1,200.[5]

It is important that the developer ensures that the administrative obligations of the OMC are met. In the event where such obligations are not met then this will affect the sale process and has the potential to thwart the sale of the units in some cases.

The third phase, the Owners-Only phase begins once the developer has finally completed the multi-unit development and has transferred all of their remaining ownership of its common areas to the OMC. Section 3 of the Multi-Unit Developments Act 2011 sets out that the developer must provide for transfer of the common areas to the OMC before the sale of the first residential unit is completed. At the Owners-only phase, the developer and their nominees usually cease to be members of the OMC and from this point onwards, the only members of the OMC are

---

5 Companies Registration Office, Company Fees Registration <www.cro.ie/Publications/Fees/Company> (accessed on the 24 January 2019).

those who are the owners of the units in the associated multi-unit development.

This three-phase evolution is one which, has been set out by the Office of the Director of Corporate Enforcement in their handbook *Company Law Handbook on Residential Property Owners' Management Companies ('Management Companies')*, and is common in the majority of management companies associated with multi-unit developments.

In any company it is vital that both members and directors should understand fully what role the company is intended to perform. Knowing what the company should be seeking to do, and should not be seeking to do, are questions that are of fundamental importance so that the company's activities however great or little they may be, can be carried on efficiently and effectively. In general, company law does not lay down what are, or should be, the activities or role of any company: management companies included. Those who incorporate the company specify at the outset what are to be its objects, which must then be set forth in the company's constitution. Thereafter those objects are capable of being modified if the members of the company, as constituted from time to time, pass a special resolution to amend the constitution. The company constitution includes the memorandum and articles of association of the company.

It is advisable for anyone connected with an OMC to obtain an up-to-date copy of the company constitution in order to gain a full understanding of the objects of the company. The constitution of a company can be obtained from the Companies Registration Office website upon payment of a fee of €2.50. Property owners should be furnished with this document as part of the unit owner's title deeds of their property.

3. Considerations for prospective owners

In a newly constructed development, when an owner buys a new house or apartment they sign two contracts, one for sale of the land or a lease in the case of an apartment and one to build the unit which is 'the building contract'. That contract is entered into with the first purchaser of a home, who is the only person who may sue under that contract. It is drafted on the basis that it will be signed under seal, for which the period for bringing proceedings is 12 years from the date of breach of contract. The agreement contains a warranty in favour of the buyer but if the home is sold during the 12-year period, the agreement does not transfer with the property and the benefit of the warranty is lost. In addition to this, if the property development company is insolvent and has no money, then that contract may be worthless. A property owner may not realise that there is a problem until it is too late to go after those who are responsible. If they do go to court or arbitration it will take money that they may not have, it will take time and if it is their home, they will be living in the property and paying the mortgage as well. In an apartment block situation, the only way that the OMC can pay for repairs is by demanding contributions from the owners because the OMC is made up of all of the owners. The repair costs can be very substantial depending on how bad the defects are and the owners have to wait until most or all of the other owners have paid before the repair work can start.

When buying a property in an OMC, an owner should inform themselves of what is involved in becoming a member of an OMC. They need to be fully aware of how apartments in particular in Ireland are owned and run and that they have a part to play in the upkeep and management of the whole apartment block. The health status of the OMC is an important area for examination. This includes looking at the financial operations of the company. This information is a matter of public record and by simply paying a €2.50 fee, any person can obtain a copy of the annual accounts of the OMC from the Companies Registration Office website.

Owners will be invited to attend and Annual General Meeting (AGM) of the OMC each year, where a number of members must agree to serve on the board of the company. They will form the decision-making body for the year, including deciding on the standards and the services for the development. In some OMCs, usually smaller OMCs, all owners are directors and this ensures that there is an equality of responsibilities and obligations among all owners. Directors will typically set the budget to achieve these standards. Directors are appointed as volunteers and there is no remuneration as is normally set down in the company constitution. At every AGM all the members of the board must resign, but can be proposed for re-election if they wish. In accordance with s 17 of the Multi-Unit Developments Act 2011, every year the board must ensure to prepare and furnish each member with an annual report on the activity within the company during the year which will include a statement of income and expenditure and a complete financial report on the company. Prior to the AGM each year every member must be shown a copy of the company's annual accounts for the previous year. The board may decide to engage various suppliers, such as a gardener, a cleaning company, etc. and the responsibility for ensuring that the development and the OMC is maintained belongs ultimately with the members and directors of the company.

A prospective owner should investigate the level of sinking-fund provision that has been set aside in the OMC prior to purchasing their property. This will give an indication as to the level of provision set aside and the scope of what the fund can provide for in the future. It should also indicate what the level of compliance is with owners paying their contribution into it. The healthier the sinking-fund the less likely it is that there will be future cash calls on owners.

Taking on the responsibilities of being a member of an OMC is not for everyone and it is important that a prospective purchaser understands these responsibilities before they join. Involvement in running the development can mean a lot of work, and if owners are not willing to get involved, then the workload will always fall to the same few committed unpaid volunteers to maintain the standards on their behalf. Being an owner in an OMC is a joint responsibility between all owners.

Before buying a unit in a multi-unit development, another area for consideration is that of the specification and design of the common areas. Generally, the more extensive the common areas, the more it will cost to maintain them. Duplexes with their own entrances to each apartment have fewer shared areas than apartment blocks with lifts, entrance halls and corridors and subsequently often have lower service charges. A further consideration is carparking issues and the use of the common areas for carparking, i.e. who can use what and when. Communal parking is regularly the cause of conflict between owners.

For prospective purchasers it is a good idea to visit the grounds at night time to check on the design, maintenance and lighting of the development. Other issues for prospective purchasers to look out for include the general maintenance in relation to the external façade of the building, the corridors, entrances and lifts and if they are due a general upgrade are there sufficient funds available in the sinking-fund to cover that or is it likely that there may be cash calls made on property owners. If the windows need to be replaced soon will the management company pay for this.

To establish the extent of maintenance required on the common areas it is important to look out for expensive features like ponds, water fountains extensive wood/timber finishes used on outside of building and inside. Features like ponds will have to be maintained by the owners. Is there easy access for emergency vehicles and are there electronic gates and/or is there electronic access? Before buying the property it is important to get further professional information about the structure of the complex, the state of repair and the frequency of planned maintenance. The estate agent (seller) will be able to give some information in relation to this. However, it is essential to get a professional chartered surveyor's report done which will be able to answer questions regarding the structure and safety. However, as they cannot do any opening up works then they cannot confirm the real truth such as fire stopping works, etc. A prospective owner should find out when the last overhaul of the complex was carried out and look to see what work ought to have been done and is still outstanding. This can have major implications on the level of service charges payable. If major work has just been completed satisfactorily, the sinking-fund may be low, but will not be needed for some of years. If no major refurbishment has been conducted for at least five to 10 years, there will be big demands on the sinking-fund and if the sinking-fund proves to be inadequate, all property owners will be expected to contribute.

Another important area of consideration for a prospective owner is that of the fire safety within the development. It is important to find out when the last fire inspection was carried out and if there are any outstanding issues with respect to health and safety. Is there a health and safety statement and is it clearly displayed? Are the fire exits free and clearly marked? Is the fire alarm panel in fault mode or normal operational mode? Are the lifts and gates working satisfactorily and when were they last serviced? The security measures that are in place will have an impact on overall costs as will a CCTV system and intercoms. There is the question of whether these components are functional and frequently checked. Is there a cleaning schedule visible and is there information displayed about who is managing the development with contact details?

The quality of the management of a multi-unit development, be it in an apartment block or a housing estate where there is a management company, is of crucial importance as it impacts directly on the level of service that owners receive, the amount of service charges payable and ultimately on the value for money being achieved on all items in the annual service charge budget. It is important to find out as much as possible initially from the person who is selling, and the solicitors. If a prospective owner is not happy with what they have discovered then they should not go ahead with the purchase. If the estate will not be taken in charge by the local authority because there is a management company it is important to check the following:

- Does the contract make reference to an OMC which manages the estate? The solicitors for the purchaser must explain all implications arising from that fact and they will also carry out searches on whether or not the OMC is still dominated by the developer and if the common areas have been transferred to the OMC. It is important to find out who the managing agent is and to conduct a background check on that firm. In particular, finding out if they are qualified, experienced and licensed to do the job and what other estates they manage. It is also a good idea to visit some of the other developments that they manage and seek references as to their competence.
- A prospective owner should find out if there is an active resident's association in place and find out about relationships between residents and the management company/agent. Are residents in conflict with the OMC, i.e. refusing to pay the annual service charges? In that case, the OMC may eventually fold and services would be suspended.
- In the case where the property is new, it is important as previously discussed, to be aware that some developers may set the service charge artificially low in the first year to make the property more attractive to purchasers. Maintenance demands may be lower when the property is new but service can be expected to increase as maintenance demands grow. In a new development there is no way of knowing what the compliance rate will be like with the payment of the annual service charge. This is a huge disadvantage because there is so much that cannot be checked out such as what the neighbours will be like and what percentage will be owner-occupier or tenant and what type of tenant.

Property owners should get involved in the running of the OMC and they should become a director at some point. Advantages of being a director include having the power to make decisions, hire and fire suppliers and appoint a different managing agent.

The success of the relationship between the property developer and the purchaser of the units in a multi-unit development will hinge upon the level of information and knowledge that the purchaser has at the time of purchase and the approach of the property developer in ensuring that the correct expertise are employed for the successful running of the OMC and smooth transfer of property in the sale of the units and, thereafter, the common areas.

Chapter 4

Implications of Being a Member of a Management Company

1. Duties and responsibilities of property owners..... 35
2. The lease agreement..... 37
3. The company constitution..... 38
4. The house rules..... 39
5. Members' register..... 42
6. Directors..... 44
7. The culture within an OMC..... 46

The duties and responsibilities of property owners in an OMC primarily arise in the context of company law and hinge upon the principle of collective responsibility. While the OMC seeks to hold all Owners to the same standard that of itself is problematic. This chapter will examine in more detail the issues which abound this arrangement which include the culture within an OMC and the competing interests of the various parties.

1. Duties and responsibilities of property owners

As the law exists, a member of any company in Ireland 'is a person who participates in the capital of the company, is registered as such and is entitled to certain rights'.[1] Every person who agrees to become a member and whose name is entered in its register of members will become a member of the company.[2] This is what property owners do when they decide to purchase a property which is part of an OMC—they are inextricably linked as an owner of a property in a multi-unit development and a member of the OMC. Very often property owners don't realise or consider that they are becoming members of a company when they buy their property in an OMC and the understanding deficit in this regard can cause problems further down the line for them and their OMC. The obligation of unit-owners to pay service charges, and the entitlement of management companies to collect them, arise fundamentally from the covenants and obligations contained

1 Office of the Director of Corporate Enforcement, *Information Book 4, The Principle Duties and Powers of Members and Shareholders*, 6.
2 The Companies Act, s 168.

in the lease agreements which both management companies and multi-unit property owners enter into in the conveyancing documents by which owners purchase their properties in a multi-unit development.[3]

Where a property owner fails in their obligation to pay the annual service charge, this hinders effective management of the development and leads to a great deal of frustration and a further administrative and financial burden for the OMC and managing agents. Good cash flow and prompt payment and co-operation between unit owners are key features of the viability of management organisations and non-payment has the potential to seriously thwart this.[4] A property owner who is a member of an OMC is in a collective responsibility arrangement whereby they find that the actions or inactions of themselves or others can have an effect on everyone involved.

One of the primary benefits of communal living in an apartment block or a housing development and being a member of an OMC is the fact that the maintenance and repair work of the common areas will be carried out by the OMC and property owners will not have to get involved in this directly. Works such as cleaning, maintaining and carrying out repairs to the common area stairwells, corridors or lobbies of their building are all the responsibility of the OMC. Equally, in a housing estate, property owners won't have to get involved in cutting the grass or maintaining the green areas of the estate. The OMC has the responsibility of carrying out all of this work on behalf of the owners. This is because property owners do not own the building, the OMC owns the building and all of the common areas which each owner has a share in. The extent of ownership for an apartment owner is said to be the first skim of plaster on the walls inside the apartment and that does not extend to the actual wall which is owned by the OMC. The OMC structure and Company Law Code provide the basis upon which members of the OMC have a say in the running of the company and how the common areas of the development are managed. Members have the opportunity to become directors giving them ultimate authority and decision-making powers within the company. Members also have a say in the form of a vote whereby they may exercise their control at company meetings although their level of involvement

---

3 ODCE, *Company Law Handbook on Residential Property Owners' Management Companies ('Management Companies')*, Dublin, 2008, 132.

4 Law Reform Commission, *Report on Multi-Unit Developments*, (LRC 90—2008).

in the running of the company is minimal by comparison to that of its directors.

A member of an OMC will have the same rights as a member of any other company under the Companies Act 2014. These rights include the right to an invitation and adequate notice of all company meetings and they are entitled to be provided with the OMCs financial statements. They are also entitled to seek explanations from company directors. Conversely, a member of an OMC also has legal obligations and duties to their OMC. These legal obligations and duties are set out in detail in the lease agreement attaching to the title deeds of their property, the company constitution and the house rules. As a consequence of the impecunious nature of the OMC, the payment of the annual service charge is one of the most contentious obligations of OMC members together with compliance with the house rules.

A person who buys a property in an apartment complex purchases their apartment on a leasehold basis. This means that they only have the lease on the property, they do not own the property. The extent of 'ownership' that a property owner has when they buy an apartment has been described as the first skim of plaster on the walls inside the apartment and the airspace inside the apartment. The owner in this case does not own the walls, windows or the roof of the building and so does not have the right to interfere with or make any material changes to the walls, windows or roofs. They cannot decide to put in a fireplace in their apartment and bore a hole through the wall for a chimney flue as they do not own the wall to do this. They cannot decide to change the glass in the windows to stained glass as they do not own the windows. The buildings are vested in the ownership of the OMC and the new property owner has a share in this OMC. The owner is duty bound by certain rules contained in any and all of the following documents which form part of the overall purchase contract of their property:

2. The lease agreement

A covenant in a lease agreement is a promise in which one party (the covenantor, the OMC) promises with another party (the covenantee, the property owner) that they will or will not engage in a specified activity. A covenant may be positive in that one of the parties promises to do something or to continue to do something. For example, the property owner promises to pay the annual service charge. A covenant may be negative or restrictive whereby the property owner agrees to refrain from doing something. For example, the property owner promises to refrain from building in a defined area or using the property for a particular purpose. Equally the covenantor agrees to provide easements to the covenantee.

Covenants were the precursor of much of the regulation that is now provided by the public law. This is not to say that covenants have lost their significance entirely. Covenants play a significant and key role in leasehold property agreements and they are an important instrument in adding to and maintaining the value of a property which is part of a multi-unit development and an OMC. Due to the nature of a multi-unit development which is communal living, it results in the coming together of individuals from all cultures, backgrounds and value systems and they must all live to a particular standard within the rules set out in the multi-unit development. The covenants in the lease agreement are set out in order to achieve this standard and to ensure that it can be enforced in law. For example, a buyer of an apartment who wishes to reside there in the long term must have some assurance that the status of the building will be maintained in that there will be no change of use or general appearance and the value of their property will not be diminished. In this regard the OMC has a responsibility to protect the value of the property and the property owner's interest.

It is essential that property owners read through and understand the contents of the lease agreement and the extensive covenants as set out therein in order to avoid potential breaches of their obligations as covenantees. There are a variety of burdens, grants, covenants, schedules, declarations, conditions and interpretations contained in the lease agreement which are binding on the parties once the contract for sale is concluded.

As part of the conveyancing of the property to the new owner, their solicitor will lodge the lease agreement with the Land Registry or the Registry of Deeds to complete the sale transaction.

3. The company constitution

The company constitution originated under the Companies Act 2014 and it replaces the term 'memorandum and articles of association'. However, the memorandum and articles of association form part of the company constitution. It is the formal document that sets out the administrative and operational rules of the OMC in accordance with company law. While this document, which has its origins in the Company Law Code relates directly to the OMC, the lease agreement, on the other hand relates directly to the transaction of the property as between the purchaser and vendor. The new property owner agrees to the terms of the lease agreement to become the new owner and thereafter a member of the OMC and is then bound by the rules as set out in the company constitution. The Companies Act and the constitution of a company together normally set out the powers of members and those powers which are delegated by the members to the directors of the company. Section 158 of the Companies Act provides that the business of the company is managed by its directors and those directors may exercise all powers of the company outside of company meetings.

There is often an overlap in provisions as set out in the lease agreement and the company constitution. For example, they both provide that the OMC has a responsibility to maintain the common areas of the development. The provisions contained in the company constitution can be amended by the members and directors of the OMC. A special resolution may be passed at an annual general meeting or an extraordinary general meeting of the company whereby a majority vote will suffice to agree to amend whatever provisions in the constitution that they wish, providing that there is no conflict with the Companies Act 2014 or any such amendments. A G1 form should be filed at the Companies Office to effect the amendment and a charge of €30.00 is payable to the Companies Office for this.

4. The house rules

The house rules adopted under s 23 of the Multi-Unit Developments Act are binding on all occupiers and owners within the multi-unit development. The Act specifies the following:

> **23.**—(1) An owners' management company may, as respects the multi-unit development for which that company has responsibility, make house rules as respects the development or part of the development relating to the effective operation and maintenance of the development and with the objective of enhancing the quiet and peaceable occupation of units generally in the development, and such house rules shall be binding on—

(a) unit owners,
(b) tenants of unit owners, and
(c) servants, agents and licensees of persons referred to in paragraphs (a) and (b).[5]

A typical set of house rules in apartment block may contain any or all of the following:

1. NOISE – You must keep all stereo, radio and TV appliances at a volume which will not interfere with or upset your neighbours' peace. This includes the playing of musical instruments, loudspeakers, mechanical noise, singing and other noise that might cause annoyance to the other occupiers of the building. Most especially, no noise should be audible outside your apartment between the hours of midnight and 9 am.
2. CONSTRUCTION WORKS – Construction work that will or may cause disturbance to your neighbour must not be carried out after 6 pm. Construction work may not be carried out on a Sunday.
3. ANIMALS – Animals are not allowed where they are found to be interfering with your neighbours' peace and where they dirty or obstruct the common areas of the development.
4. PARTIES – PARTIES ARE NOT PERMITTED ANYWHERE IN THE APARTMENT BLOCK.
5. SECURITY – Please ensure that you do not allow entry to anybody except your own personally-invited guests and visitors. Please report any suspicious loiterers to your local Garda station.
6. OBSTRUCTIONS – You must not leave bicycles, prams or rubbish of any kind in any of the common areas, for example, at the stairwell or on the footpaths. The cost to remove such an obstruction, including vehicles, will be payable by the owner. Satellite dishes are not allowed anywhere on the buildings or in the common areas.
7. PARKING – Residents and their guests are asked to park cars carefully in a manner, which will not interfere with their neighbours. Parking of boats or caravans or tractors is not permitted. Parking is only allowed in the designated parking area.
8. WASHING – Washing may not be hung out to dry over windows or balconies.

---

5 Multi-Unit Developments Act 2011, s 23(1).

9. FIRE – Residents must not tamper with the fire detectors inside their apartments. In the event of the fire alarm sounding, it is essential that all residents immediately leave their apartments and assemble in the designated areas outside the building. They should not return until such time as they are told to do so by the fire department. Do not use the lifts to exit in the event of fire.
10. EMERGENCY CONTACT – Residents are asked to keep the management company advised of the phone numbers at which they can be contacted in case of emergency, also the names and addresses of the key holders, especially if they have a burglar alarm fitted.
11. COMMON AREAS – Every effort should be made to keep the common areas and grounds clean and tidy. Residents are responsible for the immediate area outside their front door and are required to keep this area swept clean and litter free at all times.

The house rules must be adopted at the annual general meeting or extraordinary general meeting of the company where members have the opportunity to add or amend the rules by a simple majority vote. The rules are then binding on the parties providing that all proper procedures were followed and also that they are in the best interests of the OMC. For example, the imposition of a house rule stating that construction works were not permitted whatsoever would be unlawful as it would contravene the covenants of the lease agreement which states that the property owners have the right to effect repairs or refurbishment of their own apartment. Most of the listed house rules are also contained in the terms of the lease agreement and so there is a considerable overlap in this regard. However, unlike the lease agreements, the house rules can be relatively easily changed and added to at no cost while also remaining binding on the parties.

The lease agreements can be amended if the members and directors of the OMC wish to do so. The most common scenario whereby the lease agreements are amended is where a long lease is coming to an end. In this case where a solicitor is conveying a property from one owner to another, they must ensure that the lease agreement will be at least for the lifetime or more of the purchaser. If the term left on the lease is, for example, just 40 years, then a new lease must be drawn up which could be a 999-year lease. This situation will occur whereby the apartment block may have been built 50 years ago and the lease had 100 years left. What is required here is the enlargement of the lease. This transaction will typically have to be carried out for each and every property in the OMC extending the period of the lease and can only be carried out by a conveyancing solicitor. It is a long and expensive process and this is one of the main reasons why the covenants in the lease agreements are almost never amended at the will of the members and directors of the OMC.

An OMC in a housing estate or a commercial business park may also have '*Rules of the Estate*' which may vary to provide for the physical aspect of the development and what the owners wish to have included in the interest of the effective operation of the estate. These rules will also have the same binding effect as the house rules in an apartment block scenario.

5. Members' register

In accordance with s 169 of the Companies Act 2014, every company is obliged to keep a register of the company's members, their names, addresses and contact details. Section 216 of the Companies Act provides for the right of inspection. The register must be kept at a place within the State which can be the registered office of the company, its principal place of business or another place. A registered office of a company must be more than merely a post box for receiving communication, as there must be a facility for viewing company files and the members register. It is also a requirement under s 49 to have the company name clearly legible and obvious on the outside of the office or place, even if it is a residence of a director of the company. Failure to comply with s 49 is a Category 4 offence and is punishable by the imposition of a Class A fine, i.e. a fine of up to €5,000. All OMCs that are 'self-managed' are exposed to this sanction given that most volunteer directors may run the OMC from their own private residences and are not likely to have a plaque at their front door with the name of the OMC clearly legible. In addition to this, the name plaque would be moved from one director's place of residence to another as directors retire and new directors are appointed.

Typically, in an OMC where the services of a managing agent are engaged, the register of members is held on the company file with the managing agent which is normally the company's registered office. If the register is not kept at the company's registered office, the company is required to notify the Registrar of Companies of where the register is kept and of any change in that place. Section

216(8) provides as follows: 'Every such register or document shall be open to the inspection of any member of the company without charge…'

The register of members must contain the member's contact details, names and addresses. It must also contain the date that each person was entered onto the register and the date that each person ceased to be a member of the company. The register of members is an important document as it is the primary means of which a company has for knowing who the members are so that all those entitled to be notified of annual general meetings and extraordinary general meetings can be duly notified and that all company documentation such as financial statements can be forwarded to them. It is also important to clarify who is entitled to vote at company meetings. It is a member's responsibility to ensure that their details are entered onto the company register correctly and up-to-date in order to avoid a situation whereby they do not receive important company documentation such as notice of meetings. In their handbook on OMCs, the Office of the Director of Corporate Enforcement make the following comments in relation to the register of members:

> 'Another way in which the register of members is important is that it is a means by which members of the management company may seek to ascertain the necessary contact details for one another. An ability for members to get in contact with one another may be essential in order that alliances can be formed amongst members, perhaps with a view to bringing about change in the company; or, at any rate, so that the members who seek to bring about change should have at least the means to gauge the extent to which other members might be willing to support them. For example, a member who wishes to become a director of the management company might wish to write to other members (whose names and addresses he/she does not already know) for the purpose of seeking to persuade them that they should vote for him/her at a forthcoming AGM of the company. Alternatively, where some members wish to have an EGM convened for some particular purpose, (e.g. to pass an ordinary resolution) they may need to try to gain the support of at least some other members so as to satisfy the statutory pre-condition that a members' request for an EGM must come from members whose combined voting rights at general meetings of the management

company is at least 10% of the total voting rights of all the company's members.'[6]

Given that the principal duty of a member of an OMC is to pay their annual service charge and sinking-fund contributions to their OMC, it is worth noting that there are no provisions in the Companies Act which state what the level of service charge should be, nor does the Companies Act give any guidance on how the service charges should be calculated. This is provided for in s 18 of the Multi-Unit Developments Act 2011. This section of the Act sets out the rules on setting the service charge for the year, what should be included on the annual service charge budget and the rules surrounding the approval of the budget at company meetings. The Companies Act provides merely the framework within which all sorts of business may be carried on, rather than to spell out the specific ways in which companies engaged in any particular type of activity should go about running their business.

The Companies Act and the constitution of a company normally set out the powers of members and those powers which are delegated by the members to the directors of the company. Company members have the right to an invitation and specific notice periods of company meetings and all information about the company's activities both financial and otherwise.

6. Directors

OMCs are unique in company law insofar as the directors run the company in a voluntary capacity on a non-professional basis. It is common for management company directors to have no experience of acting as a company director and no experience of compliance requirements of company law. This board of volunteer directors comprises mainly of civic minded individuals who represent all members of the OMC. The OMC is merely an incorporated version of residents' associations within a multi-unit development. This paradox of voluntary, non-professional and inexperienced directors acting in a role which is governed by regulations and legislation which have sanctions as serious as prison sentences requires some consideration. Company Directors' responsibilities are wide and diverse, and they are required to act in a manner which places the company's interests

6 ODCE, *Company Law Handbook on Residential Property Owners' Management Companies ('Management Companies')* (Dublin, 2008), 44.

ahead of the director's own interests.[7] Section 16 of the Multi-Unit Developments Act sets out that a person shall not be appointed as a director of an owners' management company for life or if such appointment is for a term greater than three years. In addition to this, the company constitution will also have a provision for the rotation of directors for example:

> 'At the first annual general meeting of the company all the directors shall retire from office, and at the annual general meeting in every subsequent year, one-third of the directors for the time being, or, if their number is not three or a multiple of three, then the number nearest one-third shall retire from office.
>
> The directors to retire in every year shall be those who have been longest in office since the last election, but as between persons who became directors on the same day, those to retire shall (unless they otherwise agree amongst themselves) be determined by a lot.
>
> A retiring director shall be eligible for re-election.'

Most OMCs struggle every year to find new directors who are willing to be appointed to the board to fulfil corporate, legal and fiduciary duties as the role can be time consuming and is extremely onerous. The provisions set out above, both in the Act and the company constitution, are far removed from the reality in practice. Although directors can be protected from their exposure to liability by the OMC where the OMC puts in place a directors' and officers' insurance policy, they still run the risk of criticism from the members. Particularly where major decisions have to be made such as an urgent cash call for some emergency that has occurred where there are insufficient funds available in the sinking-fund to deal with it. In some ways, urgent cash calls may be viewed as a consequence of poor management and it is this type of scenario that an owner does not want to become embroiled in or tarnished with. Urgent cash calls in an OMC are as result of owners not setting aside sufficient funds in the sinking-fund. This sinking-fund time bomb is discussed in more detail in Chapter 5. The question of why owners do not set aside sufficient funds is one that can be examined by considering the general culture within the OMC.

---

7 ODCE, *Company Law Handbook on Residential Property Owners' Management Companies ('Management Companies')* (Dublin, 2008), 78.

7. The culture within an OMC

> 'There is nothing accidental about cultural strengths ... there is a relationship between an organisation's culture and its performance.'
>
> *Agnes Heller*

In many OMCs an independent and professional firm of managing agents are appointed by the directors to manage the OMCs day-to-day affairs. As the Managing Agent is merely appointed as a servant to the OMC, it is the directors of the OMC that have the power to instruct the managing agent on all matters of business. Given that all directors are property owners and are sometimes inexperienced in corporate governance, this arrangement exposes the possibility of biased decision making. For example, the apportionment of annual service charges may not always be set out in the lease agreements and where it is, it can sometimes be lawfully varied by the directors of the management company by passing a special resolution at a company meeting. In order for a proposal to amend the apportionment of service charges to be successfully rejected it must be disapproved by not less than 75 percent of the members present and voting at the AGM.[8] Given the low turnout and apathy of property owners in general, there is a good chance that such a proposal will succeed and the director will also succeed in amending the apportionment to their own advantage. In this case, if the annual service charge budget apportionment was to be changed from equal per unit or a set amount per unit, to apportionment on the size of the unit, and the directors unit was half the size of others, then their annual service charge could potentially reduce by half. Given that the role of the managing agent is to act as the servant to the OMC and carry out the instructions of the directors, and although they may identify this as a bad bargain for other property owners there is little that they can do. The directors have the power to make such decisions, the managing agent's interest lies in keeping their job by dutifully carrying out the wishes of the directors and, the members have the least amount of power in this situation mainly due to collective apathy. Some members of OMCs may dispute the apportionment of service charges for a long period of time in order to secure the most reduced annual service charge per year. Although there are provisions for the application of the annual service charge in the Multi-Unit Developments Act 2011 at s 18, and also in the lease agreements there still remains scope for

---

8 Multi-Unit Developments Act 2011, s 18, 4(b).

technical disputes which can vary the amount payable by any one individual property owner.

While directors can be protected by the implementation of a directors' and officers' insurance policy, there remains some circumstances where the cost of a misjudged decision cannot be indemnified. For example, a member of the OMC encroaches on the common areas by building a structure and the director's first response is to call a meeting of all members to discuss this whereby they are the subject of an enquiry. This can cause a huge amount of distress to those who have to live with each other, pitching one neighbour against another. It can create great divides and it can have a long-term effect on the quality of relationships between neighbours. If the initial approach is less confrontational then maybe relations between neighbours may not end up so damaged. It is not in the interest of the agent to prevent a director from taking certain actions even if those actions may be damaging to the best interests of the OMC because the director has the power to terminate the contract of the agent and appoint a new agent. These competing interests are all at play in the power balance within an OMC which makes navigating them more difficult.

In general, the culture within an OMC in Ireland is best described as apathetic. At one management company AGM, a property owner declared that although they owned their apartment for 20 years, they had never been to the building and asked the managing agent for directions to the building. In another case, a property owner said that he 'had not been in the building for the past 10 years'. An apathetic culture shows minimal concern for either people or performance, as individuals focus on their own self-interest. Property owners are apathetic about the implications of them being members of an OMC, in many cases they are disengaged and don't have any sense of commitment to their OMC. This is mainly evidenced by the lack of attention given to the payment of the service charges, the slow and non-payment of the annual service charge and sinking-fund levy, the poor attendance level at company meetings, the lack of replies to nomination forms for appointing a company director. A recent survey of attendance levels for the annual general meeting showed that there is an average turnout of less than 40 percent.[9]

Today, we can see that the influence of history is a deep-rooted

---

9 Survey of 30 various types of OMCs annual general meeting attendance rate in counties Galway, Sligo, Mayo, Dublin, Leitrim, Tipperary and Offaly in2017. Survey carried out by A.K. Property Services, 10 February 2018.

cause of this type of culture which stems from the Celtic Tiger era, circa 2000–2008 where the number of apartment blocks being constructed soared. Poor quality multi-unit developments were built everywhere during this period. The hangover from the notion of property developers 'raking it in' and 'creaming off' big profits from the ordinary individual who was being pushed by financial institutions to borrow large sums of money for property which ultimately lost most of its value, is the legacy which has left the reputation of the OMC in tatters and a left bad taste with most property owners. Property owners regretted their purchase, and were operating in a sphere of negative equity for so many years coupled with, in many cases, structural defects which the OMC is left with dealing with, and in most cases, to pay for the remedial works. High profile cases such as the Priory Hall in Dublin, where an apartment block of 187 apartments was evacuated due to fire safety defects, did little to improve the atmosphere and reputation of multi-unit developments and while this landmark case had the assistance of government in its resolution it was not without considerable heartbreak, suffering and losses for all of those involved.

The relationship between property owners and the property developer in many cases is one which has left the property owner with a sense of feeling hard-done-by. The outcome of that psychological contract that exposes the gap between what the purchaser had envisaged from a purchase off the plans and what the developer was to deliver, was an owner with a heavy financial burden in a market that had collapsed. The feeling that they did not get what they had paid for, and that the bargain was not met by the developer, determined their attitude to their investment. When a new property owner buys into an OMC, the existing culture can influence their attitudes and their behaviours also. This culture is at odds with the legal system (the multi-unit developments Act and the Companies Act) which is the bedrock of the OMC. The strength of this bedrock is slowly changing the culture by improving the attitudes, behaviours and values of members of the OMC as the sector matures over time.

Where an OMC is well run, has a good managing agent, no issues arising during any given year, a healthy bank balance and sinking-fund with overall good compliance of the payment of the annual service charge then it is likely that the turnout at company meetings will be very low. Where attendance figures for meetings are very high it is normally as a result of some great problems, contention, acrimony and lack of funds that motivates property owners to mobilise. It is the threat to their individual investment that they are more concerned about than the overall wellbeing of the OMC. The fact that 80 percent of apartments in the country are owned by property investors, faceless limited companies, who tend to be absent from the administration and day to day running of the company, it usually falls to the few remaining property owners who are in attendance at the annual general meeting, to either be appointed as a director or to be nominated as a director.[10] A nomination form, nominating a member of the company to be appointed as a director is usually sent to each member of the company with the notice of the annual general meeting. However, this opportunity is almost never used by members to propose a fellow member as a Director. The role of the director is seen as a thankless role with no reward. Furthermore, for self-managed OMCs that are managed by the company's Directors, in accordance with s 2 of the Property Services Regulation Act 2011, a person may not be remunerated, receive benefit in kind or any type of consideration for providing a property management service to an OMC unless they are the holders of a 'D' licence for the provision of property management services. The Act reads as follows:

> '"property service" means the provision, for consideration, in the State in respect of property located within or outside the State, of any of the following –
>
> a) the auction of property other than land
> b) the purchase or sale, by whatever means, of land
> c) the letting of land (including a letting in conacre or for the purposes of agistment), or
> d) property management services'

This stipulates that a director of a management company must hold a D licence and be formally appointed as an agent in order to receive any kind of remuneration for the work that they do when it comes to managing their OMC.

The problem of low turnout at the annual general meeting is that the numbers in attendance are so low that there is no choice in appointing a director. It is normally the same owners who attend every year and between them they keep getting re-elected as directors even when they would prefer not to be re-elected

10 Clúid, 'Request for Tenders for the Provision of A research report on Owners' Management Companies for Clúid Housing in collaboration with The Housing Agency (11 July 2017) <www.cluid.ie/wp-content/uploads/2017/07/17-07-11-RFT-OMC-research-FINAL.pdf, 16, accessed on 4 February 2018>.

but they feel that they have no choice. Some property owners may have personal and professional reasons for not wanting to be appointed as a director and that, coupled with the apathetic culture that exists within an OMC can create an administrative problem for the OMC. A person can choose not to be appointed as a director. The Office of the Director of Corporate Enforcement is explicit in this regard. They emphasise that the fact that one of the consequences of a director's resignation may be to leave the company with fewer directors than the statutory minimum, it is not of itself a legal impediment to the validity of his/her resignation. It is not the case that the 'second-last or last' director of the company enjoys any less of an entitlement to resign from his/her office than those directors who opted to resign sooner. The validity of the appointment of a director or his/her ceasing to hold office, depends on compliance with the company's articles of association, and not from the notice of the appointment/cessation being registered in the CRO.[11] Therefore, the directors may resign and leave the OMC with no directors. As most OMCs take the form of a Company Limited by Guarantee with no share capital, they must have a minimum of two directors. Where they fail in this regard, the company may be struck-off the company register. Given that the sitting directors have the best interest of the OMC in their mind, they are not likely to plunge the OMC into such a state of non-compliance and so they very often agree to be re-appointed as a director, simply because no-one else will put themselves forward.

[11] *Company Law Handbook on Residential Property Owners' Management Companies ('Management Companies')*, ODCE, Dublin, 2008, 61.

Chapter 5

The Building Investment Fund and the Annual Service Charge

1. The time-bomb sinking fund 51
2. Calculating the annual service charge 57
3. The debt recovery process 59
4. Excludable debt 68
5. Taxation 69
6. A sinking-fund case study on capital project management 70

The availability of funds in an OMC is key to the successful operation of the company and in this regard the timely collection of the building investment fund and the service charges are vital. Important information on the debt recovery process and the collection of service charges is set out in this chapter together with guidance on policies and procedures to adopt to ensure the best outcome.

1. The time-bomb sinking fund

The sinking-fund or building investment fund as it is sometimes known is a fund which is established by the OMC in accordance with s 19 of the Multi-Unit Developments Act 2011 as follows:

> (1) An owners' management company shall establish a building investment fund (in this Act referred to as a "sinking fund") for the purpose of discharging expenditure reasonably incurred on—
> (a) the refurbishment,
> (b) improvement,
> (c) maintenance of a non-recurring nature, or
> (d) advice from a suitably qualified person relating to paragraphs (a) to (c),
>
> of the multi-unit development in respect of which the owners' management company stands established.
>
> (2) Expenditure shall be regarded as being expenditure on maintenance of a non-recurring nature where—
> (a) the expenditure relates to a matter in respect of

which expenditure is not generally incurred in each year,

(b) it is certified by the Directors of the owners' management company as being expenditure on maintenance of a nonrecurring nature, and

(c) the expenditure is approved by a meeting of the members of the owners' management company as being expenditure of a non-recurring nature.

(3) The owner of each unit in a multi-unit development (including a person who is the developer or building contractor of the development) shall be obliged to make payment to the sinking fund of the amount of contribution fixed in respect of the unit concerned in accordance with this section.

(4) For the purposes of this section a developer or building contractor, as the case may be, shall be regarded to be the owner of a unit in a multi-unit development the first sale of which unit has not been completed, as and from the day on which the first sale of a residential unit in the relevant part of the development is closed.

(5) Subject to subsection (6) the amount of the contribution to be paid as respects a unit by each unit owner of such a unit to the sinking fund in respect of a particular year shall be the amount of €200 or such other amount as may be agreed by a meeting of the members as the contribution in respect of the year concerned.

(6) The obligation to establish a sinking fund and to make contributions to such fund shall apply on the happening of the later of—

(a) the passing of a period of 3 years since the first transfer of the ownership of a unit in the multi-unit development concerned, or

(b) the expiry of 18 months from the coming into operation of this section.

(7) The contributions made to the sinking fund shall be held in a separate account and in a manner which identifies these funds as belonging to the sinking fund and such funds shall not be used or expended on matters other than expenditure of a type referred to in subsection (1).

(8) Where a dispute arises in relation to whether assets of an owners' management company should properly be applied to the sinking fund account or the annual service charges account the dispute may be the subject of an application under section 24.

As the Act specifies it is a separate bank account which is ring-fenced to provide for capital expenditure of a non-recurring nature. It is important to note that the wording in the Act indicates that the sinking-fund must be held in liquid form. OMCs cannot invest sinking-funds in property or stocks or shares as this would put the funds at risk. Section 19(2) of the Act states that it must be for expenditure of a non-recurring nature. However, this conflicts somewhat with section 19(1) where it states that it is for expenditure reasonably incurred on improvement or maintenance. The problem with this, is that some commentators on the subject are of the view that the sinking-fund should not be spent on projects such as painting of the buildings as this type of a project is deemed to be maintenance of a recurring nature on the one hand, and yet, within the meaning of s 19(1) it may also be deemed to be expenditure reasonably incurred on improvement or maintenance. The Act reconciles this conflict at s 19(2)(c) where it states that the expenditure will comply with the Act whereby it is approved by a meeting of the members of the owners' management company as being expenditure of a non-recurring nature. This means that where there is a disagreement among members and directors as to what constitutes recurring or non-recurring expenditure, once the expenditure is approved by a meeting then the sinking-fund may be used.

This sinking-fund should provide for projects such as long-term planned maintenance and refurbishment such as installation and/or replacement of lifts, floor coverings, roof replacement, internal and external redecoration, etc. The fund will also cover unplanned expenses which are not covered by insurance such as legal actions, roof repairs, road repairs, etc. Prudent sinking-fund provision by OMCs is essential to the long-term sustainability of the development. There is a legitimate concern and a variety of studies which show that the majority of OMCs in Ireland today do not have adequate funds set aside and that there exists a serious deficit in sinking-fund provisions in OMCs. In their report entitled *Sinking Funds in Apartments, Meeting the Challenge,* The Society of Chartered Surveyors of Ireland note that many OMCs, in particular apartment complexes, are not adequately budgeting for future building investment needs. It is the view of The Apartment Owners' Network[1] that when, in the future, the funding crisis crystallises in an OMC it will be to the local council

---

1 Apartment Owners' Network, 'Submission to Forward Planning Section Department of Housing Planning and Local Government on Updated Draft Design Standards for New Apartments – Guidelines for Planning Authorities', 18 January 2018.

that residents will turn for financial support. Precedents for a local authority footing the bill have already been set in the context of remediation of construction defects in apartment developments. Media reports indicate that Priory Hall cost Dublin City Council ('DCC') €36.4m, approximately.[2] Reports indicate that Longboat Quay cost DCC €3.1m approximately.[3]

One of the main reasons for this deficit in sinking-funds in OMCs is due to lack of regulation of the OMC. The Multi-Unit Developments Act 2011 states that a sinking-fund must be established but it falls short of specifying what level of a fund. The level of the fund is at the discretion of the members and directors. In one case study it was shown that members and directors ranked grass cutting as almost twice as important as the sinking-fund.[4] While the setting aside of funds is at the discretion of the members and directors of the OMC, there is a conflict in that their main interest when setting the annual service charge budget and sinking-fund provision is to keep the charges as low as possible. The Law Reform Commission Report on Multi-Unit Developments recommended the establishment of a sinking-fund, however, as there is no enforcement of the Act, there are no sanctions and because there is no regulation in the area of the OMC, it is simply left to the discretion of the property owners to decide how much is set aside each year.[5]

Upon examining the sinking-fund provision in the Act, there are a number of issues that arise within the context of how OMCs are administered in practice today. On the one hand, the Act stipulates the setting up a mandatory sinking-fund but does not lay down what amount is to be set aside. It makes a recommendation of €200 per year but this is only a recommendation and not a requirement. In practice, the service charge recovery and OMC liquidity are widely accepted as the most significant and immediate financial

---

2 Olivia Kelly, 'Priory Hall refurbishment bill likely to exceed €36.4m', *The Irish Times* (Dublin, 22 November 2016) <https://www.irishtimes.com/news/social-affairs/priory-hall-refurbishment-bill-likely-to-exceed-36-4m-1.2877185>.

3 Olivia Kelly, 'Deal worth €3.1m agreed to remedy Longboat Quay defects', *The Irish Times* (Dublin, 19 December 2016) <https://www.irishtimes.com/news/environment/deal-worth-3-1m-agreed-to-remedy-longboat-quay-defects-1.2910796>.

4 Adele McKeown, *Service Charge Collection in Multi-Unit Developments*, Dublin Institute of Technology, 2016.

5 Law Reform Commission, *Report on Multi-Unit Developments* (LRC 90—2008), p 159, '*the commission recognises the need to deal with fundamental problems that might arise in a development, such as a serious deficit in building investment fund (sinking fund).*'

challenges confronting OMCs. The Law Reform Commission considered this in their report on Multi Unit Developments.[6] As far back as 2008 it was acknowledged that a high proportion of multi-unit developments in Ireland had no sinking-fund in place. A survey in 2007 by Dublin City Council noted:

> '[i]n a recent review, the adequacy of sinking-funds in a simple scheme was examined, one which did not have CCTV, underground car parking or any water or sewerage pumps. This review found that the sinking-fund amount needed for a ten-year refurbishment cycle is estimated to be approximately €420 per unit per annum.'[7]

The report goes on to say that if a sinking-fund is not built up over a period of time then property owners will be faced with large cash calls that they may not be able to afford and so the building will fall into disrepair. It is for all of these reasons cited that the Law Reform Commission recommends that there should be a clear statutory obligation on an OMCs to establish a sinking-fund. The provision ultimately set out in the Multi-Unit Developments Act 2011 is weak in that it only goes half way. It states that a fund must be set up but does not stipulate how much each year should be set aside. It states *'or such other amounts as may be agreed by a meeting of the members'*. It is this particular shortcoming that has seen this time bomb develop. As long as property owners have the discretion to set the fund as they see fit, then, given competing interests between owners who intend to sell their apartments in the short term and those who intend to remain as property owners in the long term, it is a constant battle to ensure that the appropriate amount is set aside each year. OMCs are, in practical terms, as well-off today as they were 10 years ago when that survey was completed.

In April 2018 the Apartment Owners' Network presented to the Joint Oireachtas Committee on Housing Planning and Local Government and highlighted the issue of the absence of sinking-funds in multi-unit developments stating that without urgent reform, considerable funding may be required from either local

6 Law Reform Commission, *Report on Multi-Unit Developments* (LRC 90—2008), 136.

7 Evelyn Hanlon, Private Housing Unit, Dublin City Council, *Successful Apartment Living Part 2; Survey of Service Charges, Design, Management and Owners' Attitudes in 193 Private Apartment Schemes in Dublin City*, June 2007, 16, 4.6: review of debtors and sinking funds.

authorities or national government to 'bail out' crisis owners' management companies.

The Law Reform Commission reviewed approaches adopted in other jurisdictions on sinking-funds. Sinking funds are not compulsory in all common law states (those which share a similar legal heritage with Ireland) but there is an increasing trend towards making them mandatory. Canadian provinces and Australian states and territories have specific legislative provision for the mandatory establishment of a sinking-fund.[8] Similarly, South Africa has enacted legislation requiring establishment of a general fund for every development for the purposes of, amongst other things; reasonable provision for future maintenance and repairs.[9] In England and Wales, the Commonhold and Leasehold Reform Act 2002 requires the mandatory establishment of a reserve fund in certain circumstances. Similarly, the Singapore Building Maintenance and Strata Management Act 2004 requires the establishment of a fund which covers service charges, administrative costs and all expenses normally associated with building investment funds prior to the establishment of the owners' association.

A number of elements of the legislation in these States should be noted. In the case of smaller developments, (first approach) legislation generally provides that reserve funds should be set up only at the discretion of the owners' associations. The Law Reform Commission said that they saw 'great merit in this approach'.[10]

Legislation dealing with sinking-funds in other countries varies in terms of detail on the type of expenditure to be covered. For example, s 116 of the South Australian Community Titles Act 1996 provides that the fund should be used only for 'non-recurrent expenditure' which is defined as 'expenditure for a particular purpose that is normally made less frequently than once a year'. Some legislation uses a basic, catch-all formula: 'a reserve fund shall be used solely for the purpose of major repair and replacement of the common elements and assets of the [owners' association].'[11] (Second approach.)

---

[8] Law Reform Commission, *Report on Multi-Unit Developments* (LRC 90—2008), 137.

[9] Law Reform Commission, *Report on Multi-Unit Developments* (LRC 90—2008), 137.

[10] Law Reform Commission, *Report on Multi-Unit Developments* (LRC 90—2008), 138.

[11] Law Reform Commission, *Report on Multi-Unit Developments* (LRC 90—2008), 138.

The Law Reform Commission considered that a composite of both approaches was preferable and that in the interest of best practice, guidelines should be devised which list the expenses which should be covered by the fund, this list is not and should not be exhaustive. This is ultimately the list as set out in s 19(1) a–d of the Act as set out previously.

The Commission noted the position, but did not favour the approach of that in the England and Wales Commonhold and Leasehold Reform Act 2002 whereby the directors of the 'commonhold association' (that is the equivalent to our OMC) can set up a reserve fund at the discretion of the members or in response to a 'reserve study'. This reserve study is an inspection of the common areas of the buildings which must take place every 10 years in order to determine whether the establishment of a reserve fund is necessary. The Law Reform Commission noted that a mandatory approach was preferable on three grounds:

1. When the cost of large-scale repair or replacement within the development arises, the unit owners do not have to make a large pay-out as they have accumulated funds developed over many years through relatively small annual contributions to cover such costs;
2. As evidenced by some of the problems in Ireland up to 2007 where the establishment of a fund is prudent but discretionary, it is common for developments to opt against the establishment until funds are needed urgently;
3. The existence of a mature building investment fund will prove a valuable asset tied to the property on sale of the unit and forms part of the capital value of the property.

In examining ground number two above, the current position today whereby the Multi-Unit Developments Act 2011 sets out the provision that a sinking-fund must be established but the reality is, that because there is no minimum amount to be set aside each year then OMCs remain as impecunious today as they did in 2007 when the Law Reform Commission was preparing their report. For sinking-funds in OMCs, little has changed in that regard.

2. Calculating the annual service charge

The annual service charge which is payable by members of an OMC is set to provide for all expenditure during the year within the OMC. It follows then that the amount of service charge liability that each owner will have will depend mainly on two factors. The non-exhaustive list of cost items on the annual service charge budget and the number of units in the development that will be paying to cover such costs. A simple illustration of how the budget is calculated can be seen in Budget A and Budget B, below. Budget A indicates that there are internal common area corridors and stairwells which require additional cost items such as fire alarm panel, fire extinguishers, cleaning, lifts, etc. Budget B has no such requirements. Notwithstanding the discrepancy in the number and type of costs on each budget, what is notable is that the total figure of the budget for each development can be the same but it is the apportionment of the total cost that will determine what the service charge per unit will be. Some cost items may be fixed such as auditor's fees and others may increase proportionate to the number of units in the development such as insurance and managing agent fees. Some developments will have different requirements than others. Each multi-unit development is unique in its location, size, and design, and all of these factors will determine what the annual service charge will be. It is therefore not possible to generalise about what the average service charge should or could be as there is no such thing as an average multi-unit development.

Historically, many OMCs have had a very low recovery rate of service charges which was primarily due to the lack of understanding by property owners of their obligations and lack of regulation and legislation in the area of property management. Although this situation has improved considerably since the enactment of the Multi-Unit Developments Act 2011 and the implementation of the Property Services Regulatory Authority in 2012, there still remains a need to establish effective enforcement measures to ensure that property owners are paying the annual service charges to their OMC to give efficacy to their OMC. As the law stands, service charges are recoverable as a simple contract debt in a court of competent jurisdiction and this remedy is an inappropriate remedy in this circumstance. It is inappropriate because it is a lengthy and expensive process. A well-run OMC should have a 'company policy for the collection of service charges' which sets out the rules and timeframe for the payment of the Annual Service Charge. This company policy should be discussed and approved at the annual general meeting where a resolution is passed adopting the policy which is then binding on each member. This will be followed by a 'Request for Payment – Reminder' to all property owners one month after the initial 'Request for Payment' is sent which states that if full payment has not been received or a payment plan is not in place within three months after the date of the annual general meeting, a levy may be applied. When the three months has passed the property owner will be notified that the levy has been applied and that their account will be passed to the OMCs solicitors for collection if payment has not been received. All legal costs associated with the collection of the debt will be borne by the property owner.

Budget A – 30 Apartments	
Insurance	€4,800.00
Electricity	€3,000.00
Cleaning	€2,400.00
Grounds Maintenance	€5,700.00
Fire Maintenance	€2,000.00
Refuse	€4,000.00
Lift Maintenance	€1,200.00
Eir phone line for lift	€310.00
Carpark Clamping	€600.00
Repairs & Maint.	€3,000.00
Window Cleaning	€1,050.00
Auditors Fees	€700.00
Managing Agents Fees	€7,500.00
Sundry	€500.00
Sub Total	**€36,760.00**
Service Charge p.u.	€1,225.33
Plus Sinking Fund p.u.	€250.00
Total Due equal per unit	**€1,475.33**

Budget B – 60 Townhouses and Apartments	
Insurance	€11,060.00
Auditor's Fees	€700.00
Managing Agents Fees	€15,000.00
Grounds Maintenance	€8,000.00
Sundry	€2,000.00
Sub Total	**€36,760.00**
Total Sq. Ft.	51750
Apartment sq. ft.	575
Townhouse sq. ft.	1150
Apartment Service Chg	€408.44
Plus Sinking Fund	€250.00
Total Apartment Due	**€658.44**
Townhouse Service Chg	€816.89
Plus Sinking Fund	€250.00
Total Townhouse Due	**€1,066.89**

3. The debt recovery process

In commencing the process of debt recovery for outstanding service charges, the OMC must firstly engage the services of a solicitor and ensure that they can provide the necessary accurate information in relation to the debt. After the initial letter of demand is sent to the debtor by the solicitor and the debtor has not responded, then the next step is to commence legal proceedings by issuing a statement of claim. This statement of claim will be presented to the relevant court by the solicitor.

There are three jurisdictions within which civil proceedings may be taken for debt recovery.

1. The District Court – For debts up to €15,000. There are approximately 220 District Courts throughout the country, which are administered by 44 Court Offices;
2. The Circuit Court – For debts between €15,000 and €75,000. There are 28 Circuit Courts throughout the country, each administered by its own Court Office;
3. The High Court – For debts over €75,000. There is one High Court located at the Four Courts in Dublin.

The information required for the statement of claim for the District Court is as follows:

1. A copy of the lease agreement of the property: a property owner signs a lease agreement upon the purchase of their property and is bound by several covenants including that of the payment of the annual service charge;
2. Statement of account: this statement will give details of how the debt was accumulated. It may be only one-year service charges or it may be several years of service charges that are being pursued. There may be interest added to the particular account. The provisions for adding interest to service charge accounts are normally set out in the lease agreements of each OMC;
3. Invoices: the invoices which are required are those which were initially raised and delivered to the property owner at the time that the payment was due. The total amount of these invoices should equal the amount outstanding on the statement of account;
4. A copy of the annual accounts of the OMC;
5. A copy of the letters of demand and relevant correspondence sent from the OMC to the property owner in relation to the debt;
6. The certificate of incorporation of the OMC;
7. The company constitution of the OMC incorporating the memorandum and articles of association.

In addition to this, the solicitor will be seeking information on the legal status of the debtor and all relevant information required such as the basis of claim and the address and contact details of the debtor.

Although this process is effective in some circumstances, it is simply not an efficient means of dealing with unpaid service charges and sinking-fund payments mainly because a new debt is incurred every twelve months in the form of the new service charge and a new sinking-fund contribution. The court process is a lengthy one and while an annual service charge is being pursued through the courts, by the time it is resolved and payment is received, the next annual service charge may have already been levied. Unless the property owner in question has turned over a 'new leaf' and decided to become 'compliant' the lengthy process of initiating legal proceedings in the courts must commence again for the OMC. The courts do not allow for an additional service charge, levied in the following year, to be added to a claim, therefore, a new and separate legal action must commence against the same owner. The costs associated with this type of service charge recovery are prohibitive to the average OMC. In addition to this, it can result in more than one legal action being taken against an individual property owner at any one time. Given that the process is arduous and lengthy in the first instance, to have to repeat this process over and over again is simply not an efficient remedy for the situation. This challenge of non-payment of service charges is also a major issue in other jurisdictions that have developed similar enforcement mechanisms to ours such as:

- Denial of the right to vote – This 'enforcement mechanism' is a weak one as property owners who disregard their obligation to their OMC are unlikely to attend company meetings. Those who do attend company meetings are generally compliant, engaged and active within their OMC;
- Name and shame sanctions – The effectiveness of this is dependent on the moral, ethical and civic values of each individual property owner. The property owner who is non-compliant and disregardful of their obligations normally will not possess such values in relation to the payment of their annual service charge which renders this measure ineffective. Other issues which arise here include the General Data Protection Regulation (GDPR). In some circumstances naming and shaming will be a breach of data protection law;

- The suspension of services – This can only be done in some circumstances. Suspending a car-parking service by clamping a car is only effective to those who own a car. Also, in a housing estate where the owner has the freehold of their own individual property in that the common areas do not extend into the driveway of the house, then the management company cannot encroach on their own private property to clamp their car and so there is no service to suspend here. If the house is rented to a tenant, then the management company cannot clamp a tenant's car as the legal obligation to pay the annual service charge lies with the property owner and not the tenant. A sewerage treatment plant cannot be switched to provide for only some houses in the development as its infrastructure is set up to serve all houses.

These enforcement measures are inadequate in dealing with the issue. The Law Reform Commission recommended that alternative enforcement mechanisms should be examined and developed. Although most lease agreements provide for interest being charged, The Multi-Unit Developments Act 2011 missed an opportunity to include a penalty for late payment. This sanction is used in Puerto Rico and Singapore. In Puerto Rico, 10 percent interest may be charged on any contributions which are more than 15 days overdue. In Singapore, unit owners can be prosecuted for failure to pay within two weeks of a written demand for payment from their management company, the maximum fine being a fine of $10,000 plus a sum not exceeding $100 for every day the service charge remains unpaid.[12] While the Law Reform Commission found that these measures were too Draconian in nature for the Irish situation, they allowed for the pendulum to swing too far in the opposite direction by making no provisions in this regard.

The Canadian province, Ontario, specifically targets property owners who fail to pay service charges by requiring tenants of the defaulting landlord to pay the service charge value to the OMC rather than paying rent to the landlord. Thus, the payment can constitute payment towards rent under the lease.[13] In Ireland, this type of an enforcement measure is more likely to bear results due to the high number of OMC properties that are investor owned and rented. According to Census 2016, nearly 80 percent

---

[12] Law Reform Commission, *Report on Multi-Unit Developments* (LRC 90—2008), 163.

[13] Law Reform Commission, *Report on Multi-Unit Developments* (LRC 90—2008), p 162; s 87(6), Ontario Condominium Act 1998, C 19.

of apartments in Ireland are rented; approximately 20 percent are social rented (housing association or local authority) and nearly 60 percent are rented privately. The remaining 20 percent are owner occupied.[14] Due to the high number of OMC properties that are rented, this Ontario approach is one which would be very effective in Ireland.

A forfeiture provision which is similar to a bank's right to foreclose which is typical in a commercial lease does not operate in the residential head leases in Ireland. This measure has not been part of our culture in Ireland but in Finland where it is part of their culture, it acts as a threat and deterrent to defaulters.

Given the above-mentioned lack of enforcement and measures available to the OMC in Ireland in the pursuit of outstanding service charges, the question remains as to what the equitable remedy is for the OMC. That is, the compliant property owner as against the non-compliant property owner. The lease agreements which are attached to the title deeds of each property in an OMC normally include various agreements and covenants such as:

> 'The assured easements shall be granted to the purchaser upon the conditions herein stipulated and that these presents shall contain such covenants, conditions and provisions to secure the proper management of the Estate/ Common areas in the future and to determine and enforce the purchaser's ability to contribute towards the cost of such management as are herein after contained and that the Management Company shall join in these presents for the purpose of achieving these objectives
>
> .... It is hereby declared that the grant of the assured easements is subject to and conditional upon .... the purchaser performing and observing the covenants and obligations, agreements, stipulations and restrictions on the part of the purchaser set out in the third schedule .....pay the management company said costs and expenses .. herein after called 'the service charges.'

These provisions state that the easements and privileges provided

14 Analysis of Census 2016 contained in Clúid, 'Requests for Tenders for the Provision of a Research Report on Owners' Management Companies for Clúid in collaboration with The Housing Agency (11 July 2017), available on <www.cluid.ie/wp-content/uploads/2017/07/17-07-11-RFT-OMC-research-FINAL.pdf>.

by the OMC to the property owner are subject to the property owner complying with the terms of the lease which includes, *inter alia*, to pay the annual service charge. The problem for many OMCs when they try to enforce this term of the lease agreement is that they may not be permitted to do so by the courts. For example, where an OMC restricts vehicular access to a property owner by excluding them from a database that allows a vehicular electric gate to open for users who are authorised to use the gate for access to the car park area of the apartment block. In this situation the pedestrian access is not restricted and, as such, the owner is not locked out of their property as they still have access by the pedestrian gate. This property owner can obtain an interlocutory injunction against the OMC preventing the OMC from restricting vehicular access. The cost to the OMC of defending such an action in court is generally prohibitive given the reasons why the OMC restricted access in the first place which is because the property owner in question is non-compliant with the terms of the lease agreement in that they are not paying their service charges. Non-payment of the service charges leaves the OMC in an impecunious state. What transpires in situations where there are legal battles between an OMC and one of its members is a type of circular dependency whereby on the one hand there are two parties to the action and on the other hand one of the parties has a real interest in the other party. This circular dependency can be examined in the following scenario. If we consider a hypothetical OMC consisting of 20 apartments. Each apartment service charge is €1,000. One delinquent property owner owns seven apartments and has not paid service charges for two consecutive years and has also been successful in frustrating the debt recovery process through the courts so the service charges remain outstanding. The legal fees associated with the pursuit of these outstanding service charges are borne by the OMC but with a deficit of €14,000 in the coffers, where will the money come from to pay the legal fees in the short-term? What happens is that there is either an increase in the annual service charge or a levy added to the service charges to cover this cost or both. The delinquent property owner is therefore paying their share of the legal costs incurred to take a legal action against them.

Similarly, an OMC may, seek to interrupt the easement of a power supply to an apartment due to the non-payment of the annual service charge. Liability issues that arise include the risk of personal injury and a tortious claim against the OMC even though the OMC takes steps to avoid a tortious claim where negligence can be proven by giving advance notice of a power outage for a short period of time with the intention of making the resident of the apartment aware that there will be no power during a particular period of time and giving them ample time to prepare for the outage.

As the system stands, the OMC is at risk of being successfully sued if they seek to enforce the terms of the lease agreements in these examples. This diminishes the power that the OMC has to successfully recover the service charges from delinquent property owners. In the latter case, given that the collective responsibility nature of the OMC is dependent upon the co-operation of all involved it would seem that to protect a tenant who has been well informed in advance of a short outage of power in an apartment over and above a resident who is walking down a stairs where the common area electricity supply has been disconnected by the utility company due to the fact that the OMC had no money to pay the bill, or that the buildings are not insured because the OMC has no money, then there is a greater loss to the majority of property owners than there would be for one property owner who is well informed of a slight interruption in power supply in order that the OMC may force the property owner to comply with his obligations and pay the service charge. The OMC must do everything it can to represent and protect the majority of property owners and not the minority. The law exists to protect those who abide by it and not to shield those who disregard it.

The situation concerning the enforceability of a covenant that requires a positive obligation is established in the common law case of *Halsall v Brizzell*[15] which sets out the rule in relation to housing estates where one cannot have the benefit without the burden. In this High Court case, Upjohn J held that the owner 'could not claim the benefit of the facilities without having to pay as well. He could not exercise the rights without paying his costs of ensuring that they could be exercised.' This rule was further distinguished in the House of Lords case of *Rhone v Stephens*[16] where Lord Templeman referred to *Halsall v Brizell* by stating that 'the defendant could, at least in theory, choose between enjoying the right and paying his proportion of the cost or alternatively giving up the right and saving his money.'

An international element has recently been creeping into OMCs in Ireland that is a cause of further problems for property owners

---

15 *Halsall v Brizzell* (1957) CH 169.

16 *Rhone v Stephens* [1994] UKHL 3.

when it comes to the payment of the annual service charge. There are now more OMC owners who are living abroad in the UK and Europe than ever before. The problem is when they are disregardful of their obligation in the payment of the annual service charge, there is little legal remedy available to the OMC. As we have seen, the cost of pursuing a property owner for outstanding service charges through the courts in Ireland is almost prohibitive to OMCs in that it is so costly. However, to consider pursuing a debt of outstanding service charges in another jurisdiction would be even more costly.

The impecunious nature of the OMC is a consequence of self-interest and voluntarism. A group of property owners coming together in a voluntary capacity to carry out their duties in law to their OMC requires them to set the annual service charge budget and as per the Multi-Unit Developments Act s.19(5) to set aside an amount for the sinking-fund as they see fit. The problem with this is that it is not in the interest of a property owner who intends to 'flip' their investment in a short period of time to set aside considerable sums of their own money to be availed of by the future owner of their unit. Additionally, property owners who are setting the annual service charge are mainly concerned with having the 'lowest annual service charge' and keeping the cost of running the OMC to the minimum instead of focussing on the long-term survival of the development.

While most property owners comply with the terms of their lease agreements and pay their annual service charges it is a reality that there are property owners who will always seek to frustrate the process and avoid paying the annual service charge taking desperate measures such as transferring their apartment to their son or daughter where it is neither in the interest of the vendor to pay the outstanding service charges nor is it in the interest of the purchaser to compel the vendor to pay the outstanding service charges as they are in essence 'one' and they may make an agreement for the sale to close without the outstanding service charges being paid to the OMC.

In the case of *Waterside Management Company Limited v Brendan and Asta Kelly*[17] the owners had frustrated the process for a number of years, the managing agent could not find them, they were not making any contact with their OMC or replying to any correspondence. The court heard that the managing agent had

[17] [2013] IEHC 143.

called to their home on twelve occasions to no avail. The debt on their five apartments had accrued for a period of more than five years ending with the OMC losing an appeal hearing in the High Court.

This culture in OMCs is prevalent throughout the country and stems from the building stage of a multi-unit development. At this stage, the property Developer sets the annual service charge in his/her own interest. That is, a lower annual service charge is more appealing to a prospective purchaser than a higher annual service charge. The developer's interest is selling the units in the development and there is neither an incentive nor regulation in place to ensure that an accurate and appropriate service charge has been formulated for the long-term survival of the development. Once the units are sold and the group of property owners take over to set their own annual service charge budget as officers in their own OMC they then face an uphill battle of driving against the culture of the 'lowest annual service charge' in order to build a sinking-fund which will have the capacity and financial means to cater for the required investment in the future for the OMC. Given the recession years from 2008 to 2016 there has been almost no sinking-funds set aside in OMCs and this is the main reason why so many OMCs today are characterised as a financial time bomb.[18] This poor level of sinking-fund provision amounts to a 'hot-potato scenario' being passed from the seller to the buyer of a unit each time and property owners will get burned when substantial funds for building refurbishment are required where they will face severe service charge increases and/or immediate cash calls. In situations where property owners are not in a position to pay up then the OMC faces the possibility of not having sufficient funds to meet its obligations and this will create uncertainty over the ability of the company to continue as a going concern.

What is required to address this conflict of interest is the implementation of a legal requirement for the developer at development stage to employ an independent quantity surveyor to formulate an appropriate service charge and sinking-fund levy for the OMC for the long-term viability of the development. Once the first service charge and sinking-fund levy has been set, it should then be a legal requirement that all officers of the OMC

[18] Apartment Owners' Network: Presentation to Joint Oireachtas Committee on Housing, Planning & Local Government on the 19 April 2018 from, David Rouse and Bryan Maher, Issues Impacting Apartment and Multi Unit Development. https://apartmentownersnetwork.org/?s=presentation+to+oireachtas accessed 27 January 2019.

adhere to prudent provision of such funds thereafter whereby sanctions will apply in the event that this is not complied with.

In March 2018, the Department of Housing, Planning and Local Government issued guidelines for planning authorities[19] which recommended that planning applications for apartment developments shall include a building lifecycle report which in turn includes an assessment of long term running and maintenance costs as they would apply on a per residential unit basis at the time of application, as well as demonstrating what measures have been specifically considered by the proposer to effectively manage and reduce costs for the benefit of residents. The Apartment Owners' Network note that this recommendation is being adhered to in some cases but not all.

4. Excludable debt

Outstanding service charge and sinking-fund payments are debts due by a property owner to their OMC. Like any other debt, it can be pursued as a simple contract debt in a court of competent jurisdiction. New legislation in the area of the Personal Insolvency Act 2012 sets out at s 2 that service charges are an excludable debt:

> '"excludable debt" in relation to a debtor, means any: ....
> (f) debt due by the debtor to any owners' management company in respect of annual service charges under section 18 of the Multi-Unit Developments Act 2011 or contributions due under section 19 of that Act.'

This means that when a Personal Insolvency Agreement is being drawn up for an individual, it is *only* with the consent of the OMC that the outstanding service charges can be deemed to be a debt included in a Personal Insolvency Agreement. Given the nature of the OMC where those who have carried the financial burden in the short-term for those who have not paid their service charges, it is unlikely that any OMC would vote to allow the service charge to be included in any Personal Insolvency Agreement so that they may be negotiated downwards or even written off. This is an acknowledgement by the legislature of the position that service charges occupy which is a beneficial position for the

[19] Department of Housing, Planning and Local Government, *Sustainable Urban Housing: Design Standards for New Apartments Guidelines for Planning Authorities*, March 2018, 35.

OMC considering that most other excludable debts in Ireland are State-owned debts, e.g. VAT, LPT, PRSI, local authority rates, etc.

The fact that service charge debt is treated in such a manner as an excludable debt, shows us that public policy takes into consideration the value that the payment of the annual service charge makes to the environment and those who reside in it. A poor public policy would be one where buildings were allowed to fall into disrepair throughout the wider community and as a consequence, pose a danger to those residing there and nearby. The law exists to protect us, and from this perspective it has a role to play in doing so. However, this must be balanced with the extent which the State should dictate how an individual's private property should be managed, and whether a mandatory requirement applicable to existing developments could constitute an interference with the individual's constitutional right to private property. The Law Reform Commission refer to this and note the exigencies of the common good result in necessary conditions being attached to private property ownership. For example, owners of buildings which are subject to preservation orders are limited in the changes they can make to their own private property and the requirement of planning permission before construction can take place is an example of how the right to private property is not absolute. The government at local and national level have a role to play in the operation of an OMC and must be involved, engaged and active in how these OMCs operate.

5. Taxation

While the government is not responsible for funding private property, equally it must ensure that fiscal measures which are punitive to members of OMCs are addressed. Schemes which allow for tax relief generally take the form of the rebate being received through the income tax system. The problem for the OMC in this regard is that the OMC is a not-for-profit company that is, it is not registered for income tax or corporation tax and there is no channel therefore for the OMC to avail of schemes such as the Home Renovation Incentive Scheme despite the fact that they may invest heavily on renovating the common areas of a building. As it is, the OMC must fund all capital projects in their entirety. There is no mechanism for claiming the VAT element of works back to the OMC as they are generally not registered for VAT. These works are often capital projects and involve large sums of money from the sinking-fund. This is directly disadvantageous to members of an OMC and therefore discriminatory in that it disproportionately places a tax burden on some property owners, i.e. members of an OMC, whilst providing tax relief to other property owners, i.e. those who are not members of an OMC.

6. A sinking-fund case study on capital project management

A particular apartment development comprises two apartment buildings with a total of 33 residential apartments. Built in the 1960s this OMC is operating for over six decades.

From the period 2009 to 2017 this OMC has had to carry out considerable investment projects from their sinking-fund in order to prevent the buildings from falling into disrepair.

Currently, each apartment pays an annual service charge in the amount of €1,300. This service charge has increased from €1,150 in 2009 and includes a provision every year in the annual service charge budget for €10,000 to be transferred into the sinking-fund. Service charge compliance rates are at 100 percent.

In 2009 there was some disquiet among members and Directors of this OMC. They did not trust their Managing Agent among other things and service charge recovery rates were around 60 percent. There were no sinking-funds available. A new and competent Managing Agent was appointed. A long-term plan was formulated which included a set of goals and timeframes. During the period 2009 to 2017 this OMC has funded and carried out the following capital projects from their sinking-fund:

- Re-landscaping of the green areas;
- Tarmacadam re-surfacing of roadways and carpark;
- New water tanks in both buildings;
- New roofs to both buildings;
- New windows to the common area stairwell spreading two floors of one building;
- New carpets in all common areas.

Due to the age, design and specification of the buildings, there is an ongoing requirement for such capital projects. The co-operation, confidence and acceptance of this, by all property owners is a crucial element in successfully getting projects funded and completed. The members and Directors of this OMC are considering a further refurbishment programme for the internal and external common areas where extra funds will be required and they passed a resolution at an AGM to set aside an additional €500 per unit per year for a four-year period so that a fund of approx. €70,000 will be available. This additional funding will be ringfenced and unlike the 'sinking-fund' each year it will not be used for any projects until it matures after the fourth year.

This simple practical example of how a small OMC may conduct its affairs demonstrates that although the owners set aside €303 per unit each year there still remains a considerable deficit in the funds that are required for major renewals and refurbishment. This OMC has always had the necessary funds available during those years to deal with all emergencies and carry out upgrade works to the common areas. However, they also acknowledge that by doing so, they were depleting the sinking-fund on an ongoing basis thus never having considerable funds available for a full refurbishment of the common areas and for this reason they have applied an additional levy in the amount of €500 per unit per year for a period of five years to build up such a fund for a refurbishment programme. Over a 15-year period this amounts to a sinking-fund contribution in the amount of €436 per unit per year. This contribution amount is in line with the survey previously referred to by Dublin City Council which was conducted in 2007 citing that €420 per unit per annum would be the prudent amount to set aside.

Chapter 6

The Multi-Unit Developments Act 2011

1. Introduction 73
2. A summary of sections 75
3. Areas for reform 83
4. Restoration 85
5. Law Reform Commission recommendations v the Act 86

1. Introduction

> 'An Act to amend the law relating to the ownership and management of the common areas of Multi-Unit Developments and to facilitate the fair, efficient and effective management of bodies responsible for the management of such common areas, and to provide for related matters.
>
> [24 January 2011][1]

The Multi-Unit Developments Act 2011 was signed into law on the 24 January 2011 and became fully operational on the 1 April 2011. It provides a statutory framework for the operation and governance of Multi-Unit Developments and the OMC sector. The Act applies to a

> '"multi-unit development" means a development being land on which there stands erected a building or buildings comprising a unit or units that –
>
> (a) as respects such units it is intended that amenities, facilities and services are to be shared, and
>
> (b) subject to section 2(1), the development contains not less than 5 residential units;'

This development in the law came from a need to protect property owners' rights for those who owned property in a multi-unit development. During the period 2000 to 2011 there was a huge

1 Multi-Unit Developments Act 2011.

rise in the number of multi-unit developments being built in the country. Of the 80,000 housing units completed in 2005, over 18,000 (22.4 percent) were apartment complexes, with more than 9,500 in the Dublin area alone.[2] In 2003, 44 percent of all new housing units built in County Dublin were apartments. Apartments as a housing unit were comparatively new in Ireland at the time and while there were no actual figures or statistics of the market, it was estimated that more than 10 percent of the total population were living in multi-unit developments. Today, it is estimated that a third of Dublin's housing stock is made up of apartments and this is set to rise in the coming years. The government's Project Ireland Plan for 2040 estimates that an additional one million people will live in Ireland by the year 2040 and there will be a requirement for increased living densities. Apartment living is the future of new housing in urban Ireland.

The Office of the Director of Corporate Enforcement and the National Consumer Agency had been receiving a steady stream of consumer complaints in relation to the governance and management of OMCs in the period prior to the consultation process for the Law Reform Commission's Multi-Unit Development Report and also the Office of the Director of Corporate Enforcement's publication called *'The Company Law Handbook on Residential Property Owners' Management Companies ('Management Companies')'*. This Act was to address these issues and in part it succeeded in doing so. However, seven years on, the lacunae in this law are very evident and reform of the Multi-Unit Developments Act is required.

From the property crash of 2008 to the recovery in 2016, there was little in the way of new developments being built and so evidence of the impact of the Act on the market has been scant up to now. However, with recent economic growth there has been a slow increase in the number of new developments being built. As each new OMC is established for a new development, we can now apply the provisions of the Act from the beginning of the development and in doing so the benefits and the gaps in the Act become more apparent.

The Act is developed to be applied retrospectively as well as applying to all new multi-unit developments that are built, but applying it retrospectively in some scenarios, given the lack of

2 Law Reform Commission, *Consultation Paper on Multi-Unit Developments*, LRC CP 42—2006, Dublin, p 1.

enforcement is of little value to property owners. Section 5 of the Act obliges the developer to transfer the common areas. In applying this retrospectively, if the developer has not done this and their development company is no longer in existence, then, unless the OMC initiates legal proceedings to force the developer to comply with the Act, the common areas will not be transferred. The cost of bringing an action in this regard, applying the Act retrospectively with no enforcement is of little use to Property Owners in situ prior to the Act.

2. A summary of sections

Obligation to transfer common areas

The scale of the sudden growth in multi-unit developments in Ireland in the years immediately prior to 2011 exposed the legislative vacuum that existed in the area which included a requirement for a property developer to transfer the title of the common areas to the OMC upon completion of the development. In many cases what had been happening up to this point was that the developer would continue to hold the ownership of the common areas of a development when all of the units in the development had been sold to individual owners. There were many reasons why developers did this, some reasons were more suspicious than others and the practice did little to enhance the reputation of property developers in general. Owners were sceptical of property developer's intentions in this regard. Irrespective of the impact of this on the relationship between the parties, this was a transaction which was incomplete until such time as the transfer of common areas had been effected by the developer's solicitor. From the time that the developer had started building and selling the units in the development they had given an undertaking that the common areas of the development would be transferred to the OMC. The main problem was that this was not being done in many cases.

The Act now obliges the developer as a condition of the sale of a unit in a multi-unit development, to transfer the common areas of the development to the OMC at the outset. Section 3 of the Act provides for further obligations on developers relating to certification and compliance of all works in the common areas and states that the OMC must be established in the first instance at the expense of the developer. The benefits of the Act are more clearly visible in new developments. For developments built prior to 2011, the Act imposes an obligation to have common areas transferred to the OMC within six months from the commencement of the legislation. What has transpired in practice is that this obligation has largely not been complied with. The period during and following 2011 was one of a deep recession where developers had become insolvent, banks and vulture funds took possession of developments and compliance with this provision was not their priority. One of the main failings in the Multi-Unit Developments Act was that there was no sanction imposed for failure to comply. In addition to this, the Law Society indicated that the non-transfer of common areas to a management company in such developments in compliance with the Act was not to be a blot on the title and therefore the conveyancing of such units continued as it did prior to the Act. This raises questions as to the validity of including this section in the Act if, in the first instance, there are no sanctions, and therefore little compliance, and in the second instance there are no consequences for property owners in that their property has a value as long as it can be sold.

The reality is that there remains many multi-unit developments in existence today that do not have the common areas transferred. There is no appetite for the members of the OMC to pay for the costs associated with getting the common areas transferred particularly when as they see it, it doesn't affect their investment in the OMC.

The main benefit of this section of the Act is for new developments post-2011 and considering the impact of the financial crisis and the recession during the years that followed, new multi-unit developments have been few and far between up until recently. It is for this reason that we are only now seeing the benefit of this section as it is imposed on all new multi-unit developments and it clearly enhances the position of the OMC and its members. While the Law Society may not have seen it as a blot on the title, the reality is that the title is incomplete until this transaction has occurred.

The Act introduced four separate transfer documents pursuant to s 3(1)(b), and ss 4 and 5.

a) *Section 3(1)(b)*: Transfer of the Common Areas where no residential unit was transferred before 1 April 2011;
b) *Section 4*: Transfer of the Common Areas—where any residential unit (but less than 80 percent of such units) was transferred before 1 April 2011;
c) *Section 5*: Transfer of the Common Areas where not less

than 80 percent of residential units were sold before 1 April 2011—not all units have been sold;

d) *Section 5*: Transfer of the Common Areas where not less than 80 of residential units were sold before 01 April 2011—all units have been sold).

Section 7 of the Act deals with the issue of completion of the common areas and clearly states that the transfer of common areas from the developer to the OMC does not relieve the developer from their duty or obligation to ensure the completion of the development in compliance with planning permission and other legislation. This will allay fears that many OMC members had of taking over the common areas as there was a perception that if the developer transferred the common areas then they could simply walk out on an unfinished building.

The rules on sinking funds, AGM's, calculating Service charges and debt collection

The Act provides for specific rules on the subject of the annual service charge and the sinking-fund contribution. An integral part of service charge collection is the provision of adequate, accurate and relevant information to property owners. Prior to the Act there were widespread problems in this area. One of the main causes of such a low recovery rate in the annual service charge and the sinking-fund contribution had been the understanding deficit among Owners. The Act sought to address this and in many ways was successful in that the rules are now clearly set out under s 17 of the Act which states that a specific financial report on the OMC each year is to be prepared and furnished to each and every member of the OMC. The Act is explicit in what is to be included in this report and it obliges the directors of the OMC to ensure that this is furnished to every member of the company. The report must show that the annual service charge was calculated on a transparent basis and equitably apportioned. The issue of transparency of financials was the cause of most of the complaints which were received by the National Consumer Agency prior to the Act and in this regard, the Act has been successful in addressing this.

Section 18 of the Act states that the annual service charge can only be levied providing not less than 75 percent of the persons present and voting at the general meeting of the company, disprove the proposed budget. Previous to this, owners were confused about their rights in relation to the levying of the annual service charge. It is a clear benefit that the Act is explicit on this matter.

There were a number of failings and missed opportunities in this area also. The Act states at s 22 that service charges and sinking-funds can be pursued as a simple '*contract debt in a court of competent jurisdiction.*' This provision is perhaps the most lacking in the entire Act because this means of pursuing outstanding service charges is not effective in the practical day-to-day management of an OMC as it takes a long time, is very costly and because a service charge debt re-occurs every 12 months. When an OMC pursues an outstanding service charge through the courts, very often it is not just a one-year-old debt, it is more likely to be a number of years of outstanding service charges on one particular unit. Some cases will be resolved within a year but where there is a lack of co-operation on the part of the debtor, cases can go on indefinitely and each year a new service charge is accrued on the account. The main problem is that the additional service charges cannot be added to the initial debt that was being pursued. The courts will not allow for an amount of debt to be amended once the legal proceedings have issued with the result that there may be a number of cases against the one owner for outstanding service charges.

Service charge debts should be re-categorised so as to exclude them from being statute barred and also to enable a more efficient and speedy service charge recovery than the normal contract debt collection process through the courts. Section 11 of the Statute of Limitations 1957 states that court actions for the recovery of contract debts may be brought only within six years of when the sum became due. In the case of a contract debt, the debt normally becomes due as is agreed in the terms between the parties, e.g. invoice date plus 30 days. The position in relation to court action changes where the debtor (OMC member) either acknowledges the debt after it becomes due or makes a part payment towards the debt. In these circumstances, the right of action is deemed to have accrued on the date the debt was acknowledged, or on the date of the part payment, i.e. on a later date, and giving more time to the creditor to pursue action for recovery. In the same way as the unique nature of service charges is given recognition by treatment as an excludable debt under the Personal Insolvency Act 2012, exceptional treatment should be provided by specifically excluding multi-unit development service charges from the Statute of Limitations. OMCs are funded entirely through the service charge receipts from its members. These constitute trade debtors on their balance sheet and the writing down of such debt has an impact on the robustness of the OMC. The writing down of service charge debt is ultimately funded by other members of the company, giving rise to a double payment and inequity.[3] In this regard, the Multi-Unit Developments Act missed an important opportunity to impose better suited measures for the collection of service charge and sinking-fund payments.

Section 19(5) of the Act refers to the sinking-fund provision as follows:

> '... the amount of contribution to be paid as respects a unit by each unit owner of such a unit to the sinking fund in respect of a particular year shall be the amount of €200 or such other amount as may be agreed by a meeting of the members as the contribution in respect of the year concerned.'

There are a number of problems with this section. Firstly, the amount of €200 is meaningless as it takes no account of the nature of each individual development. A sinking-fund in a multi-unit development exists to provide for major renewal and repair works. These types of works can vary from development to development depending on the design, age, type and size of the development and in this regard, there is no 'standard' or 'one size fits all'. The recent '*Design Standards for New Apartments Guideline for Planning Authorities*' issued by the Department of Housing, Planning and Local Government state at Chapter 6.13 and 6.14 that a building life cycle report should be issued at the planning stage. This will inform the OMC of what the right amount is for them to set aside each year and in accordance with the Act 'or such other amount as may be agreed by a meeting of the members', the right amount for each development will be set aside. This is an example of where the wording of the Act is broad enough to allow for such recommendations by government.[4] It is only when such a report is produced that consideration can be given for the amount that should be set aside each year in the sinking-fund. Other factors that will affect what the amount should be include the number of units paying into the fund. Secondly, the Apartment Owners' Network notes that the fact that the amount of sinking-fund

3 Apartment Owners' Network, *Submission to Review Group on the Administration of Civil Justice*, February 2018, 8.

4 Department of Housing, Planning and Local Government, *Sustainable Urban Housing, Design Standards for New Apartments, Guidelines for New Apartments*, March 2018.

contribution is to be set by the members of the OMC leaves it open to them to agree that there shall be no contribution and that this is a flaw in the legislation.[5] Thirdly, s 19(7) states that all contributions made to the sinking-fund must be held in a separate account which clearly identifies the sinking-fund and such contributions should only be used for certain expenditure specified in the Act. One of the problems with this provision is where there is a multi-unit development of six houses in an estate and the common areas comprise only of a small green area and the roadway has been taken in charge by the local authority. The only items on the annual service charge budget for this OMC are public liability insurance, grass cutting, accountancy fees and managing agent's fees. While they may have a healthy bank balance in their current account, the members of the OMC are reluctant to open a second bank account and pay additional bank charges when they do not and will not have any requirement in the future for such funds that may be required in an OMC that comprises an apartment block of 150 apartments. This section of the Act is applicable to all OMCs but it is not realistic in many cases.

Prior to the Act, apartment owners were being forced to subsidise developers who refused to pay service charges for unsold units. Section 18 of the Act rectified this situation where it states that the developer is obliged to pay the service charges for unsold units. OMCs were collapsing and individual apartment owners were facing spiralling service charges because of the failure of developers to pay service charges for the units that they were unable to sell. It was reported at the time, that in some cases, developers had taken advantage of the legislative vacuum to write discriminatory clauses into the legal documents signed by the purchasers, exempting the developer from paying service charges for unsold units. In this regard, there is a distinct benefit of s 18 of the Act.

The Law Reform Commission referred to a 'worrying trend' at the time, where developers were asking owners to pay service charges for a number of years in advance as a means of raising a large lump sum of cash. They recommended that there was a statutory prohibition on developers seeking payment of more than a year's advance on service charges.[6] The operation of this

5 Apartment Owners' Network, 'Review of Rebuilding Ireland Action Plan', Submission to Department of Housing, Planning, Community and Local Government, 11 August 2017, 10.

6 Law Reform Commission, *Consultation Paper on Multi-Unit Developments*, LRC CP 42—2006, 39.

section of the Act remains to be seen as it is the market that will dictate to what extent a property developer will have unsold units. In a situation where there are a considerable number of unsold units it is unlikely that the developer will have the money to pay the outstanding service charges and in the short term the other owners will have to pick up the tab. The real benefit of this section of the Act is that the service charges will continue to be invoiced and will eventually be paid as the liability is now enshrined in the law. Where the market is functioning normally and there is sufficient demand for the properties, it follows that the developer will be able to sell all of the units and thus avoid having to pay service charges for unsold units.

Sections 14 to 17 of the Act deal mainly with the governance within the multi-unit development and the OMC reiterating the general rules of company law as they apply to multi-unit developments. Problems that were addressed in these sections included the issue of weighted voting in favour of the developer and the rotation of directors of the OMC. The constitution of an OMC will normally comply with s 14(1) of the Multi-Unit Developments Act 2011 states as follows:

> 'one vote shall attach to each residential unit in a Multi-Unit Development to which the Owners' Management Company relates and that no other person has voting rights in respect of such determination'.

Prior to the Multi-Unit Developments Act, the voting rights of members of an OMC could be weighted in favour of the developer. This occurred in situations where an OMC incorporated as a company limited by guarantee and not having a share capital. Such a company must also have seven subscriber members of the company. The subscribers are the persons—usually nominees or associates of the Developer—who sign the documents by which the management company comes to be incorporated. In such a case, the sort of provision which may have been put in the OMCs articles of association at that time could typically have been along the lines of 'every member other than a subscriber member shall have one vote. A subscriber member shall have fifty votes'. This is just one such example of the many different sorts of weighted voting provisions which used to be found in practice. This type of weighted voting provision was controversial and the Law Reform Commission's report on Multi-Unit Developments in 2008 recommended that the one vote per unit formula is vital in the interests of clarity for the running of the OMC and this would not be possible if weighted voting was permitted.

A problem that remains with s 14(1) of the Act that deals with voting rights is, for example, in a multi-unit development of thirty units where one owner (the original developer) owns twenty-seven units and together with their spouse they are both Directors of the OMC. There are just three other owners. The voting power of the developer and their spouse who owns 27 units is such that the voting rights of the three owners is completely negated as they are in a situation whereby they must simply go along with whatever the owner with the most votes wants even in a situation whereby it is damaging to the OMC or they can be found to be non-compliant with the OMC. An owner is non-compliant where they fail to observe and obey the constitution of the company which includes among other things, the payment of their annual service charge and compliance with the house rules. Where these three owners find that the directors are in breach of the principal fiduciary duties that they owe to the company by carrying on the business of the company in a manner which is not in the best interests of the company, they may rely on s 232 of the Companies Act.[7] However, this would involve taking a civil action against the directors in the High Court and the cost of initiating such an action would normally be prohibitive for a property owner. Breaches of fiduciary duties (issues like poor management and abuse of responsibilities), do not leave a director liable for criminal prosecution and it is therefore not the responsibility of the Office of the Director of Corporate Enforcement to take an action against them.

Section 16 of the Multi-Unit Developments Act states that a person shall not be appointed as a director for a term greater than three years.[8] This will give an opportunity to the three owners to be

---

7 The Companies Act 2014, s 232(1) subject to s 233, where a director of a company acts in breach of his or her duty under s 22.

8 Multi-Unit Developments Act 2011, s 16(1): 'a person shall not be appointed as a director of an owners' management company after the coming into operation of this section if such appointment is—

(*a*) for life, or

(*b*) for a term greater than 3 years.

(2) A person who, on the coming into operation of this section, stands appointed as a director of an owners' management company, and the appointment is—

(*a*) for life, or

(*b*) for a term greater than 3 years,

shall be deemed to vacate that office—

appointed as directors and they can then effect change in the running of the OMC even in situations where the majority of votes rests with a minority of owners. This is however, a poor remedy for such a scenario especially considering that there is no enforcement of the Multi-Unit Developments Act 2011. It is manifestly disadvantageous to property owners where they find themselves outvoted to such an extent. It is in this vein that an Oireachtas Bill has been submitted to Dáil Éireann seeking to appoint an Ombudsman for the OMC.[9] An Ombudsman for the OMC would be charged with representing the interests of all members and directors of OMCs by investigating and addressing complaints of maladministration or breach of duty.

A provision under s 23 of the Act states that an OMC may 'make house rules' for the development. In an apartment block scenario in particular, it is essential that a clear set of house rules are established and furnished to all property owners. Owners then have a responsibility to impose these house rules on their tenants. These rules relate to the manner in which residents conduct themselves giving due consideration to others in the building. They are binding on the parties and it is vital that they can be enforced by the OMC when the situation arises.

3. Areas for reform

A key area for reform of the Act includes the issue of the enforcement of the lease and lessor covenants in the common interest. When an individual buys a property in a multi-unit development they make a number of covenants with the OMC on various matters and these covenants are contained in the lease agreement between the parties. While the Multi-Unit Developments Act did include some level of alternative dispute

---

(i) in the case of an appointment for life on the day which is 3 years after the coming into operation of this section, and

(ii) in the case of an appointment referred to in *paragraph (b)* on the day of the expiry of the term concerned or the day which is 3 years after the coming into operation of this section whichever is the earlier.

(3) Subject to *subsection (1)*, nothing in *subsection (2)* shall prevent the appointment or election of a person to whom *subsection (2)* applies as a director of an owners' management company at the annual general meeting of the owners' management company concerned unless this is prohibited by the articles of association or other governing document of the company.'

9 Dáil Deb, 4 July 2018; Property Services (Regulation)(Amendment) (Management Company Regulation) Bill 2018: First Stage <https://www.oireachtas.ie/en/debates/debate/dail/2018-07-04/21/spk_240>.

resolution this has, in some aspects, served to hinder the process in the collection of outstanding service charges. The inclusion of mediation in the Multi-Unit Developments Act 2011 may also have had a dilution effect on the rigidity of the covenants contained in the lease agreements and suggests that they are now somehow open to negotiation. Reform by way of an approach to the courts weighted towards the enforcement of lease covenants would improve the viability of the multi-unit development sector.

Section 24 of the Act deals with the issue of disputes arising in relation to multi-unit developments and provides for a dispute resolution process on application to the Circuit Court. Section 27 of the Act allows the court, upon its own motion, or on the request of any party, to order a 'mediation conference' with the goal of assisting the parties in reaching a settlement. Given that most OMC disputes hinge on the dispute of the payment of the annual service charge, the notion that a service charge debt to an OMC could be somehow negotiated is a principle that holds the interest of the individual supreme to the interests of the collective. Service charge debt cannot be mediated upon. House rules and terms of lease agreements cannot be mediated upon. In situations where the parties enter into mediation and do not reach an agreement and subsequently end up in court it simply has the effect of adding an additional layer of cost to the process as negotiation cannot happen where it will create an inequity to the majority of members.

In commenting on this section, Brian Hutchinson opines that this section

> 'gives tacit recognition, perhaps, to the view that court proceedings can be polarising and may make neighbour disputes worse than they were to begin with! It is peculiar, therefore, that the legislation goes on to provide that the mediator at such a conference must be a practising barrister or practising solicitor of not less than five years standing, or such other person nominated by a body prescribed by the minister. He further submits that being a practising barrister or solicitor alone does not guarantee that one has the skills or the ability to mediate in the true sense – i.e. to give due regard to the needs and interests of the parties beyond their legal entitlements – and many practitioners would probably agree. It is greatly to be feared that these private mediation conferences could descent into legitimised haggling forums where, under

> the mantle of confidentiality, there is a free for all race to the bottom. We would like to see higher standards being required – mediation training at a minimum – in the appointments to these mediation conferences'[10]

This provision in the Act raises a wide variety of questions and as it stands can only serve to have a costly and damaging effect on the OMC and the members who are often neighbours with each other.

Section 13 of the Act sets out a provision which is designed to protect property owners in the event where the property developer fails in their duty to carry out essential repairs to the common areas. This provision is somewhat linked to the era prior to the Act where developers left many sites unfinished when the property market collapsed, and the financial crisis hit. Buildings were left with unfinished common areas and in some cases, it was more than the aesthetics that were incomplete. This provision is the key to ensure that there is some remedy for OMC members where they have the right to effect essential repairs on parts of the development which are not in its ownership where those repairs are necessary for the safe occupation of a unit and they can seek to recover that expense from the person who was responsible for the work in the first place. That is usually the developer. However, in the event where the developer has gone out of business there may be little opportunity by way of recovering such a loss for the OMC.

4. Restoration

Section 30 provides for an OMC which has been struck-off the company register in accordance with the Companies Act, to be allowed within a period of six years of strike-off, to have its name restored to the company register provided that the registrar has received all annual returns outstanding. Prior to the enactment of this Act, the period allowed for such restoration was 12 months and could only be restored by a costly application to the High Court. Given the high number of OMCs that have been struck-off the company register due to the late filing of the annual return this section in the Act was vital in assisting members of OMCs in the organisation and administration of their OMC and consequently the title to their own property. A period of six years is more necessary for an OMC than other companies given that there are so many stakeholders involved. In 2011 there was a general

10 Brian G Hutchinson, 'Commercial Law Practitioner', 2011, 18(2), 22.

lack of knowledge of how an OMC operated and roles were not clearly defined for those involved. This led to a situation where there was no one taking care of the affairs of the OMC and this led to the OMC becoming non-compliant and struck-off the register. This measure in the Act provided an effective remedy in most of these cases.

5. Law Reform Commission recommendations v the Act

In their Consultation Paper on Multi-Unit Developments, the Law Reform Commission recommended the Regulation of Management Companies.[11] There was at the time, and still remains, a compelling case for the Regulation of OMCs in Ireland. In their report they refer to specific areas for regulation such as allocation of share membership, memorandum and articles of association, service charges and sinking-funds. The allocation of shares was largely dealt with in the Act where the voting rights of members are clearly established, and the memorandum and articles of association have been changed with the implementation of the new Companies Act 2014. Given that this report was issued in 2006 not all of these areas require reform now with the changes that have occurred in other areas of law. However, areas such as the regulation of OMC funds and the fact that the OMC model is built on the basis of a community of volunteers illustrates the need for regulation. The Apartment Owners' Network refer to the Commission's approach as a laissez-faire approach to regulation of the OMC.[12]

The reports which preceded the Act made recommendations for training for officers of OMCs the cost of which would be covered by the OMC itself. The commission noted the benefits that would be achieved from this such as awareness of and compliance with company law obligations. It was recognised at that stage that individuals who were volunteering their time to take on the role as a company director or secretary were often unaware of the scope of their responsibilities as company directors. This situation has not changed and no provision for this was made in the Act. Reform is needed on this matter to avoid a spate of legal actions against company officers and the potential for prosecutions from

---

11 Law Reform Commission, *Consultation Paper on Multi-Unit Developments* (LRC CP 42—2006), 75.

12 Apartment Owners' Network, 'Review of Rebuilding Ireland Action Plan', Submission to Department of Housing, Planning, Community and Local Government, 11 August 2017, 16.

the Director of Corporate Enforcement in the future. The level of exposure to liability claims for directors includes but is not limited to breaches of the Safety, Health & Welfare at Work Act 2005 where criminal convictions can be imposed with sanctions as serious as prison sentences and breaches of the Data Protection Act 2018 among others. The greatest concern being loss of life: OMCs preside over places where people live and sleep; a fire in an apartment block causing loss of life will expose any failings of any director and seek to establish negligence. The OMC structure is relatively new in Ireland, there have been no such cases to make owners realise the extent of responsibility that sits on a director's shoulders and the Multi-Unit Developments Act failed to take cognisance of this even though it had been recommended in the reports preceding the Act.

Schedule 3 of the Act contains a list of documents that must be handed over to the OMC upon completion of the development. Up to now, this information was rarely if ever provided to the OMC. This information includes completion certificates, undertakings, fire safety certificates, safety files, professionally prepared drawings, operation and maintenance manuals, warranties, maintenance contracts, results of test records, a schedule of plant and equipment, title documents, leases and all other relevant documentation. This information is a key part of the ongoing management of the common areas in a multi-unit development. It is of great benefit to the OMC that this requirement now exists in law and can be officially requested from the developers and/or their solicitors. Prior to the Act the situation was that the developer often failed in their responsibility to hand over the common areas and the handing over of documentation such as this was not something that was even considered by them in so many cases. Now, their responsibility is enshrined in law and it remains to be seen if Sch 3 is more of an aspirational appendix contained on the last page of the Act or if it has any real teeth in compelling the developer to provide the information.

In conclusion, the Act is a welcome step in the direction of providing some legal structure to OMCs. It provides protection for those buying or living in residential developments as it imposes greater legal obligations on developers and provides a reasonable framework for management practices. The Act has eliminated many of the problems which had been faced by those involved in multi-unit developments and OMCs by improving the transparency of the process through the various phases of development.

Solicitors who act for purchasers and vendors involved in property transactions within an OMC must now explain to the purchaser that he or she is now a member of an OMC and also to explain the duties and responsibilities the owner will hold as a member of the OMC. In addition to this, a new set of pre-contract enquiries called MUD ACT Precedent Pre-Contract Enquiries has been established which must be completed as part of any conveyance. Prior to the Act this level of reporting and accountability was not in place and there were serious shortcomings in this regard. The pre-contract enquiries, known as Requisition of Title must be completed by the OMC and furnished to the solicitor acting for the purchaser. They will contain replies to queries around the governance, financial and legal position of the OMC at the time of the sale. They will also seek information on potential repairs or maintenance of a significant nature that the OMC may be contemplating or planning for in the future. The enquiries will relate to:

a) All units in a multi-unit development;
b) Units in a multi-unit development in which a residential unit was not sold prior to 1 April 2011;
c) Units in a multi-unit development in which a residential unit was sold prior to 1 April 2011.

Chapter 7

The Property Services Regulatory Authority

1. **Introduction** 89
2. **Role and responsibilities** 91
3. **The Compensation Fund 2017 Report** 95
4. **Powers of PSRA** 97
5. **The Strategic Plan to 2020** 100

1. Introduction

The Property Services Regulatory Authority was established by the Minister for Justice and Equality pursuant to the Property Services (Regulation) Act 2011, which comprises 101 sections. Its establishment stemmed from the need to protect consumers and to ensure that the property services sector operates to the highest standards. Such State intervention and regulation for market efficiency is essential to address the negative externalities of the market through the setting of enforceable minimum standards.[1] This new regulatory intervention was necessary to address the problems faced by unit owners chiefly emanating from lack of supervision and regulation of the sector as set out in the Law Reform Commission's Consultation Paper[2] and on foot of a recommendation by the Auctioneering/Estate Agency Review Group in 2005.[3]

During the period up to 2011, the property market was flourishing without regulatory intervention with sharp rises in completions particularly in apartment blocks. In 2006 apartment completions were more than 50 percent of total completions in Dublin and this sharp rise coupled with a phenomenal understanding deficit and lack of supervision of service providers to the multi-unit development sector was the cause of many problems that

---

1 Padraic Kenna, *Housing Law and Policy in Ireland* (Clarus Press 2006), 63.

2 Law Reform Commission, *Consultation Paper on Multi-Unit Developments*, LRC CP 42—2006, 5.

3 Department of Justice, Equality and Law Reform, *Auctioneering/Estate Agency Review Group Report to the Minister for Justice, Equality and Law Reform* (July 2005, 7). <http://www.justice.ie/en/JELR/Pages/Auctioneering-Estate-Agency-report> accessed on 8 April 2018.

arose for both for property owners and service providers alike.[4] There was no consumer watchdog in this specific area and no government legislation for those who were acting as agents to OMCs. Problems included stand-offs over the payment of service charges by property owners, unregulated and rogue managing agents and poor service provision all of which resulted in anarchy at annual general meetings held for OMCs by owners who were ill-advised and unaware of the potential pitfalls of owning a property in an OMC or the operations of a properly run OMC. Owners described scenes at AGM's as 'ugly' where owners were pitched against each other on issues from landscaping to non-payment of service charges and where resident-run OMC committee members abdicated leaving a void until a managing agent was appointed or a new residents' association was formed. There was unrest and fallouts among neighbours and this was common in multi-unit development living prior to regulation in the sector and the introduction of the Multi-Unit Developments Act 2011 which had the effect of making life for members of OMCs more congenial.

Dublin City Council's housing department had commissioned a study into the area of private housing and multi-unit development living which lead to the production of a guide entitled *Successful Apartment Living* and strongly recommended the establishment of a regulatory body particularly for multi-unit developments stating that

> 'Dublin City Council should actively promote a new legal and operational framework for Management Companies in apartment developments to increase the sustainability and chances of success of the apartment development sector.' [5]

At that time there were numerous complaints to the National Consumer Agency and as a result they commissioned a report which identified the need for a regulator of multi-unit developments, particularly OMCs and the position of such companies in law as among the most important issues in the sector.[6]

---

4 The Law Reform Commission, *Consultation Paper on Multi-Unit Developments*, LRC CP 42—2006.

5 Evelyn Hanlon, Dublin City Council, Private Housing Unit, *Successful Apartment Living*, June 2006, 10, 5.1.

6 'Management Fees and Service Charges Levied on Owners of Property in Multi-Unit Dwellings', *Final Report for the National Consumer Agency* by DKM Economic Consultants Ltd in association with Kevin O'Higgins Solicitors, July 2006, Executive Summary.

As far back as 2005, the report to the Minister for Justice, Equality and Law Reform by the Auctioneering/Estate Agency Review Group recommended the establishment of a Property Services Regulator. Subsequently, the Law Reform Commission issued their Report on Multi-Unit Developments and recommended such a regulatory body. A significant finding of the Review Group was that the existing statutory framework for the industry was outdated, inappropriate and inadequate for the present-day market and did not provide any ongoing official supervisory, disciplinary or consumer redress system.

There was a consensus held by all parties at the time that proper organisation of the industry was necessary to protect consumers by ensuring that all stakeholders in the field understood their own obligations and duties which ought to be enshrined in law. To address these shortcomings the regulator was established to underpin a new regulatory framework in the sector. However, the Property Services Regulatory Authority which was established falls short of supervising, disciplining or providing any kind of redress for the Owners' Management Company. The Property Services Regulatory Authority regulates agents and service providers, mainly to ensure that there are no rogue operators that will run away with the money. It is an important distinction to note that the Regulator regulates service providers and not OMCs and this will become more apparent throughout this chapter. A Regulator for the Owners' Management Company has not yet been established although there are a number of proposals and submissions made to government recommending this. This is discussed further in Chapter 8.

2. Role and responsibilities

On 3 April 2012 the Property Services Regulatory Authority (the 'Authority') was established pursuant to the Property Services (Regulation) Act 2011. This new legislation replaced the Auctioneers and House Agents Acts 1947 to 1973 which have been repealed and for the first time covered Managing Agents and those involved in providing property services to OMCs in the multi-unit development sector. The main function of the Authority can be outlined as follows:

1. To control, supervise and regulate property services providers (i.e. auctioneers/estate agents, letting agents and management agents);

2. The licencing of all such services providers;
3. The establishment of a complaints investigation and redress system for consumers;
4. The setting and enforcement of standards in the provision of property services;
5. The administration of client accounts;
6. The establishment and maintenance of a compensation fund;
7. To impose sanctions on property services providers for improper conduct;
8. The creation of three public registers:
    - The Register of Licensed Property Services Providers;
    - The Residential Property Price Register;
    - The Commercial Leases Register.[7]

Section 10 of the Act states that the Authority shall consist of not more than 11 members and the Act also prescribes that the membership of the Authority must include: (a) not more than three persons who are representatives of persons who provide property services; and (b) not less than three persons who have knowledge of, or experience in, consumer affairs; and (c) one shall be an officer of the Minister.

Prior to the enactment of the Property Services Regulatory Authority, in order to obtain an auctioneer's licence a person had to lodge a bond of €12,700 in court and satisfy the district judge that they were of suitable character to be awarded the licence, that is, that they were neither a criminal nor a bankrupt. The district judge would then issue a certificate of suitability and on that basis the licence was issued. The district judge would not enquire as to the person's qualifications or experience in the field. This system was replaced with regulation whereby the Regulator takes responsibility for the licensing and regulation of all trading entities PLCs, limited companies, sole traders and partnerships who provide services such as auctioneering, estate agency, property letting and/or property management services. The regulator also has a role to develop an ongoing and adequately resourced consumer awareness and advisory programme.

The licencing of property service providers is categorised into four types of licences:

---

7 <www.psra.ie/home>.

- Licence A is for those service providers engaged in the auction of property other than land;
- Licence B is for those providing services of purchase or sale, by whatever means, of land;
- Licence C for the letting of land;
- Licence D is for those providing property management services such as Managing Agents to an OMC.

The Regulator provides a complete guide to becoming a licenced property services provider and this guide is designed to assist those seeking a licence to understand the requirements of being licenced and how to complete the necessary application forms. It gives details of all professional requirements and qualifications necessary to obtain a licence. The licence fee is determined by the class of property services provider whether it's a company or otherwise that the applicant belongs to and is unaffected by the category or number of services being licensed.

- Company €1,000;
- Independent Contractor €1,000;
- Partnership €1,000;
- Sole Trader €1,000;
- Principal Officer €100;
- Employee €100.

The impact of regulation on the sector is notable in the skills shortage being experienced by property service providers. An employer in the sector cannot now employ an individual to provide a property service of any kind unless that person is qualified and has a licence to do so. Given that the introduction of regulation happened during a period of high unemployment and extreme economic downturn, the numbers applying for licences at that time between 2011 and 2016 specifically were minimal and operations in all businesses were lean, where cost-cutting measures were more likely than recruitment drives. As the economy began its slow recovery since 2014 and is now in a period of strong economic growth (the fastest growth rate in the EU in 2017), with a vibrant property market, there are obvious requirements for more letting agents, property managers and sales agents. Prior to regulation there was no qualification process for those who wished to take up such positions and in that regard staff vacancies were easier to fill. However, regulation has changed this, and it has resulted in a shortage of skills in the sector. Sourcing suitably qualified and licenced personnel for a business in the sector is now problematic in that the only pool of resources available is that of college graduates of courses which are stipulated by the Authority which will meet the Authority's minimum academic qualification test. Examples of such courses include BSc Business in Real Estate or Diploma in Auctioneering and Estate Agency. These barriers to entry, while they have their merits, are rigid rules and do not allow any flexibility to provide solutions to employers who are faced with the current skills shortage.

Given the low number of students graduating from Irish property courses it was necessary that the regulator moved to recognise the University College of Estate Management (UCEM) undergraduate and postgraduate real estate programmes during 2018. This recognition increases the pool of human resources that Property Service Providers can draw from. An additional measure initiated by the Regulator is the implementation of a new apprenticeship programme. This programme will firstly be established in Dublin with the City of Dublin Education Training Board, and with a view to rolling it out throughout the rest of the country thereafter. This apprenticeship will be a two-year training programme with level 6 accreditation. It will require one day per week of in-house training with the remainder on-the-job learning. Applicants will achieve 120 ECTS or equivalent upon completion.[8] Employers must be accredited by Solas before they will qualify to take on apprentices. This type of apprenticeship is designed to suit school leavers as well as those who are already working in the sector but are not licenced to provide a property service.

The qualifications that applicants for a licence must meet are set out in paragraphs (a) and (b) of the Property Services (Regulation) Act 2011 (Qualifications) (Amendment) Regulations 2015 and paras (c) and (d) of the Property Services (Regulation) Act 2011 (Qualifications) Regulations 2012. They must also provide evidence of professional indemnity insurance cover, the level of which is determined by the regulator and an external accountant's certificate as part of the overall fitness and probity test for awarding licences. The Regulatory Authority is responsible for ensuring that service providers comply with their obligations under money laundering legislation. The Authority is funded mainly by the licence fees that it receives from service providers.

8 The European Credit Transfer and Accumulation System (ECTS) is a student-centred system based on the student workload required to achieve the objectives of a programme of study. Its aim is to facilitate the recognition of study periods undertaken by mobile students through the transfer of credits.

3. The Compensation Fund 2017 Report

The Authority maintains a 'Compensation Fund' in accordance with the provisions of the Property Services (Regulation) Act 2011. This fund comprises of the €100 payment by licensees on trust to the Regulator each year who must ensure that it is paid into a separate account. The Authority may invest monies of the fund in securities and they may borrow for the Fund and for the purpose of giving security in respect of such borrowing, they may charge investments of the fund. The Authority may also insure against any risk relating to the fund. According to s 77, schedule 6(6) of the Act, all costs associated with protecting and administering the fund will be paid out of the fund and they must keep all proper books of account including income and expenditure for the fund and submit the annual accounts to the Comptroller and Auditor General for audit each year.

The purpose of the Compensation Fund is to provide compensation to clients of licensees who have sustained a loss as a result of the dishonesty of a licensee. In their 2017 Annual Report the Authority notes that

> 'The Authority, where it is satisfied that a client of a Property Service Provider has sustained a loss as a result of the dishonesty of the Property Services Provider and, subject to certain conditions specified in the Act, may make a grant from the Compensation Fund to the client. At 31 December 2017, the amount standing to the credit of the Fund was over €3.1 million. During 2017, a total of 33 claims were fully or partially granted with all these claims relating to one former licensee. Two claims were refused, one of which was appealed to the Property Services Appeal Board. A decision in this appeal was pending at year end.'[9]

In order for a claim to be made, the client of a licensee must establish that he/she has suffered loss as a result of a fraud or dishonesty on the part of a licensee. The Authority commenced receiving and handling compensation claims during 2017. By the end of 2017 all grants made from the fund related to the activities of one former licensee where the vast majority of successful claims were relating to the retention of booking deposits. This was the first time that grants were awarded from the fund and given the number of claims and the amount paid out in grants,

9 Property Services Regulatory Authority, *Annual Report*, 2017, 29, Compensation Fund.

it demonstrates the disproportionate effect that the activities of this former licensee had. The Authority licensed in excess of 5,700 companies and individuals who provided property services in 2017.

It is the role of the Authority to identify those operators who are acting outside of the law without a licence. In this regard, the Authority notes just six cases to date where un-licenced individuals were operating. The Authority is not entitled to make a grant out of the Compensation Fund on the basis that a client suffered loss as a result of the negligence of a licensee. A claim for negligence or incompetence against a licensee may be made against the licensee's professional indemnity insurance policy. The Authority is not entitled to grant a claim for consequential losses or damages made by a client of a licensee they may only grant a claim in respect of monies actually lost. The Authority has a discretion to pay interest on all or any part of the amount of the loss calculated for such period of time between the date that the loss was sustained and the date that the grant is made at a rate that would be payable by a court, if the Authority considers it appropriate to do so. In the event where a licensee dies, the Authority may grant a claim notwithstanding the death of the licensee after the date that the fraud or dishonesty occurred. A grant from the Fund will not be made where a loss has already been made good by alternative means. A client must report dishonesty of licensees to An Garda Síochána. A claim for compensation from a client of a licensee must be received by the Authority in the prescribed form PSRCF 1 and within the prescribed time and it must be in writing and signed. An applicant must formally declare that the contents of the application for a grant are true. This declaration must be sworn in the presence of a Solicitor or Commissioner for Oaths and there will be a small fee for this declaration.

A claim must be made within 12 months after the loss comes to the knowledge of the client concerned. Under s 94(1) of the Act it is a criminal offence to make a false, or misleading statement or to provide false or misleading information to the Authority. A person found guilty of such an offence is liable on summary conviction to a Class A fine or imprisonment of a term not exceeding 12 months, or both. A person who is dissatisfied with the decision of the Authority concerning their application for a grant from the Compensation Fund may refer their claim to the Property Services Appeals Board within 30 days of the Authority's decision.[10]

10 Property Services Regulatory Authority website, <www.psr.ie/Website/npsra/

4. Powers of PSRA

Under existing legislation, The Property Services Regulatory Authority has the power to investigate complaints made against Property Services Providers and to initiate investigations for the purposes of ensuring compliance with the law. However, it is in this arena in particular, that there is much confusion for members and directors of OMCs. An ongoing issue in relation to this is that many of the problems which have been reported to the Authority are ostensibly in relation to the conduct and management of OMCs and their members and directors and also poor service provision by managing agents. The Authority does not have responsibility for OMCs and, as such, does not get involved with issues which arise within an OMC. The Authority does not regulate the standard of service provided by property service providers and it is this distinction which is the cause of most confusion and frustration for complaining property owners.

At the end of 2017, in total 1,205 or 76 percent of complaints received to date were concluded without a requirement for the appointment of an inspector to conduct an investigation. This compares with 862 or 67 percent of cases in 2016. In all such cases the Authority explained the reasons as to why an investigation could not be pursued. The most common reason for declining to investigate a complaint was because the subject matter of the complaint did not fall within the definition of 'improper conduct' specified in the Act.[11] 'Improper Conduct' as defined in the Act basically amounts to a service provider acting fraudulently or dishonestly—essentially running away with client monies and anything short of that, the Authority may not investigate.

Although, one of the central powers of the Authority is to investigate and adjudicate on complaints made about service providers including managing agents of OMCs, investigations in relation to the standard of service provided by a property service provider are only carried out by the Authority on their own volition and in the vast majority of cases as cited in the 2017 Annual Report (76 percent of complaints were concluded without an investigation), the Regulator does not get involved. The Regulator states that they receive an average of 300 complaints annually which relate to poor service provision by service providers, rudeness/abusive behaviour, poor communication, poor engagement on management of property.

npsraweb.nsf/page/Compensation_Fund-en> accessed 19 April 2018.

11 Property Services Regulatory Authority, *Annual Report*, 2017, 16.

In relation specifically to OMCs, the majority of complaints that the Regulator receives are in relation to the standard of service provided by managing agents and issues relating to Members and Directors of OMCs. Given that the Regulator simply does not get involved, it highlights the limited role that the Regulator plays when it comes to the real issues which abound the OMC. Property owners who complain to the Regulator about managing agents not complying with company law, or complaining that their OMC is in breach of the Multi-Unit Developments Act by failing to provide financial information to members find themselves with no redress. The Authority merely advises that 'section 95 of the Act allows for regulations to be made regarding the standards to be observed in the provision of property services by the licensees but to date no such regulations have been made' and they will then decline to investigate.

It could be said that the Regulator is little more than a toothless quango that will award a licence to a service provider if they can produce a tax clearance certificate and pay the licence fee among other things. As it is, the Regulator will award a licence to trade to a managing agent who may not be fit to trade because fitness to trade does not form part of the fitness and probity test that the Regulator sets for awarding a licence. Fitness to award a licence is distinct from that of fitness to trade. It is this particular area that property owners find confusing and frustrating when they make complaints to the Regulator about poor practice in the sector. However, this regulatory regime is constantly being developed by the Authority and the Authority has included in its strategic plan the recent roll out of the requirement for service providers to complete continuous professional development courses annually together with impending implementation of a code of standards for the sector.

Where the Regulator exercises their powers with managing agents is mainly where a service provider is operating without a licence or where a licensee is acting fraudulently or dishonestly or has essentially run away with client monies.

Any person may make a complaint, in writing, to the Authority against a service provider in relation to the provision of a service or the conduct of the service provider in the course of providing a property service. The complaint form, PSRA/COM1-12A, can be found on the Authority's website and it sets out in detail the information that is required. The Authority is required to investigate all complaints unless it is satisfied that the complaint is not made in good faith, is vexatious, frivolous or without foundation.

During 2017, the Authority received 329 complaints, a 15 percent increase on the 285 complaints received in 2016. This figure includes reports of unlicensed provision of property services.[12]

Seventy-six percent of all complaints received by the Authority in the period 2012 to 2017 were reported by the Authority to have been 'Declined/Not Accepted/Frivolous/Vexatious and Outside Remit'. This figure is reflective of the understanding deficit among property owners as to where they can turn to for redress.

The powers of the Authority's inspector are extensive in that they include the power to require any person to supply all information, records, etc., which are relevant and to question any person for the purpose of the investigation. The inspector may enter, examine and search any place at which any activity in connection with the provision of a property service is being carried on and require any service provider or any employee or agent to authorise him/her to inspect any account opened by the service provider in any bank. The inspector may be accompanied by a member of An Garda Síochána if he/she has reasonable cause to fear any serious obstruction.

The Authority has the power to sanction where they are satisfied that the service provider has engaged in 'improper conduct' and they can impose sanctions such as to issue a reprimand, warning, caution or advice to the service provider. They can revoke the service providers licence or suspend their licence for a specified period of time depending on the nature of the case. Sanctions for more serious offences include fines of up to €50,000 payable to the Compensation Fund, up to €50,000 to the Authority towards the cost of the investigation and up to €250,000 by way of a financial penalty or any combination of the foregoing.

The legislation provides for a range of offences such as providing a property service without a licence, obstructing an investigation, mismanagement of client funds, etc. Any person found guilty of such an offence is liable, on summary conviction, to a fine of up to €5,000 or 12 months' imprisonment or both or, on conviction on indictment, to a fine of up to €50,000 or five years' imprisonment or both.

---

12 Property Services Regulatory Authority, *Annual Report*, 2017, 16.

5. The Strategic Plan to 2020

In accordance with s 17 of the Property Services (Regulation) Act 2011 the Regulator is required to prepare and submit to the Minister, for approval by the Minister, a strategic plan for the ensuing three-year period. The strategic plan focuses on improving the organisational structures, systems, procedures, protocols, rules and regulations that have been established since the Authority commenced its work and which are fundamental to the long-term functioning of the Authority and ensuring that a robust regulatory framework will continue to apply in the sector.

The current plan for the period ending August 2020 focuses on:

- A continued robust regulatory framework for the sector;
- Addressing complaint arrears;
- Effective use of technology and resources;
- Improving organisational structures, systems and procedures.[13]

According to the Authority, during 2017 they carried out 700 audits with inspectors entering the premises of service providers checking on compliance rates. Compliance checks include checking that the licensee had displayed their licence in a prominent place, that there was a signed letter of engagement in place for each client, that funds were being handled appropriately, that there was a tax clearance certificate available among other things. They held nationwide seminars during the year as part of a goal of communicating with the public in the form of media advertisement campaigns and events such as the Ideal Home Show and the National Ploughing Championships. The Authority's public registers have proven very popular with the Property Price Register having over 650,000 visits to the register in 2017. Significant progress was made on the Commercial Lease Database also.

In accordance with s 18 of the Property Services (Regulation) Act 2011 the Authority may, at the request of the Minister, prepare and publish a code of practice for the sector for the purposes of setting standards for the provision of property services. Since its establishment, the Authority has set this out as one of its goals to develop a code of standards for the sector. In their strategic plan 2017–2020 the Authority sets out at Goal 2: Maintain a System of Investigation and Adjudication of Standards in the Provision of

---

[13] Property Services Regulatory Authority, *Strategic Plan, 2017–2020*, 4.

Property Services, 2.6, p 12, to develop a code of standards for all service providers in the sector and they anticipate that this goal will be delivered by the end of 2019 with the publication and implementation of a code of standards.

In advance of such a code of standards, the Authority successfully rolled out the Continuous Professional Development Programme. This Continuous Professional Development (CPD) is an ongoing duty for all licensees to undertake education and training for the purposes of maintaining professional competence. Licensees must undertake a minimum of five verifiable hours of formal PSRA CPD education in each calendar year. The accredited provider of CPD must ensure that the education and training falls within the range of categories set out in the scheme, and that it directly relates to improving standards and quality of property service provision. The following requirements must also be adequately addressed:

1. The relevance to provision of licensed property services in Ireland, with emphasis on improved quality and service provision having regard to current Irish law and regulatory practices;
2. The delivery by persons or bodies that have suitable qualifications and experience in their subject;
3. Conformity with minimum standards appropriate to the delivery of CPD in suitable locations/premises with adequate facilities and organisational structures;
4. Capability to deliver CPD on a regional basis;
5. Costs and anticipated outcomes in terms of results for participants to be clear and specific;
6. Content to be sufficiently detailed to enable the Authority to assess it effectively for accreditation purposes;
7. Recording of attendance on arrival and departure at CPD courses—issuing of certified attendance certificate to the licensees.

Letter of engagement

Section 43 of the Property Services (Regulation) Act 2011 sets out the requirement that a licensee must provide their clients with a letter of engagement. This important feature provides protection to consumers in their transactions with service providers and establishes a clear statutory basis for the standards expected of service providers including the contract terms on which the managing agent provides professional services to an OMC in a multi-unit development. The Letter of Engagement must be in the form specified by the Authority, form PSRA/S43 Form. The letter must be issued within seven working days of starting to provide, or agreeing to provide, a property service, whichever is the earlier. If the client does not sign and return the contract to the licensee within a further seven working days, the property services provider must cease, or not commence, the provision of the property service. This contract is a core element of the regulatory regime. Because of the importance of the contract the Authority drafted detailed contracts for use property services providers. The contract drawn up by the Authority is the only form of contract which may be used by property services providers.

The existing statutory framework of the Property Services Regulatory Authority as established under the Property Services (Regulation) Act 2011 has a broad scope and in relative terms it is in its infancy. Since its establishment in 2012 they have initiated just one prosecution for un licenced trading. The Authority has an important role to play in the sector and is constantly implementing new measures to improve standards, promote professionalism and ultimately protect the consumer's interest by promoting public awareness and organising information campaigns.

Chapter 8

Company Law

1. Types of companies 104
2. Governance 109
3. Directors' duties 112
4. The company secretary 117
5. The CRO 119
6. ODCE and penalties for failing to comply with company law 121

Much has been written about the complex legal structure of the OMC. The Law Reform Commission's Consultation Paper on Multi-Unit Developments in 2006 and Dublin City Council's *Successful Apartment Living* by Evelyn Hanlon in 2006 are both examples of detailed reports on the operation of the OMC citing in particular on the one hand the company law issues facing OMCs and reasons as to why the company law model does not entirely fit with the day-to-day operations of the OMC and on the other hand reasons as to why it is most suitable.

The administration, management and ownership agreement of a multi-unit development normally takes the form of a company limited by guarantee with no share capital. The exception to this may include co-ownership arrangements or housing co-operatives.

A company is an association of persons constituted for some purpose, generally to carry on a business. A registered company is an artificial legal device by which rights, powers, privileges and liabilities may be attributed to a fictional entity, equated for many purposes to a natural person. This entity acquires rights and liabilities through the acts of those who control it, its directors and its ultimate controllers, its members and shareholders.[1]

On their website, the Companies Registration Office describe a company as follows:

> 'A company is a legal form of business organisation. It

---

1 Forde and Kennedy, *Company Law*, Thomson Round Hall (4th edn, Dublin, 2008), 1, 1–01.

> is a separate legal entity and, therefore, is separate and distinct from those who run it. The company (and not the individual shareholders) is the appropriate person to be sued in the event that debts are incurred by the company which remain unpaid, despite demand. A company registered under the Companies Act 2014 becomes a body corporate as and from the date mentioned in its certificate of incorporation. The vast majority of companies incorporated also have limited liability and have to file annual returns and submit notice of change in their details.'[2]

There are many valid reasons as to why the incorporation of a company structure is the most suitable vehicle for administering an OMC and protecting the rights of individual property owners. A company is incorporated with limited liability which means that should the company accrue high debts, the liability of the owners will be limited. Given the impecunious nature of an OMC this is an important factor as there are many OMCs in Ireland carrying debts that they cannot pay due to the poor compliance rates with the payment of the annual service charge and lack of adequate sinking-funds available. A company and its members are separate personalities in law and for an OMC this enables the corporate entity but no individual owner, to hold ownership of the freehold reversion of the common areas. The OMC will own the common areas of the building and each individual owner will have a share in the common areas. As each owner is a member of the OMC this provides for a forum of democracy of ownership of the common areas and structural areas of a development. The governance of the company whereby major decisions are taken by way of resolutions at general meetings and the company accounts are presented to members at every annual general meeting provides a model that is useful to facilitate the running of an OMC in a multi-unit development situation.

1. Types of companies

Under the new Companies Act 2014 there are several types of limited companies which include a Public Limited Company (PLC). In this type of company, the liability of members is limited to the amount, if any, unpaid on shares held by them. The nominal value of the company's allotted share capital must not be less than €25,000 at least 25 percent of which must be fully paid up before

---

2 <www.cro.ie/Help/FAQs#faq2>, accessed 10 March 2018.

the company commences. It is easy to see why this model would not be the appropriate fit for an OMC in multi-unit developments. Members of an OMC do not pay money into a company for any reason other than to pay the bills of the company and provide funds for all types of repairs and maintenance works to the buildings. In this regard, OMCs are a not-for-profit company.

A Private Company Limited by Shares (LTD company) where the members' liability, if the company is wound up, is limited to the amount, if any, unpaid on the shares they hold. The maximum number of members is 149 and with such a restriction this type of company would not fit the model for an OMC where there are more than 149 units.

A Designated Activity Company (DAC)—(limited by shares). Unlike the aforementioned LTD company, this entity must have at least two directors whereas a LTD can have only one director.

A Designated Activity Company limited by Guarantee (DAC) —(limited by guarantee). The members have liability under two headings; firstly, the amount, if any, that is unpaid on the shares they hold, and secondly, the amount they have undertaken to contribute to the assets of the company, in the event that it is wound up. As with the LTD company, the maximum number of members is 149. In general, this type of company would not fit the model for most OMCs due to the restriction of members.

A Company Limited by Guarantee (CLG) (limited by guarantee not having a share capital): The liability of the members is limited to the amount they have undertaken to contribute to the assets of the company, in the event it is wound up, not exceeding the amount specified in the memorandum. As a guarantee company does not have a share capital, the members are not required to buy any shares in the company. This is the most suitable form of company structure for an OMC to take considering that the members will not have to buy shares in the company. Many charitable and professional bodies find this form of company to be a suitable vehicle and as Keane points out 'it is accordingly a suitable vehicle for associations which wish to secure the benefits of a separate legal personality and of limited liability but do not wish to raise funds from its members'.[3] Furthermore, in recognising that this type of company is normally limited to organisations which are not trading for profit, he states:

---

3 Keane, *Company Law* (3rd edn, Butterworths, 2002), paragraph 4.32.

> 'The management of such companies is normally entrusted by the articles of association to a council or a committee elected by the members rather than a board of Directors.'[4]

In their report on multi-unit developments, The Law Reform Commission stated:

> 'The Commission firmly believes, however, that the benefits of using the company law code far outweigh any perceived disadvantages. The concept of limited liability, for example, is of clear advantage to owners' management company members. The existence of a regulatory regime which protects members of the company and requires annual meetings, the presentation and transparency of accounts, and rules on corporate governance and compliance generally – and Directors' duties specifically – all operate for the benefit of the unit owner. The Commission is of the view that once a more widely understood culture of collective management and ownership becomes commonplace in Ireland, as it has in other European States and around the globe, the more the benefits of the company law code will be appreciated.'[5]

Given that OMCs play such a crucial role in most multi-unit developments it is remarkable that there are such considerable issues concerning their legal structure that remain to be addressed by the legislature and government. Many of the issues are well documented as far back as 2006 prior to the enactment of both the Multi-Unit Developments Act 2011 and the New Companies Act 2014. There were many recommendations and submissions made to the government during the consultation process for these new laws but little has changed even though the laws have been enacted. In 2006 the Law Reform Commission's consultation paper observed that legal entities under company law at the time were unsuitable for meeting the needs of not-for-profit organisations such as management companies citing the arguable incompatibility of the management company with company law. They highlighted some of the problems arising such as the lack of separation of powers.

Companies Limited by Guarantee where there is no separation of powers are unwieldy for people who hold the dual role of

---

4 ibid.

5 Law Reform Commission, *Report on Multi-Unit Developments*, LRC 90—2008.

company directors and members as they make some decisions in one capacity and other decisions in another capacity. This conflict can be detrimental to other owners in an OMC situation and it is grounded in the social values of one individual over another. A director of an OMC may be an animal lover and own a dog. If the house rules attached to the OMC state that dogs are not allowed in the apartment building, which is very common in house rules of apartment buildings, then this dog loving member of the company who is acting as a company director may have the power to amend the house rules to their liking. It would be particularly easy to do this where there is only one other director and they too own a dog. This would open the floodgates for every resident to own and keep dogs in the apartment block if they wished. The wear-and-tear effects of multiple dogs in an apartment block with limited open spaces would be very high and would, in-turn, increase cleaning costs, service charges and diminish the economic value of the apartments. Other consequences which would flow from this include a surge of issues detrimental to the peaceful occupation of the building such as dog barking complaints, dog fouling in the common areas, dog fights in the common areas, these and dog attacks on other residents are all commonplace in communal living spaces in Ireland and it is for this reason that the house rules in general state that dogs are not allowed.

Prior to the new Companies Act 2014 there was a requirement for all companies to have the annual accounts audited each year. This included OMCs and this was deemed to be almost inequitable in some circumstances where the workload and cost of auditing the annual accounts was disproportionate to the number of transactions occurring in the bank account and the level of activity in the company for the year. This was changed in the new Companies Act 2014 and there is now no requirement for an OMC to have the annual accounts audited. This provides an option for an OMC to choose whether or not they would have the annual accounts of their OMC audited. It is recommended and it is more prudent for larger OMCs to do so as it provides an additional level of checks and balances on the overall running of the company from a financial and corporate governance perspective. This new measure alleviates an unnecessary burden for smaller OMCs where it is not necessary to audit the accounts.

An OMC has limited purposes which fall short of those of a trading company and the law as it currently stands does not generally recognise this distinction. Normally an OMC is not registered for VAT. A trading company set up with the purpose of making a profit will be registered for VAT provided that the annual turnover exceeds €37,500. Although an OMC may very well have a turnover exceeding €37,500 it is not required to register for VAT. This is because of the nature of the company, it does not exist to provide a service; it exists to hold property and administer service charge payments. The benefit of this for members of an OMC is that they are not charged an additional 23 percent VAT on their service charges. In a situation where an owner's service charge is €1,500 per year, where the OMC is registered for VAT, this service charge would automatically be billed at €1,500 plus 23 percent giving the total invoiced amount of €1,845.00. The annual service charge budget will have a number of different items such as managing agent fees, electricity charges, insurance, etc. Some items have a VAT element of 23 percent such as managing agent's fees and other items have a VAT element of 13.5 percent VAT such as electricity charges, and some items have no VAT element such as insurance. In turn the OMC would claim back all of the VAT that it pays out. Private property owners are not registered for VAT and so they have no way of claiming this back. Property owners have the opportunity to claim their personal tax back at the end of the year but they must dissect the annual service charge budget to do this as they will be entitled to claim tax back on some items such as refuse charges and not on other items such as insurance.

Another consequence that flows from the issue of VAT and the OMC is that of capital expenditure projects from the sinking-fund. The OMC is not registered for VAT and because of this, for large expenditure projects such as roof replacement, the OMC can't claim back the VAT like another company would do. This skewed position is manifestly disadvantageous to property owners in an OMC compared to those who own property which is not part of an OMC. The Apartment Owners' Network[6] submits that a number of amendments to the tax law be considered so that this discrimination can be addressed. Government schemes such as the Home Renovation Scheme allows tax relief for property owners who wish to renovate their private property. This tax relief is availed of through the PAYE system. However, an OMC is a commercial entity as defined in the company law code and is not a PAYE entity and therefore does not qualify for such tax relief. This discriminates against those owning property in an OMC. Property owners in an OMC also have the need to renovate the

6 Apartment Owners' Network, *Submission to Department of Finance, Tax and Fiscal Treatment of Landlords Consultation, Submission to Tax Policy Division,* Submission 6 April 2017, p 4.

common areas of the building such as carpet replacement, roof replacement, window replacement but they are precluded from this tax relief measure due to the corporeality of the OMC.

Courtney notes that 'it cannot be overstated that under the law as it stands careful attention must be given to the maintenance of proper books of account, to the correct preparation and circulation of annual accounts and to the diligent filing of proper annual returns'.[7] In an OMC scenario, the work done is commonly undertaken on a voluntary part-time basis by people who have little or no experience or expertise in company law. The Law Reform Commission has noted that it is therefore questionable as to whether it is appropriate for management companies to use traditional forms of companies with the directorial responsibilities as a legal vehicle. The Apartment Owners' Network note that an OMC comprises a board of volunteer directors, typically civic-minded residents or owners in an apartment block or housing estate. Elected by the membership of the company these unpaid directors are charged with the primary responsibility of managing the company. This refers in particular to the upkeep of the common areas, and delivery of shared property services and of ensuring adherence and compliance with all areas of law including the onerous Safety, Health and Welfare at Work Act 2005.

2. Governance

In the context of company law, the term 'governance' means the way in which companies as organisations are run by those who own and control them. It can be contrasted with management, which signifies how a company's ordinary business affairs are conducted, although the line between overall governance and day-to-day management is not always clearly defined.[8] The common misunderstanding surrounding this issue is magnified in the OMC scenario as the management of the OMC is more often contracted out to a firm of property managing agents. The overall governance of the company remains the legal and ultimate responsibility of the directors of the OMC and therein lies the division of power between the members and the directors.

---

[7] Courtney, *The Law of Private Companies* (2nd edn, Lexis Nexis Butterworths, 2002), para 13.002.

[8] Forde and Kennedy, *Company Law*, (4th edn, Thomson Round Hall, 2008), 112, 5–01.

The annual general meeting is the best known kind of meeting in company law.[9] In accordance with the Companies Act 2014 the OMC must hold the annual general meeting within fifteen months of the previous annual general meeting. The Multi-Unit Developments Act 2011 states at s 17(5) that this meeting should take place within reasonable proximity to the multi-unit development and at a reasonable time. The Companies Act 2014 s 176(1) introduced a new rule in relation to the Annual General Meeting which sets out that the Annual General Meeting may be held inside or outside of the State. The Annual General Meeting can be held in two or more venues. What this means is that the meeting must be taking place in all places at the same time. This provides for the use of technology where members may not be able to attend at the same venue. This opens up the way for all kinds of new media to be utilised, as long as the participation is meaningful.[10] The notice period for the AGM is a minimum of 21 days and every member of the company must be notified of the meeting. Generally, the notice period for an Extraordinary General Meeting where a special resolution is tabled is fourteen days. This notice period includes the day upon which the notice is sent. If there is a dispute about the notice period, the Companies Act at s 181(3) and (4) provides as follows:

> "(3) "Where notice of a meeting is given by posting it by ordinary prepaid post to the registered address of a member, then, for the purposes of any issue as to whether the correct period of notice for that meeting has been given, the giving of the notice shall be deemed to have been effected on the expiration of 24 hours following posting.
>
> (4) In determining whether the correct period of notice has been given by a notice of a meeting, neither the day on which the notice is served nor the day of the meeting for which it is given shall be counted.
>
> (5) The notice of a meeting shall specify:
> (a) the place, the date and the time of the meeting;
> (b) the general nature of the business to be transacted at the meeting;
> (c) in the case of a proposed special resolution, the text or substance of that proposed special resolution; and

9 Thuillier, *Company Law in Ireland* (2nd edn, Clarus Press, 2015), 127
10 Thuillier, *Company Law in Ireland* (2nd edn, Clarus Press, 2015) 129.

(d) With reasonable prominence a statement that (i) a member entitled to attend and vote is entitled to a proxy (or, where it is allowed, one or more proxies), to attend, speak and vote instead of him; (ii) a proxy need not be a member; and (iii) the time by which the proxy must be received at the company's registered office or some other place within the State as is specified in the statement for that purpose."

The number of members in attendance at the AGM to make a quorum is normally provided for and can be amended in the company constitution. It is normally between two and four members and they may be present by proxy.

The business of the AGM of the company which must be covered will not vary from year to year and may include the following:

- Minutes of previous Annual General Meeting;
- Annual Report;
- Directors Reports and Financial Statements and Property Services Agreement;
- Resignation/Appointment of Directors;
- Any Other business.

The OMC has an obligation to ensure that the minutes of each company meeting are filed on the minutes file at the registered office. Failure to do so is a category 4 offence. The minutes may be recorded on a computer, the rule is that the minutes must be kept in a legible form and capable of being viewed and re-produced if required.

Section 191 of the Companies Act provides that an ordinary resolution means a resolution:

> "passed by a simple majority of the votes cast by members of a company as, being entitled to do so, vote in person or by proxy at a general meeting of the company."

A special resolution means a resolution that is

> "passed by not less than 75% of the votes cast by such members of the company concerned as, being entitled to do so, vote in person or by proxy at a general meeting of it"

This is compatible with the Multi-Unit Developments Act 2011.

Directors meetings can be a very important part of the efficient running of an OMC and generally they can be more informal than the AGM. Normally the notice period for a Directors meeting is fourteen days. The Directors are given the power to make decisions and exclusively manage the day-to-day business of the company. The companies act states that the directors of a company may meet together for the dispatch of business, adjourn and otherwise regulate their meetings as they think fit.

When it comes to decision-making in a company, the Companies Act 2014 requires that all major decisions are taken at general meetings. Section 188 states that every member whether present in person or by proxy shall have one vote save to the extent that the company's constitution provides otherwise. The constitution of an OMC will normally comply with s 14(1) of the Multi-Unit Developments Act 2011 which states as follows:

> 'one vote shall attach to each residential unit in a Multi-Unit Development to which the Owners' Management Company relates and that no other person has voting rights in respect of such determination'.

The voting rights in an OMC scenario provides a forum for the members of the company to choose to vote for something that may not be in the best interest of the company. A typical example is the vote to increase the sinking-fund for the betterment of the company. At the AGM, some members and directors may intend selling their properties in the short term and they may be reluctant to vote to adopt a hefty sinking fund levy as they will not be there to reap the benefits of it in the longer term. The result is that this company structure does not provide for the right decision for the OMC to be taken at the meeting as there is a divergence between the interest of the individual and the long-term interest of the OMC.

3. Directors' duties

Company directors' responsibilities are wide are diverse. Their duties arise primarily from two sources: statute (i.e. Acts of the Oireachtas and other legislation, e.g. EU Regulations) and common law. In an OMC situation the directors and members are one and the same and this can sometimes cause confusion. A company director stands in a special relationship to the company of which they are an officer. This special position is known as a 'fiduciary position' and the director is known as a 'fiduciary'. A fiduciary is required to act in a manner which is legally becoming of their office and which places the interests of the company ahead of their own. Directors duties are owed in the first instance to the company and not to the members, creditors or employees of the company. When a company is insolvent (i.e. unable to pay its debts as they fall due), a director will owe a duty to the company's creditors (i.e. people to whom the company owes money).

Directors' fiduciary duties are based on certain common law rules and equitable principles owed to a company by its directors. The principle fiduciary duties of a company director are owed to the company and the company alone.

The principal fiduciary duties of a company director[11] are to:

- Act in good faith in what the director considers to be the interest of the company;
- Act honestly and responsibly in relation to the conduct of the affairs of the company;
- Act in accordance with the company's constitution and exercise his or her powers only for the purposes allowed by law;
- Not benefit from or use the company's property, information or opportunities for his or her own or anyone else's benefit unless the company's constitution permits it or a resolution is passed in a general meeting;
- Not agree to restrict the director's power to exercise an independent judgment unless this is expressly permitted by the company's constitution;
- Avoid any conflict between the director's duties to the company and the director's other interests unless the director is released from his or her duty to the company in relation to the matter concerned;
- Exercise the care, skill and diligence which would be reasonably expected of a person in the same position with similar knowledge and experience as a director. A director may be held liable for any loss resulting from their negligent behaviour.[12]

---

11 Companies Act 2018, s 228.

12 Office of the Director of Corporate Enforcement, *Information Book No 2, The Principal Duties and Powers of Company Directors*, 9.

The level of exposure to liability claims against company directors of OMCs is particularly significant compared to that of any other type of company. This is because in addition to the administration, governance and management responsibilities that they bear they are also responsible in law for the buildings and the lives of the persons who come and go in them. It is important that OMC Directors ensure that they have insurance cover for such exposure by taking out a directors' and officers' insurance policy. This policy will protect them from claims made against them for actual or alleged breach of their duty, negligence, misstatements, errors and omissions.

The House of Lords decision in the case of *Salomon v Salomon* established that incorporated companies were definitively recognised by law as having the same legal existence as human beings meaning that a company was a person as far as the law was concerned and could therefore be made criminally liable under the terms of a statute. There are now numerous instances of companies being subject to criminal sanctions for breaches of statutory duties under health and safety legislation, competition laws and the Companies Acts. In 2001 the Company Law Enforcement Act established the Office of the Director of Corporate Enforcement with the specific power to enforce the penal elements of the Companies Acts.

Claims such as personal injury claims are made against the OMC but it is the directors of the OMC who are named on the action as they are the controlling mind of the company. Although, the controlling mind theory is limited in its utility when it comes to attributing criminal liability to companies, if the prosecution can identify an individual who is sufficiently senior and sufficiently involved in the day-to-day activities of the direction of the company, which directors of OMCs are, then those directors may be prosecuted in a criminal liability charge or a corporate manslaughter charge. The Law Reform Commission has published proposals to reform the area of corporate manslaughter and note that a significant difficulty which must be overcome in formulating a test for corporate manslaughter is the 'paradox of size'. Cases of corporate manslaughter will necessarily involve organisational problems and failure of management. Where systems are badly constructed and clear chains of responsibility are not in place, accidents will be more likely to occur. A conviction may be based on the size of the entity. The larger and more complex the company structure is, the easier it will be for it to avoid liability. This difficulty is well illustrated in the following two cases. In

R v Kite and OLL Ltd[13] a one-man company was convicted of manslaughter when the managing director was convicted. This contrasts with the outcome of *R v P & O European Ferries (Dover) Ltd*[14] which arose from a ferry disaster in Zebruggee harbour in which 193 people died. The report of the official inquiry noted that 'from top to bottom the body corporate was infected with the disease of sloppiness'. Notwithstanding the findings of the formal investigation that the company's procedures were severely lacking, the company avoided liability as no one human person could be found liable for manslaughter. The lack of a clear system of responsibility, which was the cause of the disaster in the first place, also led to the dismissal of the case.

For an OMC the serious end of the scale when it comes to such an issue is that of loss of life due to fire. A person who is a director of an OMC can be found to be negligent in their duty to maintain fire safety equipment where such equipment is not maintained and is faulty. Where a direct link can be made to show that the loss of life was because the fire safety equipment was not maintained, a director is at risk of being charged with corporate manslaughter due to negligence.

The failure of an OMC to file an annual return with the Companies Registration Office on time can lead to a company being struck-off the register of companies.[15] Section 343(11) of the act states as follows: 'If a company fails to comply with the requirements of this section, the company and any officer of it who is in default shall be guilty of a category 3 offence.'

In addition, fines of up to €5,000 can be imposed on a conviction for breach of the annual return filing requirements. Once an OMC has been struck-off, it has no legal existence and until such time as the company is restored to the company register there is no value in any of the properties in the development as they cannot be sold while the status of the OMC is 'dissolved'. In this instance a company director is exposed to a claim from an owner for loss of a sale. But for the director's breach of duty would the owner have been able to close the sale of their property.

The 2008 *Company Law Handbook on Residential Property Owners' Management Companies* by the Director of Corporate Enforcement states that, in general, directors are obliged to carry out their

---

13 *R v Kite and OLL Ltd* (1994) Winchester Crown Court.
14 *R v P & O European Ferries (Dover) Ltd* (1991) 93 CR APP R 72.
15 The Companies Act 2014, ch 13, s 343(11).

functions with skill and diligence. However, a director need not exhibit in the performance of his or her duties a greater degree of skill than may reasonably be expected from a person of his or her knowledge and experience. Neither is the director bound to bring any special qualifications to his or her office, and so if the members of a company are content to appoint a person without any special skills or previous experience as a director of their company, they cannot afterwards complain that the director was not as skilful as they might have liked. On the other hand where a person has particular skills or competences they are bound to bring them to the boardroom table of any company of which they are a director. So, for example, if one of the directors is a qualified accountant, he or she will be under a somewhat higher duty than the non-accountant directors to ensure that the accounting obligations of the company are properly discharged.[16]

The above position may be a source of comfort for some volunteer directors but the social conscience position is also worth some serious consideration. In a situation where there is a fire in an apartment block and there is loss of life. The OMC will be investigated rigorously by several state bodies and insurance companies. Questions and responsibility will be laid squarely at the door of the directors in the first instance. In the event where there was a breach of their duty giving rise to a successful negligence claim, the directors will be found to have blood on their hands.

The important issue here for inexperienced volunteering officers of OMCs is the risk to exposure in an area of law that places such punitive burdens on a civic-minded individual who volunteer to become a director or secretary of an OMC. In their report on multi-unit developments, the Law Reform Commission noted that 'when individuals agree to be a director of an owners' management company, they are often unaware of the scope of their responsibility as company Directors'.[17] This report was published in 2008 and the evidence is that there is little improvement in the situation.

The introduction of legislation and regulation in the area since this report has simply added to the lack of understanding and lack of knowledge that directors and officers of OMCs have. As

---

16 *Company Law Handbook on Residential Property Owners' Management Companies ('Management Companies').*

17 Law Reform Commission, *Report on Multi-Unit Developments*, LRC 90—2008, 86.

far back as 2008 the Commission recommended that officers of OMCs should receive training, the cost of which would be covered by the company itself. The benefits of this training would include heightened awareness of and compliance with company law obligations. It would also tackle the understanding deficit surrounding OMC membership. This issue of training has also been highlighted by The Apartment Owners' Network in recent submissions to the Department of Housing Planning and Local Government.[18]

4. The company secretary

In the OMC context the company secretary is normally a member of the company and can also be a director of the company, appointed by the membership to carry out the duties and function of the company secretary. Every company is required by law to have a company secretary. The duties of the company secretary are defined in company law. Their main functions are normally to oversee the company's day-to-day administration and to ensure specifically that the company complies with the law and observes its own regulations. While many OMCs appoint a managing agent to manage the day-to-day administration of the company, and the managing agent may carry out the administrative functions, it is only upon instruction by the company directors and secretary that they do this, and in this regard, the managing agent is not acting as company secretary in law but as agent to the company secretary.

Every person should, on or before appointment as a company secretary, familiarise themselves with the duties and obligations attaching to the position. Generally, no formal qualifications are required to become the secretary of a private company. However, the directors of all companies have a duty to ensure that the person appointed as secretary has the skill necessary to discharge his or her statutory and other legal duties and such other duties as may be delegated to the secretary by the directors.

Certain persons are ineligible to hold office as a company secretary, such as a person who is under the age of 18 years, an undischarged bankrupt and a person disqualified from acting as

---

18 Apartment Owners' Network, 'Submission to Forward Planning Section, Department of Housing, Planning and Local Government on Updated Draft Design Standards for New Apartments – Guidelines for Planning Authorities<https://apartmentownersnetwork.org/>, 18 January 2018, 6, accessed 10 March 2018.

a director. The first secretary of the company must be named in the statement delivered with the constitution to the registrar for registration. Subsequent appointments to the office of company secretary are in accordance with the constitution of the company.[19] These appointments are normally made at the annual general meeting of the OMC.

A number of duties are imposed on the company secretary by the Companies Act. However, few of these are the secretary's exclusive responsibility. Rather, they tend to be tasks which may (or are required to) be performed by the secretary and a director of the company. They include signing the annual return (which is also required to be signed by a director of the company).[20]

A company secretary, as an officer of the company, is under an indirect duty to comply with the company's obligations under the Companies Act 2014. A company secretary is in default where he or she authorises or permits a default to take place in breach of his or her duty as a secretary. Where a secretary, in purported compliance with any provision of the Companies Act, answers a question, makes a statement, produces a document, knowing the answer, statement or document to be false, or is reckless in the conduct of his or her duties; he or she is in breach of the Companies Act. The secretary is obliged to disclose certain information for inclusion in the Register of Directors and Secretary and the Register of Directors' and Secretary's Interests. The information that must be disclosed is: where the secretary is an individual: the name, residential address, date of birth. Where the secretary is a corporate body: the corporate name, its registered office, the registration number and the country where it is registered. A company secretary is under a duty to exercise due care, skill and diligence in the performance of their duties. The secretary can be held liable for any loss arising as a result of their negligence. However, the secretary need not exhibit in the performance of their duties a greater degree of skill than might reasonably be expected from a person with their level of knowledge and experience. [21]

In addition to the duties imposed specifically by statute, a company secretary may be allocated important administrative

---

[19] Office of the Director of Corporate Enforcement, *Information Book No. 3 The Principal Duties and Powers of Company Secretaries*, 7.

[20] ibid.

[21] Office of the Director of Corporate Enforcement, *Information Book No. 3 The Principal Duties and Powers of Company Secretaries*, 7.

duties, which will vary depending on the nature and size of a company. These may include, for example: keeping the company's minutes of board meetings, keeping, and making available for inspection, the company's registers on behalf of the directors, including, *inter alia*, the register of members, register of directors and secretaries, register of directors' and secretary's interests and ensuring that documents are filed with the Registrar of Companies within the prescribed time limits, such as the company's annual and other returns, communicating with the company's members, for example notifying the members of meetings of the company, details of proposed resolutions to be considered at meetings, circulating them with copies of the annual financial statements, etc., delivering copies of special and certain other resolutions passed by the company, administering share transfers, ensuring that the board's decisions are properly communicated.

As with the role of the director, the role of the company secretary is a burdensome one for those who put themselves forward as a volunteer with little knowledge or experience. It is in this context that a review of the company structure of an OMC was undertaken in great detail by the Company Law Review Group prior to the enactment of the new Companies Act 2014. However, we see now following the enactment of the new law that little has changed when it comes to the operation of the OMC within the confines of what is set out in the Companies Act. The most notable changes in the Act include a company not now having to audit the annual accounts, a change of the company name from LTD to CLG, replace the memorandum and articles of association with a new company constitution and issue new certificates of incorporation. According to Courtney, Company Law was carefully designed to ensure transparency for all users of company law.[22] The Companies Act is the largest piece of legislation ever enacted in the history of the state, there are 1,448 sections and 17 schedules and the problem with its application to OMCs is that one size, notwithstanding how big it is, does not fit all.

5. The CRO

It is important for those involved in the day-to-day management of an OMC to understand the role and function of the Companies Registration Office and its importance with regards to company

[22] Dr Thomas B Courtney, Chairman, Company Law Review Group, 28 March 2017 <www.clrg.org/CLRG/Publications/Annual%20Report%20 Company%20Law%20Review%20Group.pdf> accessed 10 March 2018.

compliance. The Companies Registration Office is the central repository of public statutory information on Irish companies and business names. The CRO operates under the aegis of the Department of Business, Enterprise and Innovation. The CRO has a number of core functions which include:

The incorporation of companies and the registration of business names. It is the statutory authority for registering new companies in the Republic of Ireland. The office also registers business names. A business name is a trading name which differs from the names of the persons or the company who own the business.

The receipt and registration of post incorporation documents. Companies, and to a lesser extent business names, have an obligation under law to file certain documents with the CRO. These documents include details of changes of registered office, changes of company officers (director or secretary), or a number of other changes which affect the company. Companies are also required to file annual returns, and in most cases they must also file annual accounts. The CRO also keeps details of mortgages and charges imposed on companies.

Unfortunately, not all companies comply with their obligations to file documents. The CRO can take a number of measures to deal with companies who fail to file their annual returns, including prosecution of the company or directors, or striking the company off the register.

Companies who fail to file annual returns may be struck-off the register of companies. If a company is struck-off, the protection of limited liability no longer exists and individuals can be held personally liable for any debts incurred after strike-off. Also, the assets of such a company will become the property of the State. While it is usually possible to reinstate companies which have been struck-off, this can be an expensive process. Companies wishing to avoid such a fate should ensure that their annual returns are filed on time. In 2004 there were 1,401 companies struck-off for failing to file returns, this increased to 9,514 in 2005. The dramatic increase is mainly due to the introduction of the *Integrated Enforcement Environment System* in late 2004. In 2016, 8,302 companies were struck-off the register for their failure to file annual returns. The programme of enforcement is ongoing.

Almost all of the information filed with the CRO is available for public inspection, usually for a small fee. Certain vital information, such as company name and registered office address, may be checked free of charge on the web search facility. A more detailed synopsis of a company is available by ordering a company printout or a copy of any document filed. This again can be obtained using the web search facility and a charge applies. Details of business names are also available using the search facility. Some basic statistics are available in the annual report.[23]

6. ODCE and penalties for failing to comply with company law

The Office of the Director of Corporate Enforcement was established by the government in 2001. Its primary function is to enforce company law and it has a range of enforcement powers in responding to allegations of company law breaches. The mission of the office is to improve the compliance environment for corporate activity in the Irish economy by encouraging adherence to the requirements of the Companies Act, and bringing to account those who disregard the law.[24]

Breaches of certain obligations in company law can have serious consequences for a company, company director or any other person who is responsible for those breaches. Those consequences can include court proceedings against those who are considered to be responsible for the breaches. A person who is unsuccessful in defending a legal action will usually be subject to some form of penalty. They will usually also have to pay their own legal costs and the costs of the person who started the proceedings. There are court imposed penalties for criminal offences and also civil penalties.

There are two types of criminal offences:

- A summary offence, which is considered to be less serious and is dealt with in the District Court before a judge only; and
- An indictable offence, which is generally a more serious offence. Depending on the circumstances, it may be prosecuted either in the Circuit Court before a judge and jury or in the District Court if the District Court judge agrees to do so.

In general, the highest penalties on conviction are:

23 <www.cro.ie/about> accessed 10 March 2018.

24 <www.odce.ie>.

- €1,905 and/or 12 months in prison for each summary and indictable offence prosecuted in the District Court; and
- €12,697 and/or five years in prison for each indictable offence prosecuted in the Circuit Court.[25]

The ODCE are also responsible for enforcing the provisions of the Companies Act where civil penalties include sanctions such as disqualification, restriction and strike off. Section 838 of the Act states that a person may be disqualified from being appointed or acting as a director or other officer, statutory auditor, receiver, liquidator or examiner or being in any way, whether directly or indirectly, concerned or taking part in the promotion, formation or management of a company.

Automatic disqualification by way of a court order occurs where a person is convicted on indictment of any offence under the Companies Act or any other enactment in relation to a company as prescribed; or any offence involving fraud or dishonesty. A disqualification undertaking is a new administrative procedure which provides that a person has an option to submit to disqualification without the need for a court hearing and the Director of Corporate Enforcement may, at their discretion, accept this disqualification undertaking. One of the benefits of this is the avoidance of expensive court costs.

The provisions relating to the restriction of company Directors apply to insolvent companies, i.e. companies that are unable to pay their debts as they fall due. When a company goes into liquidation or receivership and is insolvent, a director of the company who fails to satisfy the Director of Corporate Enforcement or the court that he or she has acted honestly and responsibly may be restricted for a period of up to five years.[26] As with disqualification, there is a new administrative provision which gives a person the option of submitting to a restriction without the need for a court hearing and the Director of Corporate Enforcement may, at their discretion, accept this restriction undertaking.

A company may be penalised for non-compliance by being struck-off the company register. In such an event, ownership of a company's assets automatically transfers to the State. In an OMC

---

25 Penalties for Breaches of Company Law, Office of the Director of Corporate Enforcement, 2.

26 The Office of the Director of Corporate Enforcement, 2015, *Information Booklet No 2, Company Directors,* 'The Principal Duties and Powers of Company Directors under the Companies Act', 22.

scenario, this means that the common areas of the development would be owned by the State and ownership will remain with the State until the company is restored to the company register. The most common reason for strike-off in the context of the OMC is failure to file the annual return on time.

Company law in the context of the OMC is both comprehensive and extensive. It is important for all those involved in an OMC to have an understanding of the role of the various bodies involved so as to avoid any pitfalls.

Chapter 9

Receivers and the OMC

1. Introduction 125
2. Appointment of receivers 125
3. Benefits to OMCs of receiver appointment 128

1. Introduction

Receivership is a process which is used by a bank or a secured lender in accordance with the rights conferred in a charge or mortgage document, to sell assets such as a property which was promised to them if they failed to pay the loan secured against the property. This process is almost exclusively used by banks and is a procedure of last resort for the lender in their efforts to realise the repayment of a loan. A receiver may also be appointed by the High Court and is therefore an officer of the court, having a duty to act responsibly and take their instructions from the court. A receiver may be appointed by deed under seal on behalf of a bank and is then a fiduciary for the bank in that they owe a duty of good faith and a general duty of care to the bank and also to those who have guaranteed the debt that gave rise to the receivership, in respect of exercising their powers of sale. Once a receiver is appointed, floating charges crystallise and become fixed. This prevents the company from dealing with the charged assets without the receiver's consent.[1]

2. Appointment of receivers

It is important to look at the issue of receiverships within the context of the OMC given the impact that the recent avalanche of receiverships has had on members of OMCs and the risks and consequences associated with being a member of an OMC in such a scenario.

Many OMCs will have more units than owners. It is a common scenario where one owner will own more than one unit or own several units within a development. The effect of this is that the

1 Michael Forde and Hugh Kennedy, *Company Law* (4th edn, Thomson Round Hall, 2008), ch 24, 775.

liability for the payment of the annual service charge and the sinking-fund payment rests with one entity and relies upon this entity remaining solvent to be able to pay the annual service charges and sinking-fund contributions. Where this entity is in financial difficulty and cannot pay its debts then the negative impact of this on the other members of the OMC is multiplied. This was particularly problematic in the aftermath of the Celtic Tiger era when the financial crisis hit in 2008. The property market collapse had more of an impact on those owners who owned numerous properties than those who owned a single unit. Yet it was those single-unit owners that carried the catastrophic burden of debt for the multiple of properties owned by those who were unable to pay their debts as the non-payment of the annual service charge and sinking-fund payments left a hole in the company's finances year after year. What followed in many of these cases was the appointment of a receiver by the banks to these properties. The OMC is an unsecured creditor in this scenario and receivers owe no duty to unsecured creditors. In cases where receivers were appointed it was primarily because the value of the asset had collapsed and there was no money in the property until the property was sold. This meant that in many cases in the intervening years while waiting for the property to be sold, the receiver did not have funds to pay the annual service charges. In most cases OMCs were frequently unsuccessful in extracting the annual service charge from the receivers in the intervening years.

An example of an apartment block comprising 30 apartments where one owner owns eight apartments and a receiver is appointed by the lender to sell all eight properties. The added complication that these properties may be the subject to tax relief would make it inequitable to proceed with the sale of the properties until the tax relief has expired after possibly a 10-year period from the initial date of sale leaving the OMC without any service charges being received for these properties in the intervening years. This represents a total of 64 service charges un-recovered over an eight-year period in a development of just 30 apartments. Given the collective responsibility nature of the OMC it will fall to the other 22 units in the OMC to carry this financial burden in the short term while waiting for the outstanding service charges to be recovered upon the close of sale. It is important that the directors of the OMC ensure that interest is applied to each account as a means of retribution for carrying this financial burden. In cases such as this one, it is more likely that there will also be other individual units in the development that will have defaulted on paying their service charges and this will have the result of increasing the burden of debt on other members of the OMC.

In some cases, receivers may have paid some service charges in the intervening years but it may only have been on a piecemeal basis where the funds in the property allowed. For example, where the apartment was rented and there was rental income being received.

These types of scenarios caused severe funding problems for OMCs during a period of great economic crisis. It fell to individual property owners to fund losses as great as this in the short-term while waiting for receivers to sell the assets. In cases where interest was applied to the debt, the amount eventually payable by the receivers was considerably higher. To illustrate this point, we consider a scenario where a receiver is appointed over an apartment which was mortgaged in the amount of €180,000. The value of the property plummeted to €40,000. The annual service charge on the property is €800 per year with interest and penalties amounting to €200 per year. Where the service charge is not paid for eight years then the loss suffered by bank will have increased by 25 percent due to the delay in payment. This is a compound debt scenario and was a feature of OMC properties in receivership during the economic recession period from 2008–2015. In these cases, the bank lost out by not paying the service charges in the intervening years and incurred further costs and the OMC members lost out in that they were left carrying the financial can in the short-term while the OMC had no cash reserves for capital projects.

As the overall economy and the property market recovers and until the next cyclical downturn occurs, a situation where the value of the asset is less than the debt due on the mortgage is unlikely. In most cases now, when a receiver is appointed over a property by a bank they will contact the OMC and they will provide the deed of appointment. They will then be seeking the co-operation of the OMC with regard to documentation such as insurance indemnities and requisitions. It has become more common now that receivers will pay service charges while they are waiting to sell the properties and they will engage with managing agents in a more open and transparent manner than they did during the recession years of 2008–2015.

3. Benefits to OMCs of receiver appointment

One of the benefits of a receiver being appointed over properties in an OMC is that there is a degree of certainty that the outstanding service charges will be paid. This is compared to a property owner who is in financial difficulty retaining ownership of their properties and not being able to afford to pay the annual service charge. A property owner with multiple properties in one OMC who does not pay the annual service charge and allows the debt to mount year on year may be pursued by the OMC through the normal debt collection process through the courts. This costly and slow process for the OMC only adds to the debt burden of other members of the OMC. Even in a case where the owner is brought before the courts it may be determined from the owner's statement of means that they only have the means to pay a certain amount per month to the OMC which may not be sufficient to ever clear the debt given that service charges are incurred each year. It is for this reason why it is better if a receiver is appointed over these properties on two counts. Firstly, the full amount of the outstanding service charge will be received by the OMC upon the close of sale and secondly a new and functioning property owner will be in place and those service charges will be more likely to be paid each year thereafter.

While a receiver may be appointed by way of equitable execution the courts have found that where a judgment debtor does not hold an equitable interest in a property a receiver cannot be appointed by way of equitable execution. This was confirmed in the case of *Waterside Management Company Limited v Brendan Kelly and Asta Kelly*[2] where the judgment debtor (the OMC) does not hold an equitable interest but a legal interest. The background to this case is interesting as it demonstrates the problems with the current legal structure surrounding the collection of annual service charges and the need for reform in this area.

In this case the management company sought to appoint the managing agent as a receiver over rents due to the owner of five apartments within an OMC. The management company was granted judgment in the sum of €9,684.05 together with costs. Following on from this an execution order was extracted against the goods of the owner but returned by the Sheriff marked *nulla bona*. The managing agent averred that she had called to the owners' address at least 12 times after having sent correspondence

---

2 IEHC [2013] 143.

to this address, all without response, and that the owners no longer lived at this address and were not in contact with their OMC.

In the Circuit Court the judge agreed to appoint the managing agent as receiver by way of equitable execution over so much of the rents payable by the tenants in occupation of the five apartments.

The owners of the five apartments appealed this decision in the High Court and were successful on the basis that the Circuit Court judge erred in appointing the managing agent as receiver by way of equitable execution over the rents due from the apartments as this remedy is only available where the judgment debtor had an equitable interest in the receivership property. They further argued that the management company failed to seek an examination following the judgment in aid of execution in the District Court, pursuant to Ord 53 of the rules of that court and that the Circuit Court order would have the effect of making the managing agent a landlord over the properties in accordance with the Residential Tenancies Act 2004 as defined in s 5 thereof and that the Managing Agent did not have the intention nor the ability to carry out these duties. In addition to this, they successfully argued that the appointment of a receiver would violate their right to earn a livelihood.

The management company asked the court to consider whether it was 'just and convenient' to appoint a receiver by way of equitable execution given the inappropriateness of an instalment order as a remedy in this case, in particular by reference to purported difficulties with locating, serving and contacting the owners.

The findings in law of the court amounted to the fact that the appointment of a receiver by way of equitable execution may be reserved to circumstances where the debtor holds an equitable interest in property which is not capable of being attached by the ordinary process of enforcement. As the sum in question was a relatively small one, appointing a receiver by way of equitable execution over the rents payable would be disproportionately prejudicial towards others holding an interest in the properties in question and the judge was of the belief that the appointment of a receiver could not be deemed 'just and convenient' in this case.

In this case, the OMC had lost the appeal but while the managing agent had experienced severe difficulties in making contact with these owners before this hearing, the owners had appealed the decision of the Circuit Court and there now remained no problems in serving them as they were represented at the appeal hearing. The OMC could now pursue them for the outstanding debt. By this time the outstanding service charge had increased to in excess of €30,000, the cost of which is borne by all other members of the OMC until such time as it is recovered.

What the management company sought to do by appointing a receiver was a powerful remedy for OMCs seeking to recover outstanding service charges and the decision of the High Court was disappointing as it leaves OMCs with no other option but to embark on more costly and less effective means to recover outstanding service charges. This further highlights the need for reform in the area of the recovery of outstanding service charges.

Chapter 10

Company Strike-Off and Restoration

1. **What is a company strike-off? ... 131**
2. ***Heidlestone*: strike-off and restoring an OMC to the Company Register ... 133**
3. **Transfer of common areas where the developer is not trading ... 144**
4. **Section 30 restoration of a company to the Company Register ... 146**

1. What is a company strike-off?

All companies including OMCs have to comply with certain requirements under the Companies Acts[1] and the filing of the annual return is one such requirement. Strike-off occurs by administrative act of the Registrar of Companies when certain statutory circumstances prevail such as the failure to file the annual return for one year to the companies registration office.[2] According to the Companies Registration Office over 11,000 companies are being struck off on average each year.[3] In the case of an OMC this has a detrimental effect on the operation of the company and more importantly on the title of each property within the OMC as it threatens the continuation of the legal existence of the OMC. This will have the effect of making the individual properties in the development unsaleable until such time as the OMC is restored to the Company Register.

Section 725 of the Companies Act 2014 states that strike-off is also possible where the CRO has reasonable cause to believe that a company does not have at least one director who is resident in the State. Given the poor attendance levels at AGMs for OMCs and the level of apathy among property owners when it comes to their OMC, this is a significant risk for an OMC. Also, where there are no persons recorded in the CRO as directors of the

---

1 Companies Acts 2014.

2 Companies Acts 2014, pt 12, ch 1, s 726(a).

3 Companies Registration Office, 'Information Leaflet No 28, Strike-Off and Enforcement', May 2017, 1.

company and where the Revenue Commissioners notify the CRO that the company has failed to deliver specified particulars of its business to the Revenue Commissioners within 30 days of having commenced business may also lead to strike-off.

Strike-off is something which is eminently avoidable because it cannot occur where a company is up-to-date with filing its returns, is carrying on its business and has the appropriate number of directors (including at least one director resident in the State) and delivers the required statement to the Revenue Commissioners. In accordance with s 728 of the Companies Act 2014, strike-off is always preceded by a notice from the CRO sent to the Company's registered office in which the company is informed that it is at risk of strike-off and invited to take the appropriate steps (e.g. by filing outstanding returns, by delivering the appropriate Revenue statement) to avert the threat. The contents of the notice will state the following:

a) that the issue of the notice is the first step in a process that may lead to the company being struck-off the register;
b) state the ground or grounds for striking-off being invoked by the Registrar;
c) state that the company will be dissolved if it is struck-off the register;
d) state that each director of the company at the date that the notice is sent is liable for disqualification if the company is struck-off the register (this does not apply to companies in liquidation);
e) specify the remedial step;
f) specify the date on or before which the remedial step must be taken (28 days);
g) state that failure to take the remedial step on or before the date so specified may result in the Registrar giving public notice of an intention to strike the company off the register. The date to be specified for the purposes of subs (1)(f) shall be a date falling not less than 28 days after the date of the notice.[4]

At this stage, it is still possible for an OMC to avoid strike-off by delivering to the Registrar all annual returns that the company has failed to make. If the Registrar does strike-off the company it will be dissolved under s 733(2) of the Companies Act 2014.

4 Companies Registration Office, 'Information Leaflet No 28, Strike-Off and Enforcement', May 2017, 2.

Where an OMC has been struck-off, s 30 of the Multi-Unit Developments Act states:

> '... provided that the registrar has received all annual returns outstanding, if any, from the company, the company may be restored to the company register.'

and

> ... Upon the registration of an application under subsection (1) and on payment of such fees as may be prescribed, the company shall be deemed to have continued in existence as if its name had not been struck off.'[5]

Following strike-off of a company, the company ceases to exist as a legal entity as and from the date on which notice of its strike-off is published in the CRO Gazette. The date of this publication is the date on which the company is dissolved pursuant to the Companies Act 2014. One of the effects of this will be that service providers, banks and contractors will not want to do business with a dissolved company and it will make trading almost impossible.

Consequences for directors of a company which is dissolved may include that a disqualification order may be made against them by the High Court on the application of the Director of Corporate Enforcement. The liability of company directors and members continues and may be enforced in their personal capacities as they lose the protection of limited liability where the company has been struck-off the company register. It is much more sensible for an OMC to comply with its legal obligations and ensure that the company does not become eligible for strike-off.

2. *Heidlestone*: strike-off and restoring an OMC to the Company Register

The correlation between company strike-off and the ownership of common areas is an important one when it comes to the position of the OMC. Section 25 of the State Property Act 1954 maintains that where a body corporate holds property that it does not dispose of prior to its dissolution, immediately upon such dissolution, the property vests in the State. However, there is an exception to this principle and it is where the property is held on trust for another person as is the case for the common areas of an OMC.

---

5 Multi-Unit Developments Act 2011, s 30(1)(2).

In the initial stages of construction, the common areas of a Multi-Unit Development will remain in the ownership of the development company during the period while the developer is onsite and is developing and selling the units in the development. As part of the conveyance which is completed by the developer's solicitor, the Multi-Unit Developments Act 2011 obliges the developer to transfer the common areas to the OMC. The benefit of this obligation rests with the OMC. Notwithstanding this and for a variety of reasons, there still remains numerous OMCs throughout the country where the common areas have not yet been transferred. In a situation where the property development company has been struck off the company register the course of action for the OMC may be to seek to rely on the Trustee Act 1893 as in the case of *In the matter of Heidelstone Company Limited.*[6]

Once it can be established that a trust is created between the owners of the individual units and the former development company in respect of the common areas then s 26 of the Trustee Act 1893 may be relied upon which provides that where a trustee entitled to or possessed of any land cannot be found, the High Court may make an order, termed a vesting order in the act, vesting the land in any such person, in any such manner, and for any such estate as the court may direct. The High Court in *Heidelstone Company Ltd* held that a "trustee who cannot be found" includes a dissolved company.

This case is of significant importance for all OMCs who are seeking to have the common areas of their development transferred where the original property development company is dissolved. It is also relevant to those OMCs that are dissolved as it was acknowledged by Laffoy J in this case that it was the particular circumstances of the case which gave rise to it being more cost effective to incorporate a new OMC instead of restoring the original OMC to the company register.

In this high court action, the OMC was successful in getting the common areas transferred from the dissolved development company to a new OMC which they incorporated because the original OMC was dissolved.

6 *In the matter of Heidelstone Company Limited and Courtview Management Limited*, [2006] IEHC 408.

The **Heidelstone** *case summary*

IN THE MATTER OF HEIDELSTONE COMPANY LIMITED

AND

COURTVIEW MANAGEMENT LIMITED

IN THE MATTER OF THE TRUSTEE ACT 1893

APPLICATION OF PAUL BOOTHMAN,PAULINE BOOTHMAN,MARY GOGGINS,PHILIP DONNELLY,ESTHER WALSH,ANNE WALSH,VALERIE BYRNE,JOHN CASHMAN,AILEEN FORBES BYRNE,HERBERT DARLINGTON AND RAYMOND FREELEY

AND

COURTVIEW MANAGEMENT (NO. 2) LIMITED

This application arose out of the manner in which the sale of apartments and townhouses are structured. Both the vendor company and the management company had been struck off the register of companies for failing to make returns and dissolved without the scheme of disposal having been fully implemented. It was held by Laffoy J that the Court did have a power pursuant to s 26 of the Trustee Act 1893 to vest the interest of the vendor company and/or the management company in a new management company which had been incorporated by the applicants.

In her judgment delivered on the 24 November 2006, Laffoy J, accurately predicted that the problem which the applicants were seeking to address would be encountered with increasing frequency in relation to the sale of apartments and townhouses in developments carried out during the previous decades. It is a problem which was finally dealt with in the Multi-Unit Developments Act 2011 which provides for the transfer of common areas.

Generally speaking, apartments are sold by way of long lease, the internal shell only of the apartment being demised to the purchaser. As part of the scheme of disposal the vendor will have procured the incorporation of a management company with a memorandum and articles of association which provides for the apartment owners having control of the company once all of the apartments have been disposed of. The vendor will have entered into an agreement for the sale of the common areas, which generally include the external common areas such as car parking areas, the structure of the building and the internal common areas, at a nominal price but subject to the leases of the apartments. In this way, the apartment owners, through the medium of the management company, should eventually become the owners of the common areas.

In the case of townhouses with external common areas a similar type of scheme has been adopted with the variation that, since the enactment of the Landlord and Tenant (Ground Rents) Act 1978, townhouses may only be sold by way of outright conveyance of the fee simple or assignment of the leasehold interest. So, in the case of a townhouse development, what the management company should ultimately acquire is the fee simple or the leasehold interest in the external common area subject to the easements and rights in favour of the purchasers of townhouses created by the conveyances or assignments to them.

In such developments the full implementation of the scheme of disposal by the apartment or house owners assuming control of the management company and by the common areas being conveyed to the management company is an essential element in completing the title of each apartment owner and house owner. If this becomes impossible because of the dissolution of the vendor company or the management company, or both, the title of each apartment owner and house owner remains incomplete. That is the position in which the applicants (the owners) in this case found themselves in.

In this case both the vendor company and the management company had been struck off the register of companies for failing to make returns and were dissolved without the scheme of disposal having been fully implemented. The relief sought by the applicants in this case to remedy that difficulty was an order pursuant to s 26 of the Trustee Act 1893 (the Act of 1893) vesting the interest of the vendor company and/or the management company in a new management company which had been incorporated by the applicants.

The judge considered that the approach adopted by the applicants was the correct approach and granted the relief sought.

In considering the case, the judge stated that she had no doubt that where, as part of a scheme of disposal of apartments or townhouses, a vendor incorporates a management company to manage the common areas and enters into an agreement to transfer the common areas to the management company on the completion of the sales of the apartments and houses, the management company becomes the owner in equity on the completion of the sales of all of the apartments or houses, as the case may be, subject to the terms of the agreement and subject to payment of any nominal sum provided for therein. On the completion of such sales, the vendor thereafter merely holds the legal estate as trustee on behalf of the management company.

Section 25 of the Act of 1893 provides that the High Court may, whenever it is expedient to appoint a new trustee or trustees, and it is found inexpedient, difficult or impracticable to do so without the assistance of the court, make an order appointing a new trustee even if there is no existing trustee, and s 26 empowers the court to make a consequential vesting order in favour of the new trustee or trustees. Section 26 also provides that in the other circumstances set out in that section, one of which is where a trustee entitled to or possessed of any land cannot be found, the court may make an order, which is called a vesting order in the Act, vesting the land in any such person, in any such manner and for any such estate as the court may direct.

The applicants in this case were the majority of the owners of apartments and townhouses in the development known as Courtview at Castle Avenue, Clontarf, Dublin. The original developer and vendor of apartments in Courtview was the company first named in the title of the case (the First Company), which procured the incorporation of the Second company mentioned in the title of the case (the Second Company) to manage the common areas. The development area comprised two Victorian houses situated at Castle Avenue, Clontarf, numbers 50 and 52 Castle Avenue, and the ground at the rear which had a separate road frontage to the rear. The original plan was that No 50 Castle Avenue would be developed as eight apartments, No 52 would be developed as eight apartments and ten new apartments would be constructed on the ground at the rear of numbers 50 and 52.

The original scheme of disposal was part implemented and effected as follows:

(1) The First company procured the incorporation of the Second company as a company limited by guarantee and having a share capital on the 11 October, 1985. The primary object for which the

Second company was established, as set out in its memorandum of association, was to

> ". . . acquire the Lessor's interest in certain parts of the lands situate at Courtview, Castle Avenue, Clontarf, in the City of Dublin and to hold the same as an investment for the benefit of the lessees of the flats erected thereon and to acquire common areas of the said lands for the benefit of the owners of residential units thereon."

It was also provided that an object of the company was to manage the apartments, to provide management services to the common areas, and to collect the service charges. The memorandum of association also provided that no person should be admitted to membership of the Second company other than the subscribers thereto and the lessees of the apartments comprised in the development. The subscribers to the memorandum were the two Directors of the first company each of whom subscribed for one ordinary share of IR£1 in the share capital of the second company.

(2) By an agreement dated the 21 January, 1986, made between the First company of the one part and the Second company of the other part (the Management Company Agreement), the First company agreed to sell the entirety of the development (the Estate) to the Second company at the price of IR£1 subject to and with the benefit of the leases to be granted of the apartments on the Estate and subject also to an option reserved to the vendor. The Management Company Agreement was in the form normally used for this type of development and it provided for completion of the purchase within three calendar months of the completion of the development or on the 31 December 1990, whichever should be the earlier. The only unusual feature was the option clause under which the first company reserved the exclusive option to retain out of the Estate the building No 50 Castle Avenue together with all necessary easements over the remainder of the Estate.

(3) The eight apartments in No 52 were disposed of by leases, all in the same form, which were created between March, 1986 and October, 1986. Each lease was made between the first company of the first part, Second company of the second part and the purchaser/lessee of the third part and created a term of 500 years from the 1st January, 1985, at a nominal yearly rent of IRE1 (if demanded). It was recited in each that the first company was seised of the estate in fee simple in possession subject to the Management Company Agreement but otherwise free from encumbrances. It

was further recited that the First company had agreed to convey all its estate right title interest in the Estate as soon as leases in the same form had been granted in respect of all of the apartments subject to and with the benefit of the leases and subject further to the option but otherwise free from encumbrances. While the recital did not specifically state that the agreement was with the Second Company, that was clearly the case. What was demised was the internal shell of the apartment together with the usual easements, rights and privileges. Each lease was in the form normally used for this type of development.

The original development plan was not fully implemented. In 1987 the First company sold off the rear area of the Estate, with the participation of the second company, to Langarth Properties Limited (Langarth). Langarth developed that area by the construction of five houses. The houses were disposed of by conveyances made in 1988, each being made between Langarth of the first part, the Second company of the second part and the purchaser of the third part. Each conveyance recited that, as part of the scheme for the disposal and future management of "the Estate", Langarth had agreed to convey all its estate, right, title and interest in "the Estate" to the Second company as soon as conveyances of the houses to be erected on "the Estate", had been granted, subject to such easements, rights and privileges as were granted or were intended to be granted to the purchasers of the houses. In this context "the Estate" meant the land at the rear of numbers 50 and 52 Castle Avenue, known as Courtview which corresponded with the land conveyed to Langarth by the First Company. The participation of the second company in each conveyance was for the purpose of assuring all its estate, right, title and interest in the house site being sold to the purchaser. This participation was necessary because of the rights of the second company under the Management Company Agreement. Each conveyance recited that the purchaser was a member of the second company.

A further change to the original scheme of disposal took place in July 1987, when the option reserved in the Management Company Agreement was exercised, which had the effect of taking No 50 Castle Avenue out of the scheme. As a result of the foregoing changes, the Estate within the meaning of the Management Company Agreement was reduced and comprised of No 52 Castle Avenue with adjoining unbuilt-on land which is the property that was the subject of this application. This property is further referred to as the Varied Estate.

The complications arising from the variation of the original development plan and the original scheme of disposal were dealt with by the court as follows:

(i) The first eleven applicants on the application had procured the incorporation of the last named applicant, Courtview Management (No 2) Limited (the New Management Company), a company limited by guarantee with a share capital. Its objects were to acquire the Varied Estate subject to the leases of the apartments in No 52 and to manage it, collect the service charges and such like in conjunction with the management of the external common areas on the property conveyed to Langarth in 1987. The New Management Company was incorporated on 16 June 2005 to be controlled by the owners of apartments in No 52 and the owners of the houses at Courtview. Its memorandum of association, in essence, replicated the memorandum of association of the Second company in all material respects.

(ii) Three of the five owners of houses developed and sold by Langarth on the property acquired by it were applicants on this application. The owners of the remaining two houses did not participate.

In a grounding affidavit sworn on the 19th May, 2006, the first applicant averred that they "had taken no part good, bad or indifferent in relation to this and the judge noted that the first applicant would not be prejudiced in any way by the order that she was to make in this case. However, the judge considered that they should be informed by letter from the applicants' solicitors of the intention to make the order and that they should be advised that unless they objected to the making of the order by informing the applicants' solicitors of their objection within two weeks of the date of that letter, the order was to be perfected. If they objected, the matter would be re-listed to hear their objection.

Alternatively, on production of an affidavit from the applicants' solicitors proving that this requirement had been complied with and that they had either indicated that they had no objection or not responded, the order was to be perfected.

There were some external common areas around the houses developed by Langarth and Langarth were going to convey that area to the New Management Company.

(iii) In relation No 50 Castle Avenue, on the direction of the court, the applicants' solicitors wrote to the director of the First company and the Second Company, requesting that he either confirm in writing that he has no objection to the application or, alternatively, that his legal advisors contact them. By letter dated 15th November, 2006, to the applicant's solicitors, the director set out his understanding that the application was "to effectively regularise matters at 50 and 52 Castle and the 5 townhouses at the rear of the same". He consented to the application and indicated that he welcomed it.

The order that the judge was going to make in this case would not be perfected until such time as the applicant's solicitor's letter of the 8th November, 2006 and that letter of 15 November 2006, were exhibited in an affidavit sworn by the applicants' solicitors and filed in court.

The evidence put before the court was that searches in the Registry of Deeds from 1985 to 2006 did not disclose any conveyance from the First company to the owner of No 50 and the judge took care to ensure that the vesting declaration she would make was worded in such a way as not to prejudice the owner at the time of No. 50 Castle Avenue and to preserve any easements and rights it was intended should be enjoyed by that property over the Varied Estate.

The First company was struck off the register of companies and dissolved with effect from 26 October 1990, and the Second company was struck off the register and dissolved with effect from 19 May 1993, in each case for failure to make annual returns.

The judge noted that the owners had, since the mid 1990's made Herculean efforts to regularise the position for the owners of the apartments and houses at Courtview. They engaged in correspondence with the office of the Chief State Solicitor between April, 1997 and November, 1997. The outcome of that correspondence was that the Minister for Finance was not prepared to exercise his power under s 31 of the State Property Act 1954 (the Act of 1954). The explanation for this refusal was given in a letter dated the 8 May 1997, from the Chief State Solicitor to the applicants' solicitors in the following terms:

> "As you are aware, under the provisions of s. 28 of the State Property Act 1954, where a body corporate holds property which it does not dispose of prior to its dissolution, immediately upon such dissolution that property vests in

> the State. An exception is property held by the dissolved body corporate upon trust for another person. The agreement of the 21st February, 1986, between Heidelstone Company Limited and Courtview Management Limited appears to amount to a trust. As you will appreciate, until this property has passed to the State the powers of the Minister for Finance under section 31 of the State Property Act, 1954 do not come into force. In that event it might be possible for you to bring an application under the Trustee Acts."

The applicants gave notice of these proceedings to the Chief State Solicitor and furnished a copy of the special summons and grounding affidavit and exhibits, including the correspondence with the Chief State Solicitor in 1997. There was no intervention by any State authority in these proceedings.

On the facts of this case Laffoy, J found as follows:

(a) At and immediately before the date of its dissolution, the First company held the Varied Estate in fee simple upon trust for the Second company by virtue of the provisions of the Management Company Agreement. While no evidence was adduced that the nominal consideration of IR£1 was paid to the First Company, it was the view of the judge that this may be overlooked in reliance on the *de*minimis principle. The *de*minimis principle is a legal doctrine and a latin expression meaning that the law does not concern itself with trivial issues.

(b) At and immediately before the date of its dissolution, the Second company held its beneficial interest in the Varied Estate for the benefit of the lessees of the apartments in No 52 holding under the leases created by the First company in 1986 carved out of the fee simple. Those lessees or their successors, who were applicants on this application, were the ultimate beneficiaries of the Varied Estate.

(c) Both the legal estate of the First company and the beneficial interest of the Second company were subject to the leases of the apartments in No 52 and also to such easements, rights and privileges in favour of No. 50 and the purchasers of houses on the property conveyed to Langarth in 1987 as were created by virtue of the scheme of disposal.

(d) The beneficial interest of the owners of the apartments in No 52, by their consensus, would now be held by the New Management Company and regulated by it.

The judge took into regard, the attitude adopted by the Minister for Finance, who properly concluded in 1997 that the State has no claim to the Varied Estate under the Act of 1954, and considered that the court did have the power to make a vesting order under s 26 of the Act of 1893.

In addition, the judge made an order vesting the Varied Estate in the New Management Company in fee simple and for all other estate, right, title and interest as the First company and the Second company had therein at the respective dates of dissolution, subject to the leases of apartments in No 52 Castle Avenue created by the First company and subject also to such easements, rights and privileges for the benefit of No. 50 Castle Avenue and the lands conveyed to Langarth in 1987 as subsist thereover.

In commenting on this case, Laffoy J, noted that it was not inconceivable that prior to 26th October, 2010 an application might have been brought under s 12B(3) of the Companies (Amendment) Act, 1982 to have the First company restored to the Register of Companies. If such an application were successful, the First company would be deemed to have continued in existence as if its name had not been struck off. However, she was of the view that possibility did not in any way militate against the making of the vesting order that she had made, because the restored First Company's interest in the Varied Estate would be subject to the trusts which had been clearly established in evidence, even if the vesting order were not made and the restored First company could be compelled to execute a conveyance which would have the same effect as the vesting order.

Finally, the judge stated that she was satisfied that, having regard to the circumstances of the case, it was probably more cost effective and was certainly a more clear cut solution to the title problem to procure the incorporation of the New Management Company rather than seek to have the Second company restored to the register of companies.[7]

---

7 *In The Matter of Heidelstone Company Limited and Courtview Management Limtied, In The Matter of The Trustee Act 1893, Application of Paul Boothman, Pauline Boothman, Mary Goggins, Philip Donnelly, Esther Walsh, Anne Walsh, Valerie Byrne, John Cashman, Aileen Forbes Byrne, Herbert Darlington and Raymond Freeley AND Courtview Management (No. 2) Limited,* IEHC 408, [2006]

3. Transfer of common areas where the developer is not trading

Where an active and trading development company has failed, refused or neglected to transfer the common areas within the statutory specified time limits, the OMC may rely on s 24 of the Multi-Unit Developments Act (Ord 46B of the Circuit Court Rules) for the purposes of compelling compliance with the relevant section of the Act. Applicants to such proceedings are those as defined by s 25(1) of the act and include, among other things, the OMC and any/or individual members of such a company. Persons outside the section may apply to the Circuit Court on an *ex parte* basis under s 25(2) for permission to proceed under the Act.

The problem for many OMCs of being faced with this scenario of having to compel a developer to transfer the common areas is the significant cost of the action. Given that this action must be taken in the Circuit Court, the OMC would be faced with funding the action initially. It is likely that by virtue of the fact that the Act imposes an obligation on the developer to transfer the common areas that the OMC would obtain an order for costs if the application were successful. The minimum costs of such an action would be in the region of €5,000 for solicitor's costs and €2,500 for barrister's costs. In the event of the case being successful, it is most likely that costs would be recovered from the developer. In assessing the costs of such an application and the likely recovery of same, one has to have regard to the financial status of the developer, i.e. are they of sufficient financial standing that it is likely that they will be in a position to pay any costs awarded and if not, can the OMC afford to pay.

Due to the lack of enforcement of the Multi-Unit Developments Act, an action to compel the developer to transfer the common areas is particularly adversarial in nature and such a form of adversarial litigation will carry with it the usual risks associated with adversarial litigation. In contrast to this is an action taken under the Trustee Act 1893, where an OMC will be simply seeking the assistance of the High Court to rectify a problem with the title of their property where the developer or title holder for the common areas of their development no longer exists, that is, that the company status of the developer is struck-off the company register and status dissolved at the Companies Registration Office as was the case in *Heidelstone*.

The appropriate course of action for redress for OMCs where the common areas have not been transferred will depend on the status of the original developer or the title holder to the common areas and it will also depend on the status of the OMC on the company register. Most property development companies that built apartment blocks and established OMCs prior to the Multi-Unit Developments Act 2011 will be dissolved at CRO. The 2011 Act introduced a number of safeguards to ensure that the common areas are transferred in advance of any difficulties arising. Section 3 of the Act states that no unit may be sold without: (a) the establishment of a management company at the cost of the developer; (b) the transfer of the legal interest of the common areas to the management company; (c) certification of compliance with fire safety to be provided to the management company; and (d) the developer to enter into a contract with the management company outlining duties and obligations, that is, the management company agreement. Section 4 of the Act provides that the transfer of common areas, in cases where s 3 does not apply, must be completed within six months of the commencement of the legislation.

The ability to restore a former developer company to the Register of Companies pursuant to s 738 of the Companies Act 2014 does not militate against an application pursuant to s 24 of the Trustee Act 1893 when dealing with a dissolved development company. Indeed, the latter may be the more prudent course of action, particularly where the development company is financially unsound or where it is not possible to take effective control on restoration.[8]

4. Section 30 restoration of a company to the Company Register

In the case of *Heidelstone*, it was found to be more cost effective and a more clear-cut solution to incorporate a new OMC than to seek to have the old OMC restored especially since the common areas had not been transferred at that stage. This will not be the case for most OMCs that are struck-off. Laffoy J noted that

> 'having regard to the circumstances of this case, it was probably more cost effective and it is certainly a more clear cut solution to the title problem to procure the incorporation of the new management company rather than seek to have the second company restored to the register of companies.'

---

8 Dean Regan, 'Title Fight, Common Areas in Multi-Unit Developments', Law Society Gazette, Ed 38, July 2017.

Where the common areas of the development have been transferred to the OMC and subsequently the OMC is struck-off the company register, it will normally be more efficient to restore the company to the register than to incorporate a new OMC. In *Heidelstone* restoration was not the appropriate option because among other reasons, the common areas were not transferred but it may be the best option in other circumstances where the common areas are transferred and the OMC may be restored to the company register in accordance with s 30 of the Multi-Unit Developments Act 2011.

Where an OMC has been struck-off under s 733 of the Companies Act 2014, s 311 of the Companies Act 1963 or was struck-off under s 12 of the Companies Amendment Act 1982, it may apply for restoration by filing Form H1-OMC within six years of the date of dissolution. A fee of €300 is payable but if the dissolution is within one year of application for restoration, the filing of form H1 will be sufficient using the restoration process available under ch 2 of pt 12 of the Companies Act 2014. In addition to this, all outstanding annual returns together with financial statements must accompany the application. These financial statements must relate to an individual financial year and may not be amalgamated with the accounts for another financial year or years.

Since 1 June 2017 all annual returns are filed electronically at a fee of €20 plus the relevant late filing penalties. Late penalties can be considerable depending on the period of time which has elapsed since the company last filed their annual return. It is a combination of the late filing penalties and accountancy fees which give rise to the high cost of such an exercise and this is why it is much more sensible and economical for a management company to comply with its legal obligations in the first instance and ensure that the company does not become eligible for strike-off.

Late penalties are charged at €3 per day for every day that the company has been late in filing the annual return. This cost increases to a maximum of €1,200 per annual return. The Registrar must be satisfied that the relevant sections of the Companies Act is being complied with before they will restore the company to the register. The form H1-OMC is for Owners' Management Companies only and cannot be used to administratively restore a company struck-off the register by the Revenue Commissioners. It must be accompanied by the relevant certificates before restoration can be effected.

Form H1-OMC may be signed by a member of an OMC, however, it is necessary for each annual return of the OMC to be signed by a director and the secretary of the company and for the financial statements annexed to each return to be certified by two of its directors. Administrative restoration is not possible if more than six years have elapsed since the date of the company's dissolution. The company's date of dissolution may be ascertained by checking the search facility on the CRO website. The OMC cannot be restored to the register unless the accountant's/solicitor's certificate accompanies the H1-OMC form, as well as the certified copy of the deed of transfer of the common areas or a part thereof in respect of the multi-unit development in relation to which the OMC was incorporated. 'Certified copy' means a copy of the deed of transfer that has been certified by a solicitor as a true copy of the original deed.[9] Where an officer of an OMC completes Form H1 within the first 12 months of the dissolution, it is not necessary to file Form H1-OMC. However, where a restoration application is made between one and six years after the dissolution, the officer of the company must complete Form H1-OMC. Form H1 is valid only for the first year since the dissolution of the company and has less requirements than the Form H1-OCM. If a member of the company is making the application to restore the company then Form H1-OMC must be completed. Form H1 will be rejected where not all of the necessary documents have been filed.

In a multi-unit development, the title of each property is incomplete where the common areas are not transferred. Following the enactment of the Multi-Unit Developments Act 2011 it was suggested that the effect of the legislation which states that the developer has an obligation to transfer the common areas, is to render the apartments unsaleable where the common areas were not transferred. In practice, there is some confusion as to what effect the non-transfer of common areas has on the saleability of a property within an OMC. Barrister Dean Regan notes in his article, 'Title Fight' in the Law Society Gazette in July 2017 that the non-transfer of the common areas 'will have ramifications for the future sale and transfer of such properties'. However, this is not the case in practice, particularly with properties sold prior to the Act. The Law Society of Ireland issued a practice note on the matter stating:

'There is no statutory restriction on selling apartments

9 Companies Registration Office, Notes on completion of Form H1-OMC <www.cro.ie>.

> where the transfer of common areas has not yet taken place where the apartments were completed before 2011. The Act does not provide for any sanction of non-compliance. Prior to the Act the titles of both new and second hand residential units in Multi-Unit Developments were regarded as good and marketable on the basis that there was an enforceable contract to transfer the common areas to the OMC at the appropriate stage of the development, and many such sales were completed since the Act became law and many sales continue to be completed regardless of this obligation. The 2011 Act does nothing to detract from or weaken the position of a unit owner in a development governed by sections 4 and 5, transfer of common areas.'[10]

The position that many OMCs find themselves in throughout the country today one where the original developer of their multi-unit development has gone out of business and the development company which they had set up to sell the units in the development is status dissolved at CRO while the common areas of the development are still not transferred. In most cases this problem relates to properties which were constructed and first sold prior to the Multi-Unit Developments Act 2011. Section 3 of the Act precludes this situation from arising now, as, a unit in a multi-unit development cannot be sold unless the common areas have been validly transferred by deed. There are a lot of property owners and members of OMCs who therefore have incomplete titles on their properties.

The question that arises here is, where is the incentive for the members of the OMC to rectify the title of the common areas of multi-unit development complexes by effecting the transfer of common areas since the value of their investment is not affected? On the one hand it is important to have the title to the property complete but the position of most property owners in this situation today is, if the cost of doing so is prohibitive and there are no ramifications of not doing so, then why would they seek to incur considerable Circuit Court costs to effect the transfer of common areas? There are various scenarios in which these issues may be dealt with all of which depend on where the title to the common areas rests. It is estimated that one third of all OMCs in Ireland fall

---

[10] The Law Society of Ireland, 'Practice Note, Effect of the Multi-Unit Developments Act 2011 on existing developments', 4 November 2011, <www.lawsociety.ie/Solicitors/Practising/Practice-Notes/Effect-of-the-Multi-Unit-Developments-Act-2011-on-existing-developments/#.W2SIqChKiyI>, accessed 3 August 2018.

into this category whereby the original development company is dissolved and the common areas are not transferred.[11]

The future prospects for these OMCs where the common areas are not transferred and the development company is dissolved is uncertain. There are a number of proposals by various groups in relation to the matter. Regulation of the OMC is one such proposal which has been examined in more detail in chapter 8 of this book. If the government enact legislation to establish a new and separate regulatory body for the OMC, then it is possible that the rectification of the title of all these properties could form part of their remit.

The Apartment Owners' Network note in their written statement to the Joint Oireachtas Committee on Housing, Planning and Local Government that, currently, the Multi-Unit Developments Act and the Property Services Regulatory Authority fall within the remit of the Department of Justice and Equality. They propose that as the sector has developed and grown it should fall under the Department of Housing, Planning and Local Government and not that of Justice and Equality.[12] It is a possibility that this government department may then have the responsibility of dealing with the issue of transfer of common areas where the original development company is dissolved. A type of 'property amnesty' could also be introduced whereby an allowance is made for a simple transaction to occur to effect the transfer of common areas to their rightful owners, the OMC. This would deal with the problem and rectify hundreds of thousands of title documents across the country and would therefore comply with the implementation of the scheme of disposal which is provided for in the Multi-Unit Developments Act 2011. Given the shortcomings of the Multi-Unit Developments Act in many areas, perhaps an overhaul of the Act could include a section which will adequately deal with this issue.

---

11 A survey of 30 OMCs throughout Ireland, carried out by A.K Property Services, 30% of OMCs do not have the common areas transferred and the original development company is dissolved.

12 Apartment Owners' Network, Written Statement to Joint Oireachtas Committee on Housing, Planning & Local Government, Issues Impacting Apartment and Multi-Unit Developments, 19 April 2018. https://apartmentownersnetwork.files.wordpress.com/2018/04/aon-jochplg-statement-2018-04-19.pdf

Chapter 11

Insurance and the OMC

1. Introduction 151
2. Insurable perils and uninsurable perils................ 153
3. The claims process.. 156
4. Avoiding insurance pitfalls 162
5. Airbnb and insurance 163
6. Case studies 165

1. Introduction

This chapter deals with the issue of insurance policies for OMC's and gives detailed information on the various types of insurance policies, factors which affect the cost of the policy, insurable perils and non-insurable perils. Every insurance policy has an excess and the excess is the amount of money which the property owner must pay towards the claim that they are initiating. An insurer will have many types of excesses within a policy in particular an apartment block insurance policy and these are discussed in more detail in the following pages. The appointment of a loss assessor by the OMC is a matter for consideration for the OMC when a loss has been suffered and Owners should be aware of what is involved in these circumstances.

The insurance of a property against damage was historically effected by means of a 'fire' insurance policy, which could be extended to cover other specific perils. The modern approach is to arrange an 'all risks' or 'accidental damage' policy which is generally described as material damage insurance. Insurance companies ascribe different titles to such policies for marketing purposes, but the intention is that whatever the policy is called, it should provide for a wide range of perils.[1] Insofar as Irish law is concerned, 'all risks' cover does not mean literally cover against all risks. Such cover does not include damage which is inevitably due to ordinary wear and tear or inherent vice.

One of the most important items on the annual service charge

1 Austin J Buckley, *Buckley on Insurance Law* (4th edn , Round Hall, Dublin, 2016), 16-01, ch 16, 980.

budget of an OMC is the cost to provide adequate insurance policies. Depending on the nature of the development, the number of insurance policies that may be required can vary and may include Material Damage Buildings Insurance, Directors' and Officers' Insurance and Lift Engineering Insurance. Each insurance policy will set out the definitions of cover. The definition of Buildings will vary from policy to policy and will normally encompass the following:

> 'buildings and services including outbuildings, garages, swimming pools, tennis courts, patios, terraces, drives, footpaths, walls, gates, hedges, fences and fixtures and fittings including fitted wooden or laminated flooring and any fitted kitchen, bathroom or bedroom units and their integrated appliances excluding aerials, satellite aerials and their fittings or masts.'

The insured must have an insurable interest in the subject-matter of the insurance policy. This means that the insured must have an economic interest and a relationship of proximity to the subject-matter insured. For an OMC, the insured is the OMC and the OMC's interest is each of the apartments and the common areas that make up the entire building. Where the common areas of an apartment block have not been transferred to the OMC the OMC will still have an insurable interest. This interest is derived from the fact that the common areas are held in trust for the OMC and so they have a legal right to insure them. Buildings insurance policies for multi-unit developments are commercial insurance contracts and are different from a private home insurance policy for properties that are not part of a multi-unit development. Both will provide for similar risks but some insurance companies that provide cover for private houses may not offer commercial insurance products for OMCs.

Indemnity is the controlling principle in insurance law.[2] What is meant by an indemnity is that a loss must have been suffered by the insured. This is an essential prerequisite as the purpose of the policy is to restore the insured to the position they were in before the incident or accident occurred which gave rise to the claim. The principle of indemnification plays a considerable role in dealing with difficulties arising with insurance contracts but only where the computation of the loss is an issue.[3] Once

---

2 Brett LJ in *Castellain v Preston* (1883) 11 QBD 380 at 386; 52 LJQB 366.

3 Attracta O'Regan Cazabon, *Insurance Law in Ireland*, Round Hall, Sweet & Maxwell, 1999 ch 1, 17.

the OMC has paid the premium it is the Insurance Company's liability to provide an indemnity. The amount of indemnity will not automatically equal the sum insured under the policy. This sum simply represents the upper limit of the insurance company's exposure in the event of a successful claim and the insured will not be entitled to recover more than the actual sum insured. For an OMC it is essential therefore, that the level of indemnity and the sum insured are both adequate to cover a full re-instatement cost in the worst-case scenario. Formulas for calculating the sum to be insured can be accurately assessed by a qualified building surveyor and therefore exposure to a risk of underinsurance will not be an issue for an OMC that has accurately calculated the re-build cost of the buildings. Conversely, when it comes to directors' and officers' insurance, the extent of a claim may be more ambiguous. If the level of indemnity on such a policy is for €500,000 then depending on a very broad range of scenarios, this may be sufficient and it may not. The methods of calculating what the limit of indemnity is in this type of policy is much less scientific in this regard.

All insurance premiums are calculated based on the level of indemnity and the claims history. Thereafter, there are several other factors which will affect the premium for each individual policy. In this regard, no two policies are the same. If the building is in a location which is prone to flooding then this will have a considerable impact on the premium as the risk of a claim is higher.

2. Insurable perils and uninsurable perils

The buildings are normally insured against damage by fire, flood, lightning strike, explosion, earthquake, water or oil escape, terrorism, vandalism, subsidence, theft and many other insurable perils which will be stated in the policy document. Business interruption cover may include alternative accommodation costs and loss of rent receivable. Public liability cover has a typical limit of up to €6.5 million for any one claim. Employers liability cover has a standard limit of €13 million for any one claim. This would cover claims made by any self-employed tradesmen engaged by the management company. However, each peril may have conditions attached and not every policy will have the same conditions. For example, insurers may not provide cover in the event of a lightning strike if they find that lightning conductors in the building are not in place and where it can be shown that they should have been in place. Also, it may not be possible to succeed in a claim for escape of water where the apartment is unoccupied depending on the exclusions and warranties contained in the policy. It is therefore imperative that the OMC has procured the appropriate scope of cover for the individual requirements of their OMC. While the OMC will provide buildings insurance, owners should be aware that they should provide have their own contents insurance policy to cover the contents of the apartment. A contents insurance policy will cover furniture and other contents which are not fixed. The point at which the buildings cover stops and contents cover starts can sometimes be ambiguous and it has been a critical part of negotiations between insurance loss assessors and insurance loss adjusters. It will be dependent upon various warranties and exclusions in the policy. In some cases, all white goods such as washing machine, dryer, fridge are deemed to be contents but oven and hob are not. However, where the oven and hob are not built-in appliances then they are deemed to be contents. Equally in most cases, a tenant's personal belongings such as laptops, clothes, etc. will not be covered under a landlord's contents policy in cases where the apartment is rented, and the tenants should ensure to cover their own personal belongings.

There are many instances where a loss may not be covered. The general principle of insurance is that it provides financial cover against a possible eventuality such as accidents and/or incidents of an unexpected nature. In general, structural defects in apartment blocks are not an insurable peril and insurance companies will seek to firstly establish whether the loss was caused by a structural defect or not. General wear and tear on a property will not be covered and any loss which is as a result of a gradual process such as water seeping in over time and where the main loss is because of lack of maintenance of the property would usually not be covered. A simple example of such a scenario is where a seal on a bath or shower fails and this is not detected by the owner of the property and results in water damage to the apartment beneath, this will generally not be covered under the terms of the policy.

Insurance companies vary in the scope of cover that they provide. They sell their policies in a competitive open market where OMCs shop around for the best scope of cover and the most competitive premium available to them. The cover that the insurance company will offer and the risks that they will provide for will depend on the marketplace. One insurer may provide cover for a property in an area liable for flooding while another insurer would not be prepared to take on that risk. This means that for some OMCs they will have a larger number of companies to tender the contract of insurance out to and others may be restricted depending on the risks that they are seeking cover for. However, insurance companies regularly change the scope of what they provide cover for and the market changes very often. At one time the water damage excess for apartment blocks was the same as the material damage excess. This has changed considerably in the past 10–15 years as the number of water damage claims in apartment blocks increased dramatically. Now all buildings insurance policies will have a variety of excesses with the highest excess usually for water damage claims. It is important for an OMC to shop around regularly at renewal as the market is constantly fluctuating. Insurance companies can refuse to insure an apartment block if they decide that they do not want to take on the risk. While an insurance company will normally pay out for the cost of the material damage, they will not normally pay out for costs associated with the stress that a property owner suffers or expenses such as travel and time that the property owner has incurred due to the incident.

Most if not all apartment block policies incorporate an underinsurance clause also known as an average clause which makes the policyholders responsible for the proportion of the value at risk which is not insured when compared against the sum insured. An example is where an apartment block buildings sums insured stands at €1.5 million but the actual cost of reinstatement is €3 million. The effect of this underinsurance is that any claims admitted by the insurance company will only be proportionately paid in the amount of 50 percent making the policyholders responsible for the balancing 50 percent. This is a significant exposure for an OMC. At the annual general meeting of the OMC each year, owners are constantly seeking ways to reduce the cost of each item in the budget and given that the reduced sums insured will result in a lower premium, the OMC should not be tempted to reduce an overhead by exposing themselves to such underinsurance. OMCs must be certain that they insure their buildings for the full re-instatement value to avoid such exposure as it is well acknowledged that it is within the control of the insured policyholder as opposed to the insurer to do so. It is recommended that an OMC employs a qualified building surveyor to establish the correct re-build cost of the buildings.

All lifts in multi-unit developments require an Independent Thorough Examination every six months as part of the Safety Health and Welfare at Work Act 2005 and as described in the

Safety Health and Welfare at Work (General Application) Regulations 2007 which states that a safety inspection, called a Regular Thorough Examination, is to be carried out by an independent competent person. The purpose of this requirement is to develop a thorough examination method which has proven to enhance the safety of lifts, thereby reducing the risk of safety-related incidents or accidents such as trapping, crushing, slipping, falling, cutting, pinching, etc. This inspection must not be confused with the regular maintenance which is carried out by the lift maintenance company as it is additional and independent of that. The emphasis is on impartial and independent. It may include a '60-point safety check' on lifts which has been developed in conjunction with the Dutch 'Liftinstituut' who are world-leading safety experts in relation to lifts and other vertical movement equipment. Where there is a claim against the OMC for an incident or accident with a lift, this claim may not be covered in the event where this examination had not been conducted. Only companies that are accredited with an ISO 17020 accreditation are deemed to be 'competent' to carry out these inspections. It is most common that the engineering divisions of insurance companies provide this service to OMCs. This legislation exists to place the burden on the duty holder (the OMC) to safeguard all passengers in the lift and to control the way in which they use and maintain the lift.

Directors' and officers' insurance is particularly important in an OMC scenario given that many directors and officers in an OMC act in a voluntary non-professional basis and often may not have any experience of being a company director. As the role is so onerous with the weight of the Companies Acts, it follows that they should be protected where possible against any claims that are made against them. This type of insurance policy provides indemnity for the directors for any decisions that they make which may give rise to a legal action against them. The excess on such a policy can be considerably high given the cost of defending such an action. Intentional illegal acts, however, are typically not covered under a directors' and officers' policy. Claims on a directors' and officers' policy are very rare and this is reflected in policy premiums.

3. The claims process

When it comes to property insurance claims, the different types of claims that can be made varies greatly. By far, the most common type insurance claim in an apartment block is that of escape of water or a water damage claim. Property owners are sometimes confused about the roles of the various actors in such a circumstance and given that there is usually general upheaval and emotion involved it can prove to be a difficult period for those owners.

In the event of a claim, the role of the OMC is to ensure that there is adequate cover in place. For small issues which are contained within the confines of an apartment, the OMC does not get involved in repairs or remedial works. The property owner will usually take responsibility for this. In this regard, the property owner depends on the OMC to have the proper scope of cover in place to provide for the claim which they will make on the insurance policy.

Insurance policies for OMCs are commercial contracts and for this reason they must be procured through an insurance broker. The Managing Agent has a duty of disclosure and utmost good faith to insurers and is responsible for providing the broker with all of the relevant material facts about the development to the broker. The insurance broker is then responsible for providing the appropriate scope of cover.

Clarke discusses the duty to disclose and notes that the duty to disclose all facts that a reasonable insurer would think material to the risk requires a lot of the insured; he is required to know what the insurer thinks material.[4] Kenny J in the Supreme Court, in *Chariot Inns Ltd v Assicurazioni Generali SPA & Coyle Hamilton, Hamilton Philips*[5] stated the test thus:

> 'It is not what the person seeking insurance regards as material, nor is it what the insurance company regards as material. It is a matter or circumstance which would reasonably influence the judgment of a prudent insurer in deciding whether he would take the risk and, if so, in determining the premium which he would demand. The standard by which materiality is to be determined is objective, not subjective. The matter has, in the last resort, to be determined by the court: the parties to the litigation may call experts in insurance matters as witnesses to give evidence of what they would have regarded as material

4 Robert Clark, *Contract Law in Ireland* (8th edn, Round Hall, Dublin, 2016).

5 *Chariot Inns Ltd v Assicurazioni Generali S.P.A. & Coyle Hamilton, Hamilton Philips,* [1981] ILRM 173.

> but the question of materiality is not to be determined by the parties.'

The managing agent should bring it to the attention of the members and directors of the OMC where a building surveyor is required to establish the correct buildings sums insured. If the managing agent fails to disclose all material facts it could invalidate the insurance cover.

In the event of a claim, the managing agent will liaise between the property owners affected, the loss assessor and the insurance company while the claim is progressing. The insured is the OMC and so the settlement or payout will be paid directly to the OMC. The managing agent will then pay this out to the affected owners.

Generally, the managing agent does not get involved in carrying out repairs to the inside of any of the apartments but where there is damage to common areas they will arrange for the necessary repairs. In the event where the entire building is affected then the OMC should arrange for a suitably qualified project manager to arrange, oversee and sign off on all works to the building.

Where there is damage caused to the building of the OMC from a third party, the managing agent will liaise with the third party. For example, where an adjoining building which is not part of the OMC has a water leak which is causing damage to the building of the OMC, the managing agent will liaise with the owners of this adjoining building to resolve the leak and the OMCs insurers will seek compensation from the adjoining building's insurers.

The role of the insurance company is to simply make the payment to the OMC.

The apartment owner will use the insurance payment to pay for all of the costs which they have incurred to rectify the damage and they will arrange for all such repairs to be carried out to the inside of their apartment.

As with all other aspects of shared living, the efficient resolution of incidents and accidents in a multi-unit development hinges very much upon the co-operation of the parties involved. If a water leak emanates in one apartment caused by a failed outlet pipe which is concealed underneath a bath and flows down into the apartment beneath, then the level of co-operation from the owner of the overhead apartment to resolve the issue will depend on the level of damage caused to the apartment beneath and vice versa. If the owners act quickly and co-operate then there will be minimal damage. If they are disregardful of their responsibilities this can have a delaying effect to the fixing of the leak causing additional damage to the apartment or unit beneath. Property owners have a duty to mitigate their loss and to act quickly and while most property owners act responsibly, not all property owners do. The loss suffered to a commercial unit on a ground floor can be considerably higher than that of an apartment as the loss of business is an added cost.

The claims process begins when a property owner reports the incident to the managing agent. This is usually the property owner who is suffering the damage of the water leak such as water coming down from the apartment overhead.

The managing agent will investigate the issue and immediately notify the insurers of a potential claim. Liability incidents of any nature need to be advised to insurers as soon as is reasonably practical as insurers will need to undertake their own investigations taking photographs, interviewing witnesses and taking witness statements while the information is fresh. Delays in reporting of incidents to insurers may have the effect of negating cover.

Whether the OMC chooses to make a claim on the insurance policy or not depends on the size of the potential claim and the excess on the policy. If it is a small water leak that is easily fixed with only a water mark on the ceiling of the apartment below then the only cost is the cost of re-decorating the ceiling and the water damage excess on the policy may be much greater than the cost of the repair works. In this case there is no claim and the property owner takes responsibility for redecorating their own ceiling.

Where the cost of the damage caused is estimated to be greater than the policy excess it is prudent for the OMC to appoint an insurance loss assessor. An insurance loss assessor will represent the OMC in the claim to ensure that the maximum legitimate entitlement is secured from the insurance company in the interest of the property owner who has suffered the loss. Suitably qualified Insurance loss assessors know and understand the policies in force and are in a position to vindicate policy-holders rights. An insurance loss assessor will negotiate with an insurance loss adjuster who is appointed by the insurance company to act in their interest with regards to the amount of the payout. The loss assessor will negotiate with the loss adjuster and agree on a settlement figure for the amount of the claim. They will administer the claim and gather the required information such as date and time of loss, description of loss, estimate of loss and photographic evidence. The amount that they agree upon will be the value that they believe the claim should be. The actual loss may be different to the settlement amount, however, that is a matter of opinion.

The loss assessor's fees are paid by the policyholder and they are normally based on a percentage of the settlement figure plus 23 percent VAT. The problem with this is that there is an incentive for the loss assessor to inflate the claim so that their commission is higher. It is in the loss assessor's interest to secure the highest possible settlement figure and this results very often in the settlement amount being greater than the loss suffered. Often this is where the excess is absorbed. Where there is more than one apartment that has suffered a loss then the settlement figure will be apportioned in accordance with the size of the loss for the individual apartments. The loss assessor will advise on such apportionment.

Once the managing agent has notified the insurers of a potential claim and appointed a loss assessor to represent the OMC in the claim, the loss assessor and the loss adjuster will meet at the affected apartment to survey the damage. This meeting normally takes place within a week of the insurance company being notified. After this meeting the property owner is free to carry out the repair works. In some cases, the property owner may not be in a financial position to carry out repair works until the insurance payment has been received.

The insurance company will firstly have to confirm their acceptance of liability and this can take a number of weeks. It can typically take anywhere between 1–3 months for a settlement figure to be agreed between the parties and between 6–9 months for the insurance company to make the payment.

In some cases, property owners are advised by the loss assessor not to effect any repairs until the settlement figure has been agreed. However, in practice this is not always the best thing to do. If property owners have a duty to mitigate their loss and they are paying for alternative accommodation while repairs are being carried out, then it follows that to mitigate their loss they would have to arrange to have the repairs carried out sooner rather than later to reduce the cost of alternative accommodation.

The advice not carry out any works until they know how much the settlement figure is, so as to avoid overspending, is contrary to the general rule in insurance which is to put the person into the exact same position that they were in before the incident/accident. This rule is vastly ambiguous in that it is almost never possible to be in the exact same position afterwards. Where a twenty-year-old kitchen is destroyed by fire and is to be replaced as part of an insurance claim, then a new kitchen leaves the property owner better off after the fire.

The relationship between the settlement figure and the loss suffered is problematic in that the loss suffered is subjective. The insurance company will use statistical techniques and mathematical skills to quantify the loss for the property owner but it is subject to what the loss assessor thinks and what the loss adjuster thinks the value of the claim should be. In considering the loss assessor's advice, if the cost of the repair works to the apartment are dependent upon the amount of the settlement figure then it indicates that the property owner will either be in a better or worse position after the claim and this conflicts with the rule that the purpose of the policy is to restore the insured to the exact same position that they were in before the incident or accident occurred which gave rise to the claim and that the person should be no better off and no worse off after a claim.

The insurance settlement may be made by the insurance company to the OMC in a number of payments and at various stages. In the event of a substantial claim where property owners incur considerable unforeseen sudden costs such as alternative accommodation, the insurance company will normally make an interim payment to cover such sudden costs while the claim is being processed and this will be after the insurance company accept liability and can often be before a settlement figure is agreed.

When the loss assessor and loss adjuster agree on a settlement figure, the insurance company will present a settlement offer to the insured. In most cases they will offer two options, a cash settlement offer and a re-instatement offer. In a scenario where the agreed settlement figure is in the amount of €18,000 the insurers may offer a cash payment of €10,000 and not hold anything back for retention or an interim payment of €12,600 with the retention of €5,400 being released once all of the works have been completed and vouched by means of VAT invoices. It is common for the property owner to accept the latter option and thereafter not to seek the retention.

Retention is important for insurance companies so that they can be sure that the works that were agreed to by the insurance company or their loss adjuster are executed in full and that the amount of the claim payment is not subsumed into some other work which fell outside the scope of cover or were not part of the claim as stated. The insurance company will have an expiration date on the retention and if it is not claimed by that date, then it is lost.

If a property owner is not satisfied with the settlement offer that the insurance company present to them the loss assessor may negotiate further on their behalf. Thereafter, if the property owner is still not satisfied with the amount being offered, the matter can then be referred to Insurance Arbitration to resolve within a specified period of time. The appointed arbitrator will determine such matters in which the insured and underwriters fail to agree, and they will make an award thereon. This award will be made in writing and it will be final.

4. Avoiding insurance pitfalls

As previously noted, it is important that the reinstatement costs for apartment block insurance policies are accurately calculated by a suitably qualified surveyor. Commercial insurance contracts such as apartment block insurance policies differ from contracts in general, in that they are contracts of '*uberrimae fides*' or contracts of utmost good faith whereby the insured must not only refrain from making false representation of material facts, but they are also duty bound to disclose all material facts which are known to the insured but not to the insurer. The principle case in which this rule was discussed was *Abbot v Howard*[6]_where Foster B stated:

> 'In no contracts, does it appear to me, that the parties deal on so unequal terms, as in contracts of insurance. One party has all the information, and the other is perfectly ignorant. It is with reference to this view, that the principle has been clearly established, that the inequality of knowledge ought to be rectified as much as possible, before the contract is entered into. It may be asked, – Must a party, before effecting an insurance, give a minute detail of every trifling incident of his whole life? The answer is

6 (1832) Hayes 381 at 423.

> – Those incidents and occurrences which are trifling, he need not communicate; but he is bound to give information of every *material* circumstance, and none else. The deciding upon their materiality, is the province of the Jury: and, by that doctrine, the interests of the party insured will be little endangered.'

A warranty is a term in the contract of insurance whereby the insured vouches that certain statements of fact made by them are entirely accurate or that they will perform a specific obligation in a given manner. In an OMC this may amount to a scenario whereby the OMC agrees to maintain the common areas of the development and they fail to do so by not replacing light bulbs or attending to defects on stairwells which have the potential to be found to be the central cause of the incident or accident. This would constitute a breach of such warranty and the insurer is entitled to repudiate all liability under the contract from the date of the breach irrespective of the materiality of that breach to the contract or to the loss arising from it. Clauses in such insurance policy wording may be as follows:

> 'whilst this policy insures you against a wide range of contingencies it does not insure you against every possible loss for example it is not a maintenance contract and it is a condition of this Policy that the Premises is kept in good repair and that reasonable steps are taken to avoid damage'.

5. Airbnb and insurance

The use of the units in a multi-unit development, in particular an apartment block is normally set out in the planning guidelines and it will normally be for residential use. Although there is no original condition on this, planning authorities have decided in a number of cases that ongoing use of an apartment for short-term holiday lets is a material 'change of use' and as such, requires the owner to apply for approval for this.[7] Guidelines issued by the Department of Housing, Planning and Local Government state that planning authorities should be proactive in ensuring short-term letting activity complies with the planning code and the

7 Department of Housing, Planning and Local Government, 'Circular: Guidance on Planning Applications for Short Term Lettings' <http://www.housing.gov.ie/sites/default/files/publications/files/circular_pl10_aph3_2017.pdf>, accessed 11 May 2018.

guidelines have noted the negative impact of short-term letting on the long-term letting market. This may preclude the use of the unit for short-term Airbnb rentals. Such use may be deemed to be commercial use and this should be disclosed to the insurer so that the appropriate level of cover is provided. In general, OMCs will resist the use of apartments for Airbnb as short-term lets are often associated with noise, parties and lack of consideration for neighbours as well as wear and tear on the common areas such as scuffing of walls from suitcases, etc.

Under the planning code, all development, including a material change of use, requires planning permission unless exempted under the Act or the associated regulations. However, there is a specific exemption in art 10(4) of the Planning and Development Regulations 2001 (the Regulations) for, within certain limitations or restrictions, development which consists of the use of a house for overnight guest accommodation, which, therefore, does not require planning permission. This exemption is typically or traditionally relied upon in the context of the provision of B&B-type accommodation. It is important to note that, for the purposes of art 10(4), 'house' does not include a building designed for use or used as two or more dwellings or a flat, an apartment or other dwelling within such a building. In other words, apartments do not benefit from this exemption.

In a situation where an apartment is rented out for example for two nights at the weekend to a group of revellers who through their own negligence are the cause of a fire in the building, it is possible that the insurance company may not provide cover on the basis that the use of the apartment contravened the terms of the policy.

Personal injury claims are provided for under the public liability section of the policy in a multi-unit development and unlike material damage claims they are very rare. A public liability policy will be in place even where there are no buildings insured through the OMC for example, a housing estate with an OMC will have a public liability policy in place to indemnify all owners against any personal injury claims. One of the problems that OMCs face when it comes to a personal injury claim is the length of time that it takes for such a claim to be settled. In some cases, it can take up to eight years for such claims to settle and in the intervening years the insurers may place a reserve on the policy while the claim is being negotiated and investigated. The amount of the reserve is decided by the insurers and can be as high as €100,000.

The effect of this reserve on the renewal premium is considerable as the renewal premium is higher.

6. Case studies

Case studies of insurance claims provide important information about various issues which can arise when a claim is being processed and help others to avoid the pitfalls which they may otherwise encounter.

In a small apartment block of 20 apartments a fire broke out in the middle floor and spread to the roof and adjoining apartments. All units were affected with 10 units being badly damaged. The units were a timber frame construction with standard finishes internally and externally. There was a mixture of owner-occupied and tenanted units. The fire brigade were on site for eight hours and Garda Forensics attended site the following morning. Nobody was injured. The OMC had cover for Buildings and Landlords' Contents with extensions for Alternative Accommodation and Loss of Rental Income. Tenants contents were not insured by the OMC, this is normal practice as the OMC could not recover on behalf of a tenant.

Once the Gardaí confirmed they had no interest in the site, insurer's loss adjusters had access to the site together with the OMC's appointed loss assessor. Insurers appointed their own forensic investigator on day three. The loss assessor advised tenants and owners not to disturb the scene until the investigation was complete. The investigator completed their report and five weeks later the insurers confirmed their acceptance of liability.

If the insurers repudiated liability the OMC may have required a further forensic investigation and this would have the effect of delaying the process. The two main issues which developed were:

1. The actual cause of the fire
2. The fire-proofing of the timber frame construction.

The OMC had no financial resource to contribute and could not support the owners who were affected most of whom were young first-time buyers with big mortgages. Those that were tenanted lost their tenants because they had to live somewhere. The owners were now under severe financial pressure and personal stress.

Insurers accepted liability on week seven and paid an interim stage payment to assist the owners financially. The owners then had to meet to discuss and agree on their approach for re-instatement which included the following:

(a) Structural survey and scope document;
(b) Design & planning permission;
(c) Tender phase;
(d) Agreement of and appointment of contractors;
(e) Project supervision.

The insurance claim also involved, surveys, schedules, invoicing and proofs of:

(a) Landlords' contents losses;
(b) Occupiers' alternative accommodation costs;
(c) Loss of rental income costs;
(d) Fire service fees;
(e) Engineer and architect's costs.

What is not covered under the policy is the excess of €5,000 and loss assessor's fees. These costs will be borne by the OMC.

The entire case took 18 months to conclude because of the reinstatement time. The fire-proofing of the timber frame construction proved to be of a proper standard. The managing agent of the OMC and the insurance broker had proper cover in place and the policy disclosures and claims history were also very good. Insurers established that the fire started in a washing machine and they sued the manufacturers under the rules of Subrogation. This case went on for a further three years with insurers getting most of their money back and some of the other uninsured costs were also paid in the liability claim.

Chapter 12

Landlord and Tenant Law in the Residential and OMC Context

1. Introduction ... 167
2. The Residential Tenancies Act 2004 ... 170
3. Landlord obligations ... 171
4. Tenants' obligations ... 174
5. Part 4 tenancy ... 177
6. Notice periods ... 180
7. The Residential Tenancies Board ... 181
8. Dispute resolution ... 183

1. Introduction

According to Census 2016, apartment living in Ireland is dominated by renters with nearly 80 percent of apartments being rented. Of this 80 percent, approximately 20 percent are social rented (housing association or local authority) and nearly 60 percent are rented privately. The remaining 20 percent are owner occupied.[1]

A persuasive correlation exists between the sharp rise in the number of apartment developments in Ireland and the sharp rise in the number of landlord and tenant relationships. Figure 1 shows the growth of this market in recent years.[2] Given the critical national need for housing supply in the market this trajectory is set to continue in the coming years as there is an acceptance that urban areas such as Dublin need to be built upwards rather than outwards and this will result in several new apartment blocks being constructed.

1 Clúid Housing in collaboration with The Housing Agency, Analysis of Census 2016 contained in Requests for Tenders for the Provision of a Research Report on Owners' Management Companies, 11 July 2017, available at <www.cluid.ie/wp-content/uploads/2017/07/17-07-11-RFT-OMC-research-FINAL.pdf>.

2 Residential Tenancies Board, 'Rent Index, Quarter 1, 2018', <https://onestopshop.rtb.ie/images/uploads/general/RTB_Rent_Index_Q12018_Final.pdf>.

Figure 1 – RTB Rent Index – National Q4 2007=100

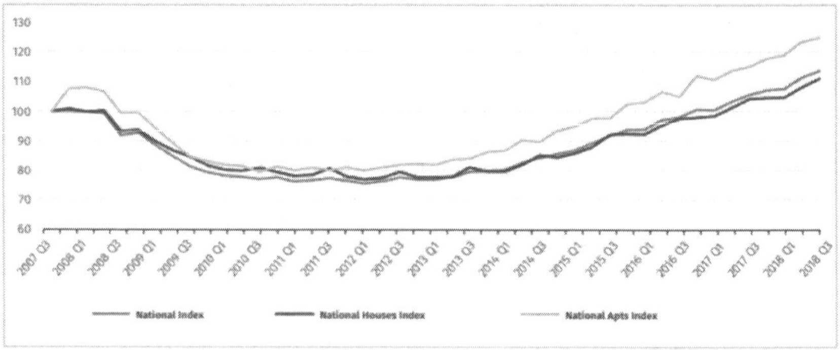

The law on landlord and tenant is founded in contract and is complex and wide covering commercial and residential tenancies. In the context of the Owners' Management Company in Ireland the majority of the law in its application to this area relates to the Residential Tenancies Act 2004. This chapter will deal specifically with the rights and obligations of landlords and tenants in the residential context of landlord and tenant law.

Wylie refers to the starting point for the law of landlord and tenant as the almost unique provision in s 3 of Deasy's Act otherwise known as the Landlord and Tenant Law (Amendment) Act 1860, which provides:

> 'The relation of landlord and tenant shall be deemed to be founded on the express or implied contract of the parties, and not upon tenure or service, and a reversion shall not be necessary to such relation, which shall be deemed to subsist in all cases in which there shall be an agreement by one party to hold land from or under another in consideration of any rent.'[3]

In 1999 the government launched the Commission on the Private Rented Residential Sector. The Commission's focus was to address the controversial issue of security of tenure, the supply and quality of accommodation, the investment return and market considerations and the development of the sector.

The Commission's overall vision for the sector was

---

3 JCW Wylie, *Landlord and Tenant Law* (3rd edn, Bloomsbury, 2014), ch 2, 30.

> '... a vibrant, thriving, well-managed and diverse sector which satisfactorily meets a range of housing needs, provides an adequate supply of secure, affordable, good quality accommodation and operates within a regulatory framework which protects the interests of tenants and landlords'.[4]

Twenty years later, most people would argue that we are far from such a vision with constant reports of tenants being evicted from their homes by landlords who are in breach of the rules set out by the Residential Tenancies Board ('RTB') or finding some way around the rules so that they can increase the rent with a new tenancy. The shortage of housing supply in the market gives rise to increasing pressure on the sector. What was envisaged by Gladstone's government of 1880, with the enactment of the Land Law (Ireland) Act 1881 which provided for the 'three F's': fair rent, fixity of tenure and freedom of sale could hardly be seen as effective in some cases in the current rental market in Ireland. In 2017 there was an 88 percent increase in applications to the Residential Tenancies Board from tenants querying a rent increase and a 20 percent increase in the number of disputes submitted to RTB on the previous year.[5]

Landlord and tenant law in Ireland has a history of being extremely technical and complicated and the establishment of the PRTB has made some strides in clarifying the law. The development of the law in this area and the enactment of the Residential Tenancies Act 2004 brought necessary reform to landlord and tenant law which seeks to address the challenges faced by letting agents, landlords and legal practitioners within the private sector. The Residential Tenancies (Amendment) Bill 2018 was given approval for publication by Government on the 11 December 2018. If successfully enacted, this Bill will have significant implications for landlords. The Private Residential Tenancies Board (PRTB) was established in 2004 as an independent body on a statutory basis under this Act to support and develop a well-functioning rental housing sector and provide for an appropriate balance of rights between the landlord and tenant. In addition to this, one of the more dynamic provisions of this new Act was the introduction of a part 4 tenancy which provides improved security of tenure to tenants and applies where a tenant has been renting a property for

4 Commission on the Private Rented Residential Sector, *Commission on the Private Rented Residential Sector Report*, para 8.1.1.3.

5 Residential Tenancies Board, *Annual Report*, 2017, ch 5, 40.

at least six months and has not been served with a valid notice of termination, in general, they will automatically acquire security of tenure and can stay in the property for a number of years. The Private Residential Tenancies Board changed its name to the Residential Tenancies Board (RTB) on 7 April 2016 when among many amendments, approved housing bodies (generally known as Housing Associations) were brought under its remit by the Residential Tenancies (Amendment) Act 2015.

2. The Residential Tenancies Act 2004

The application of the Act is dealt with by s 3 of the Act as subsequently amended. Subject to numerous exceptions, the Act applies to every dwelling which is the subject of a tenancy. This includes a tenancy created before the passing of the Act. The Act does not apply to any tenancy which exceeds a term of 35 years regardless of whether the tenant may or may not be able to acquire the fee simple to the property. It is important to firstly establish the existence of a landlord and tenant relationship and the finding of a 'tenancy' as defined in the Residential Tenancies Act 2004 which states that a tenancy is defined as including a periodic tenancy and a tenancy for a fixed term, whether oral or in writing or implied, and where the context so admits includes a sub-tenancy and a tenancy or sub-tenancy that has been terminated.[6] Failure to meet this criteria may mean that some other type of relationship exists such as a licence agreement which is simply permission and generally falls outside the remit of the RTB and of the legislation. Neither the landlord nor the tenant in this situation can avail of the rights set out in the legislation or can refer a dispute to the RTB. It is important to distinguish between a tenancy and a license and examples of situations where a tenancy does not exist, and which are exceptions to the Act include the following:

a) A person staying in the property as a holiday letting agreement, Airbnb or hostel type of accommodation;
b) A person sharing a house or apartment with its owner under the rent-a-room scheme;
c) A person occupying accommodation under a formal licence arrangement, where the owner is not a resident, where the occupants are not entitled to its exclusive use and the owner has continued access to the accommodation;
d) Where a person is living with the spouse, parent or child

---

6 Residential Tenancies Act 2004, s 5(1).

of the landlord and there is no written letting agreement in place;

e) Where a person is a tenant in local authority housing.

Section 3(1) of the Act states that the Act applies to every dwelling which is the subject of a tenancy including those that were created before the passing of the Act. However, there are various exceptions listed in subs 3(2). It is not possible to contract out of the provisions of the Act and even in the absence of a written tenancy agreement the statutory obligations apply. Section 4(1) of the Act defines a dwelling as a property let for rent or valuable consideration as a self-contained residential unit and includes any building or part of a building used as a dwelling.

Exceptions to the application of pt 4 of the Act provide that pt 4 shall not apply to a dwelling which is one of two dwellings within a building that, as originally constructed, comprised a single dwelling, and the landlord resides in the other dwelling. However, in order for s 25 to operate the landlord must, in accordance with subs 25(3), opt in writing for pt 4 not to apply by means of a written notice to the tenant, such notice to be served before the commencement of the tenancy. Section 25 does not operate to prevent the remaining parts of the Act from applying to residential tenancies.[7]

3. Landlord obligations

Landlords are obliged to register every tenancy of a dwelling rented by them with The Residential Tenancies Board (RTB). The proposed Residential Tenancies (Amendment) Bill 2018 includes making it a criminal offence for landlords that fail to register and update tenancies with the RTB. Sanctions of up to €15,000 may apply. Section 12 of the RTA 2004 sets out many of the landlord's obligations to the tenant in detail and this includes the peaceful and exclusive occupation of the dwelling. It is common for a tenancy agreement to include a covenant that the landlord will allow the tenant peaceful occupation of the property without interruption providing that the tenant complies with their obligations and the terms of the tenancy agreement. Prior to the enactment of the Residential Tenancies Act 2004, s 41 of Deasy's

7 Dr Gabriel Brennan, Michelle Linnane, David Soden and Sean Brodie, *Landlord and Tenant Law*, Law Society of Ireland (6th edn, Oxford University Press, 2013), ch 6, 61.

Act implied a covenant that the tenant was to have the quiet and peaceable enjoyment of the property without interruption from the landlord. This covenant could only be invoked by the tenant and only on the condition that the tenant was compliant in their own obligations. In *Whelan v Madigan*[8] it was held that a tenant could not rely on s 41 because at the time of the disturbance of her enjoyment, the tenant owed a substantial amount of money to the landlord in rent arrears.

Section 12(1)(a) of the Residential Tenancies Act 2004 changed this position whereby the landlord is now obliged to allow the tenant of a dwelling to enjoy peaceful and exclusive occupation of the dwelling irrespective of whether they are complying with their tenancy obligations or not. In *Boyne v Hanaway*[9] the landlord entered the property without the tenant's permission at a time when the tenant was present in the property. The tenancy tribunal determined that the landlord was to pay the sum of €4,500 in respect of damages for his (and his wife's) unlawful entry into the property, including their threatening behaviour during that episode and for breach of the tenant's right to peaceful and exclusive enjoyment of the property. This award was made by the tenancy tribunal notwithstanding the fact that the tenant was €5,250 in arrears of rent. The tribunal also directed that the tenant was to pay the arrears of rent of €5,250 to the landlord but that the tenant was entitled to set this sum off against the damages of €4,500 awarded to them, leaving the sum of €750 payable to the landlord.

Prior to the Residential Tenancies Act 2004 ('2004 Act') there was a requirement that there must be some physical interference or interruption of the tenant's property, but since the introduction of the 2004 Act text messages and letters can now also constitute an interruption of the tenant's peaceful enjoyment of their property.

A landlord is obliged to carry out repairs and maintenance to the structure of the dwelling and all such repairs as are from time to time necessary and ensure that the structure complies with housing standards as prescribed under s 18 of the Housing (Miscellaneous Provisions) Act 1992 (s 12(1)(b)(i)). Landlords will need to be familiar also with the provisions of the Housing (Standards for Rented Houses) (Amendment) Regulations 2009 (SI 2009/462)—'Houses' being widely defined in the Regulations.

---

8 [1978] ILRM 136.

9 TR49/DR1262/2008, 14 October 2008.

The Residential Tenancies Board have issued information to all landlords on this subject in regard to their obligations such as the guide on minimum standards for rented residential accommodation. The list is not exhaustive and includes issues such as lighting and fire safety.

Landlords must keep the structure of the dwelling insured against loss, damage and destruction in accordance with s 12(1)(c) of the 2004 Act. They must also take out liability cover for at least €250,000 if the policy is attainable at a reasonable cost.

A landlord is obliged to return or repay promptly any deposit paid by the tenant (s 12(1)(d)) and to reimburse the tenant for all reasonable and vouched-for expenses incurred by the tenant for repairs to the structure or interior for which the landlord is liable. However, this applies only where the landlord refuses to carry out such repairs when requested and the postponement thereof poses either a significant health risk to the tenant. The obligation to return the security deposit does not apply in situations where there are arrears of rent or there are costs to the landlord of restoring the dwelling where the tenant is in breach of their obligations under s 16(f) and causes a deterioration to the dwelling beyond normal wear and tear. Tenancy tribunals have awarded tenant's compensation for the landlord's failure to return the deposit promptly. In *Azad v Sinnathambi*,[10] the landlord was directed to pay the tenant the sum of €900 which was the amount of the deposit and a further sum of €400 for the landlord's breach of obligation to promptly return the deposit to the tenant. The burden of proof rests with the landlord to establish the reason for retaining the deposit. In the case of *Lawlor and Anor v Ryan*[11] the landlord claimed that he was entitled to retain the deposit to cover costs of restoring the house to the condition it was in when it was first rented to the tenant. The tenancy tribunal stated that the onus of proof is on the landlord to prove that the security deposit should be retained by him and stated the following:

> '[A]s the Appellant Landlord produced no documentary evidence to support his case, and as the onus is on him to produce compelling reasons why the tenant's money should not be returned to her, the Tribunal finds in favour of the Tenant.'[12]

---

10 TR16/DR234/2008, 1 October 2008.

11 TR07/DR711/2007, 23 February 2007.

12 Una Cassidy, Jennifer Ring, *Landlord and Tenant Law, The Residential Sector* (Round Hall, 2010, ch 5, 103).

If a landlord engages the services of an agent to act on their behalf, they are obliged to furnish to the tenant the name of the agent and provide particulars of how the tenant can contact the landlord or agent.

If the dwelling is part of a multi-unit development such as an apartment complex, the landlord is obliged to forward to the management company any complaint in writing made by the tenant to the management company and also any replies back from the management company.

In addition to the obligations specified in s 12, the landlord is expressly prohibited under s 14 from penalising a tenant for referring any dispute between the parties to the Residential Tenancies Board, for giving evidence in any proceedings under pt 6 to which the landlord is a party and for making a complaint to a Garda in relation to any matter arising out of the occupation of the dwelling. A tenant cannot be penalised for giving notice to their landlord of their intention to carry out any or all of the above. Section 14 states that a tenant is penalised if they are subjected to any action which adversely affects their peaceful enjoyment of the dwelling. Subsection (3) concerns a reasonable inference that certain otherwise lawful action on the part of the landlord in fact constitutes penalisation; and subs (4) states that s 14 is without prejudice to any other civil or criminal liability to which a landlord may be subject for doing a thing prohibited by the section.

An obligation on landlords in respect of third parties is imposed by s 15 of the Act. Under this section, landlords owe a duty of care to each person who would be directly and adversely affected by a failure to enforce an obligation of the tenant under the tenancy. Such cases will be referred to the Residential Tenancies Board. Landlords are under a duty to ensure that the actions of all lawful occupiers of and visitors to the dwelling do not result in the peaceful enjoyment of their property by any third party (including co-tenants) being reduced. This means that the neighbour of a tenant in breach of their obligations by behaving in an anti-social manner, may seek redress against the landlord before the RTB.

4. Tenants' obligations

Section 16 of the Residential Tenancies Act 2004 sets out the tenant's obligations in detail. In summary these are:

a) Pay rent when due to the landlord or their agent (s 16(a)(i));
b) Pay charges or taxes imposed by the agreement, except where to do so is unlawful or in contravention of any other enactment (s 16(a)(ii));
c) Not to cause the landlord to be in breach of their statutory obligations under any enactment. This provision makes specific reference to '...regulations under s18 of the Housing (Miscellaneous Provisions) Act, 1992'. These are the Housing (Standards for Rented Houses) Regulations 2008 (SI 2008/534) which set out minimum standards for rented dwellings, as well as the Housing (Rent Books) Regulations 1993 (SI 1993/146) (s 26(b))
d) Allow access to inspect the dwelling at reasonable intervals to the landlord or any person(s) acting on their behalf, on a time and date agreed in advance (s 16(c));
e) Notify the landlord or their agent of any defect requiring repair to enable them to comply with their obligations under any enactment in regard to the dwelling or tenancy (s 16(d));
f) Allow reasonable access to the landlord or any person(s) acting on their behalf for the purposes of carrying out any works for which the landlord is responsible (s 16(e));
g) Not to cause any deterioration in the condition of the dwelling. Normal wear and tear is expressly disregarded in determining whether the tenant is in compliance with this obligation. In this respect the length of time elapsed since the tenancy commenced, the extent of occupation that the landlord could have reasonably foreseen, and 'any other relevant matters' shall be taken into consideration (s 16(f)). While it is difficult to state in a given case precisely what will amount to 'normal' wear and tear, it may be noted that the RTB has published a website note on the topic of normal wear and tear as regards items of furniture. This note includes a reminder to landlords of their right to carry out regular inspections of the dwelling and its contents.

   In the event of non-compliance with s 16(f), the tenant is obliged to take such steps as the landlord may reasonably require to restore the dwelling to the condition it was in at the commencement of the tenancy (subject to the matters to be disregarded in para (f) and mentioned above) or to defray any costs incurred by the landlord as a result of their taking any reasonable steps for that purpose (s 16(g));
h) Not to behave or allow other occupiers of or visitors to the

dwelling to behave in an anti-social manner (s 17 defines anti-social behaviour.) This paragraph refers expressly to behaviour not only within the dwelling but within the vicinity of it (s 16(h));

i) Not to act or allow other occupiers of or visitors to the dwelling to act in a way which would result in the invalidation of a policy of insurance in force in relation to the dwelling (s 16(i)). If any such act results in an increase in a policy premium, the tenant is obliged to pay the increased element to the landlord. This expressly includes each further premium falling due for payment that includes the increased element (s 16(j)). Section 17(4) clarifies the meaning of 'increased element' to allow for a proportional increase or reduction in future policy premium payments due.

j) Not to assign or sub-let the tenancy without the written consent of the landlord, which consent may be withheld at their discretion. This discretion amounts to an absolute right on the part of the landlord; in such an event the tenant may simply terminate the tenancy in accordance with s 186 and having regard to notice provisions (s 16(k));

k) Not to alter or improve the dwelling without the written consent of the landlord, which consent again may be withheld at their discretion except where such alteration or improvement consists only of repairing, painting and/or decorating, in which event consent may not be unreasonably withheld (s 16)(1)). Section 17 defines 'alter and improve' to include changing the locks and adding to or altering the building or structure, including any building or structure that is subsidiary or ancillary to the dwelling;

l) Not to use the dwelling or cause it to be used for any purpose other than as a dwelling without the written consent of the landlord; again, such consent may be withheld at the landlord's discretion (s16(m));

m) Notify in writing the landlord of the identity of each person (other than a multiple tenant) who, for the time being, resides ordinarily at the dwelling (s16(n));

In regard to s 16(k), (l) and (m), s 17(3) expressly provides that the landlord shall be entitled to any reasonable disbursements incurred by them in deciding upon the tenant's request, to include cases where consent is refused.[13]

---

13 Dr Gabriel Brennan, Michelle Linnane, David Soden and Sean Brodie, *Landlord*

5. Part 4 tenancy

The part 4 tenancy is one of the most dynamic provisions introduced by the 2004 Act in that it radically changed the law on security of tenure. It is broken into various chapters. Section 28(1) states that where a person occupies a dwelling for a period of six months and no notice of termination has been served, then that tenancy will continue for a period of four years from the commencement of the tenancy or the relevant date (whichever is latest). The provisions of part 4 place on a statutory footing a minimum period of security of tenure for tenants that cannot be contracted out of and which is implied into every tenancy or lease agreement. The termination of this tenancy is subject to s 34 which provides for termination of a part 4 tenancy by a landlord. This can be done on one of two ways. Either the landlord will have the required grounds for termination and the required notice will be served including the appropriate notice period or the termination will be after four years and the required notice will be served including the appropriate notice period. The grounds on which a landlord may terminate a part 4 tenancy are stipulated in the Act as follows:

1. The tenant has failed to comply with any of their obligations and unless the failure provides an excepted basis for termination the tenant has been notified of the failure by the landlord and that notification states that the landlord is entitled to terminate the tenancy if the failure is not remedied within a reasonable time specified in the notification and the tenant does not remedy the failure within a specified time;
2. The dwelling is no longer suitable to the accommodation needs of the tenant and of any persons residing with him or her having regard to the number of bed spaces contained in the dwelling and the size and composition of the occupying household;
3. The landlord intends, within three months after the termination of the tenancy to sell the property;
4. The landlord requires the dwelling for his or her own occupation or for occupation by a member of their family. The notice of termination must include a written statement specifying the identity of the intended occupants (if not the landlord) and their relationship to the landlord and the expected duration of that occupation. The landlord

and Tenant Law, Law Society of Ireland (6th edn, Oxford University Press, 2013), ch 6, 66.

is required to offer the dwelling back to the tenant in the event where the dwelling is vacated by the intended occupants within the period of six months from expiry of the period of notice or where a dispute has been referred to the RTB under pt 6 for resolution and the determination of the RTB is that the notice was invalid;

5. The landlord intends to substantially refurbish or renovate the property in a way which requires the dwelling to be vacated for that purpose (and, where planning permission is required for the carrying out of that refurbishment or renovation, that permission has been obtained) and the notice of termination contains a written statement specifying the nature of the intended works and that the landlord is required to offer to the tenant a tenancy of the dwelling if the contact details requirement is complied with and the dwelling becomes available for reletting;
6. The landlord intends to change the use of the property to some other use (and where planning permission is required for that change of use, that permission has been obtained) and the notice of termination contains a written statement including the nature of the intended use and that the landlord is required to offer to the tenant a tenancy of the dwelling if the contact details requirement is complied with and the dwelling becomes available for reletting.[14]

When it comes to the termination of residential tenancies, it is important to note that a part 4 tenancy can be terminated by mutual agreement of the parties under s 69 of the Act.

The Residential Tenancies (Amendment) Bill 2018, includes providing powers to RTB to investigate and sanction landlords who engage in improper conduct including non-compliance with the rent increase restrictions in rent pressure zones. These sanctions will see the maximum fine going from €3,000 up to €15,000. The Bill also proposes significant amendments to the part 4 tenancy including increasing the maximum fines for the contravention of the 2004 Act by landlords from €3,000 to €15,00. It will make it a criminal offence for landlords to implement rent increases that contravene the law or that do not adhere to new definitions of a substantial change. A new legal definition of substantial change to the property will be set out. This is to address the problem of landlords using refurbishment of the property as a loophole in the law to evict tenants to simply get new tenants

---

[14] Residential Tenancies Act 2004, s 34.

who will pay a higher rent in a market where there is a shortage of rental accommodation. The Bill seeks to significantly extend the notice periods for tenancy terminations by landlords.

In contrast to the landlord's legal position, the tenant may terminate a part 4 tenancy prematurely for no reason. However, if termination arises by virtue of the landlord's default, s 68 sets out that in certain instances the tenant should first give written notice to the landlord to remedy the failure within a reasonable time. Where no remedy is forthcoming, the tenant will rely on s 68 as regards the appropriate notice period. The notice of termination should clearly set out the reason for the termination if the tenant is relying on s 68.

According to s 39(1) a part 4 tenancy shall terminate on the death of a tenant. This does not act to deprive the other multiple tenant or tenants of the protection of that part 4 tenancy.[15] The exceptions to this are set out in subsection 3, as amended. This provides for any one of four classes of person to elect in writing to become a tenant or tenants of the dwelling. These are:

i. A spouse or civil partner of the tenant;
ii. A person who was not a spouse of the tenant but who was the tenant's cohabitant within the meaning of s 172 of the Civil Partnership and Certain Rights and Obligations of Cohabitants Act 2010 and lived with the tenant in the dwelling for a period of at least six months ending on the date of the tenant's death;
iii. A child, stepchild or foster child of the tenant, or a person adopted by the tenant under the Adoption Acts, 1952 to 1998, being in each case aged 18 years or more; or
iv. A parent of the tenant.

Chapter 4 (ss 40–42) sets out, under s 41 the right to further a part 4 tenancy where a tenancy continues to the end of the four-year period without service of a notice of termination by either party. This is called a 'further Part 4 Tenancy' and commences on the expiry of the four-year period. It shall continue in being for four years provided that the landlord does not serve a notice of termination under either s 34(a) or s 42 of the Act.[16]

---

[15] Chapter 6 of RTA 2004, s 52.

[16] Dr Gabriel Brennan, Michelle Linnane, David Soden and Sean Brodie, *Landlord and Tenant Law, Law Society of Ireland* (6th edn, Oxford University Press, 2013), ch 6, 75.

6. Notice periods

Chapter 3 sets out in detail the notice periods that apply to the parties based on the duration of the tenancy in question. Section 65 clarifies s 62(1)(f) and states that the period of notice itself need not be specified in the notice of termination. Either party may choose to give a greater notice period than is required under s 66, subject to the s 65(4) rule (if the duration of the tenancy concerned is less than six months, a period of notice of more than 70 days may not be given in respect of it).

The notice of termination must contain certain elements in order for it to be valid. The RTB issue draft notices on their website www.rtb.ie. When a landlord is issuing a notice of termination there can be very minor technical errors or omissions which could deem the notice of termination to be invalid. There can be many reasons why a notice is deemed invalid such as date of service not specified or not correct. The notice did not state that any issue as to the validity of the notice or the right of the landlord to serve it must be referred to the RTB within 28 days from the receipt of the notice. The notice did not specify termination date or grounds for termination or was not accompanied by a statement/ statutory declaration where required. The RTB note that some 24 percent of all notices received were invalid in 2017. Changes in the legislation in 2015/16 which introduced a 'slip rule', allow an RTB appointed decision maker to overlook a minor error in a notice of termination, once the error does not prejudice the notice itself, and which would otherwise be valid. In 2017, of the 411 notices of termination deemed valid, the 'slip rule' was only applied in 26 cases.

In order for a notice of termination to be valid it must:

a) Be in writing;
b) Be signed by the tenant or landlord or their authorised agent, as appropriate;
c) Specify the date of service;
d) State the grounds for termination (where the tenancy has lasted for more than six months or is a fixed term tenancy);
e) Specify the termination date and also that the tenant has the whole of the 24 hours of this date to vacate possession;
f) State that any issue as to the validity of the notice or the right of the landlord to serve it must be referred to the RTB within 28 days from the receipt of the notice;

g) Be accompanied by a statement/statutory declaration where required.

The first day of a period of notice is the day after the notice is served. The notice periods depend on the length of the tenancy and the reason for issuing the notice in some circumstances. In some cases, such as when a landlord intends to sell a property, they will be required to submit a statutory declaration with the notice of termination. The RTB have samples of Statutory Declarations on their website at www.rtb.ie. Sample Statutory Declarations must take a specific format and must be signed in the presence of a Commissioner for Oaths, Practicing Solicitor, Notary Public or Peace Commissioner.

Required notice periods of termination by landlord

Below are the notice periods a landlord must give a tenant. Column A provides the notice periods as they currently stand pursuant to s 66, Table 2 of Residential Tenancies Act 2004 (the '2004 Act') as amended, by the Residential Tenancies (Amendment) Act 2015 (the '2015 Act'). Column B provides the notice periods in the Residential Tenancies (Amendment) Bill 2018.

	A	**B**
Duration of Tenancy	**Notice Period per 2004 Act**	**Notice Period in 2018 Bill**
Less than 6 months	28 days	28 days
6 or more months but less than 1 year	35 days	90 days
1 year or more but less than 2 years	42 days	120 days
2 years or more but less than 3 years	56 days	120 days
3 years or more but less than 4 years	84 days	120 days
4 years or more but less than 5 years	112 days	120 days
5 years or more but less than 6 years	140 days	140 days
6 years or more but less than 7 years	168 days	168 days
7 years or more but less than 8 years	196 days	196 days
8 or more years	224 days	224 days

7. The Residential Tenancies Board

The Board came into existence as a statutory body on 1 September 2004. The RTB's main functions are set out at s 151 of the 2004 Act and include the resolution of disputes between tenants and landlords in accordance with the provisions of pt 6 of the Act. To maintain a register of private residential tenancies and tenancies of approved housing bodies. To provide a dispute resolution service for tenants and landlords including approved housing bodies and to carry out research into the private rented sector. It also provides policy advice to the government on the private rented sector including developing and publishing guidelines for good practice for landlords and tenants in the private rented sector. Recent publications include guides on 'Being a good tenant', 'Being a good landlord' and 'Dispute Services and how they work'.[17]

The register

The National Register of tenancies maintained by the RTB provides important and accurate data on the rental sector in Ireland. They share information with the Department of Employment Affairs and Social Protection and the Revenue Commissioners.

All landlords are required by law to register their tenancies within one month of the tenancy commencing and failure to do so will lead to late penalties and/or a criminal conviction with fines up to €4,000 plus costs and or six months' imprisonment.[18]

According to the RTB the benefits of registration for the landlord is the access to the dispute resolution services as there is no fee for mediation and a fee of only €15 for adjudication if the application is made online, and €25 if the application is sent by post. A landlord cannot access the RTB dispute resolution process unless they are registered, however a tenant will have their application for dispute resolution accepted by the RTB whether the landlord has registered the tenancy or not. Other benefits of registration include the fact that the landlord will be able to claim mortgage interest relief for their property and claim the registration fee as an allowable expense.[19]

It is important for the tenant in the property that the landlord is registered with the RTB as they will often need proof of their tenancy for various state agencies such as colleges and banks etc. The Residential Tenancies (Amendment) Bill seeks to allow the RTB to publish rental amounts in its register. This final

---

17 Residential Tenancies Board, Being a good tenant, A guide to the Residential Tenancies Act, August 2017, Residential Tenancies Board, Dispute Services & How They Work, RPC009170_EN_PR_L_1

18 The Residential Tenancies Act 2004, s.134(1)

19 https://onestopshop.rtb.ie/register-a-tenancy/why-register/ accessed 22nd February 2019

amendment in the Bill seeks to provide tenants with the right to access information on the amount of rent paid by the previous tenant of the property, before their own tenancy commences. This register will be available to tenants who want to investigate whether the Rent Pressure Zone provisions are being adhered to by their prospective landlord. The key measures and reforms are designed to enhance enforcement powers for the RTB, provide greater security of tenure for tenants and further underpin the operation of the Rent Pressure Zone arrangements.[20]

8. Dispute resolution

According to s 76(4) of the Act, a licensee has the right to bring an action to refer a dispute to the RTB for dispute resolution services, where the landlord has refused consent to the licensee becoming a tenant of the tenancy. This is the only circumstance where a licensee can refer a dispute to the RTB as the RTB does not have jurisdiction to deal with any other disputes referred by licensees.

One of the main focuses of the Commission on the Private Rented Residential Sector's report was that of dispute resolution between landlords and tenants. Disputes in the area involved more than mere issues with fixtures and fittings within the property. The more serious disputes were in relation to the return of security deposits, evictions and levels of rent. One of the problems was the lengthy period of time that dispute resolution was taking with complex court proceedings. This system was not a practical solution for landlords or tenants with the result that disputes were very often not addressed and although the parties may have been victims of an injustice there was little recourse by way of a remedy. The RTB now have a specifically designed and more speedier dispute resolution procedure for both landlords and tenants. The RTB deal with disputes through mediation, adjudication or by way of a tenancy tribunal hearing and has largely replaced the courts in dealing with disputes. In Q1 2018 the RTB dealt with 1,900 disputes. Of this number 57 percent were taken by tenants and 42 percent were taken by landlords. The remaining 2 percent were third parties such as neighbours or others affected by a tenancy. Seventy percent of landlord disputes related to rent arrears and overholding. Thirty percent of tenant disputes related to deposit retention. Rent arrears/rent

---

20 http://merrionstreet.ie/en/News-Room/Releases/Statement_by_Minister_Eoghan_Murphy_on_the_Residential_Tenancies_Amendment_Bill.html> accessed on 31 January 2019

arrears and overholding remains the most common issue referred to the RTB for dispute resolution. In 2017, applications for rent arrears/rent arrears and overholding accounted for 27 percent of all applications received for dispute resolution. Rent arrears can be a significant problem for landlords and tenants. Overholding occurs when a tenant fails to leave the rented property where a landlord has issued a valid Notice of Termination. Where a tenant does not vacate the tenancy following receipt of a valid Notice of Termination, they must continue to pay rent, however, this does not imply a recognition of an ongoing tenancy. In 2017, the RTB received 1,547 applications for dispute resolution that related to rent arrears, and rent arrears and overholding. There were 626 cases where determination orders were issued for rent arrears and rent arrears and overholding in 2017. Some 77 percent of Notices of Termination served for rent arrears, (or rent arrears and overholding), were found to be valid. The issue of rent arrears and overholding is significant in the sector. The total amount of awards in relation to arrears was over €1.6 million in 2017 with an average award of €3,400 per landlord.[21] This picture is consistent with the shortage of supply in the market place and the fact that tenants have little or nowhere else to go.

The steps in the process for a dispute

A landlord or tenant can log a dispute with RTB either online or by postal application form. The cost of the online application is €15, and the postal application is €25. There is no fee for the Dispute Resolution of Mediation.

Parties may choose either adjudication or mediation to resolve their dispute where both alternatives usually involve a hearing with the parties and either an independent adjudicator or mediator in attendance. Some cases are processed by submitted evidence only. In 2013 the RTB introduced a telephone mediation option in addition to the meetings already offered, to provide a more convenient option for those using the mediation service. The RTB consider mediation to be one of the more efficient ways of dealing with disputes and achieving mutually agreeable resolutions. Telephone mediation is a convenient way to address disputes quickly and effectively where an impartial, trained mediator works with both sides. Both sides are individually contacted by telephone and, through a series of calls, the mediator facilitates the parties in coming to an agreed resolution within a short period

---

21 *Residential Tenancies Board Annual Report, 2017,* ch 5, 40.

of time. Telephone mediation does not rule out other options if an agreement is not reached. This process is a lot quicker than the adjudication process and it is less formal, less adversarial and requires less paperwork. Parties may also opt for a face to face mediation hearing. In 2017, 5,823 new applications for dispute resolution were received by RTB, only 1–2 percent of registered tenancies accessed the Dispute Resolution Service and almost half of all cases were processed and closed within 4–8 weeks.[22]

Once an application for dispute resolution is made, a case number is then assigned to each case and can be accessed online by entering the case reference number where additional information and evidence can be uploaded.

At an adjudication hearing, an adjudicator will enquire fully into all matters relevant to the dispute and consider the testimony and evidence provided by both the parties in dispute. Either party may send a representative or make a written statement if they cannot attend on the day of the hearing, but they must inform the RTB of this in advance. If the case respondent chooses not to attend the hearing, the case can proceed in their absence and the adjudicator's determination will be binding on them if the applicant's claim is upheld. Following the hearing, the adjudicator will prepare an adjudication report which will contain the determination. This report is sent to the parties who have 10 days within which to submit an application for appeal to an RTB tribunal, it forms the basis for a legally binding Determination Order by the Board of the RTB.[23]

The RTB cannot advise the parties as to whether they should opt for adjudication or mediation. Mediation is the quickest and easiest route if both parties agree to engage in the process, however, generally where the parties have been in dispute for some time and have failed to reach agreement it is less likely that mediation will be a realistic solution in these cases.

Third party disputes

A landlord owes a duty to each person who could be potentially affected by their tenants negative or anti-social behaviour and of them being found in breach of their obligations under a tenancy. This duty is imposed on landlords by s.15(1) of the Act. This duty is

22 *Residential Tenancies Board Annual Report, 2017*, ch 5, 34.
23 <www.rtb.ie/faq>, accessed 13 August 2018.

owed to certain third parties who may have no connection with the tenancy concerned. In subs (1) 'person who could be potentially affected' means a person who, it is reasonably foreseeable, would be directly and adversely affected by a failure to enforce an obligation of the tenant were such a failure to occur and includes any other tenant under the tenancy mentioned in that subsection. This third party may bring an application for dispute resolution to the RTB pursuant to s 77 of the Residential Tenancies Act 2004. Before such a complaint may be referred to the RTB, the following conditions must first be satisfied:

> 'the referrer of the complaint is or was directly and adversely affected by the landlord's alleged breach of duty of s.15(1) and before submitting the complaint, the referrer took all reasonable steps to resolve the matter by communicating or attempting to communicate with the relevant parties or former parties of the tenancy concerned. This condition does not require the referrer to institute or threaten to institute legal proceedings against the parties or former parties of the tenancy.'

In the case of *Horgan v Walsh and Anor,*[24] a third party referred a dispute to the PRTB against the owners of a neighbouring dwelling. In its decision, the tenancy tribunal said that it did not consider that the third party had complied with s 77(2)(b) of the RTA 2004, in that he did not take all reasonable steps to resolve the matter and in particular did not approach the tenants directly, in whose hands the tenancy tribunal said that the remedy for the third party's complaints lay.

The most common operation of s 15 and s 77 of the Act in practice arises from disputes with tenants of a dwelling who are acting in an anti-social manner causing noise disturbance to their neighbours. In *Dunne v Farrell*[25] a neighbour to a rented dwelling made a complaint to the PRTB in relation to the behaviour of the tenants of that dwelling. The neighbour alleged that the tenants in the dwelling had engaged in anti-social behaviour, with many cars calling at late hours to the house, by leaving dirt and rubbish in the garden and by being personally intimidating to her. In evidence given by the landlord, he said that he did not dispute that his tenants had engaged in anti-social behaviour but claimed that he had made many attempts to rectify the situation.

---

24 TR84/DR 719/2007, 17 April 2008.
25 TR52/DR444/2007, 13 July 2007.

The landlord said that he had called to the rented dwelling on a number of occasions to ask the tenants not to make noise at anti-social times, that he had spoken to An Garda Síochána and the Residents' Association to whom complaints had been made and that he had issued two notices of termination to the tenants who ultimately vacated the property. Notwithstanding this, the tenancy tribunal determined on the evidence before it that the landlord had breached his obligations under s 15 of the Residential Tenancies Act 2004 and was directed to pay the third party the sum of €1,000 in damages.[26]

[26] Una Cassidy and Jennifer Ring, *Landlord & Tenant Law, The Residential Sector* (Round Hall, 2010).

Chapter 13

Regulation of the OMC

1. Introduction 189
2. Regulating the OMC 189
3. Funding for regulation 203

1. Introduction

The Multi-Unit Development and apartment sector in Ireland is a growing sector and taking this into consideration there exists a real need for regulation of the sector. In examining this further this chapter will expose the importance of regulation of the OMC and the costs associated with such regulation.

2. Regulating the OMC

The EU28 Figures in the table below show where Ireland is in terms of the numbers of the population that live in multi-unit developments. Compared to our European counterparts, Ireland has the lowest number of people living in flats or apartments and given the huge demand for accommodation in our larger cities the trend in the future must be for multi-unit developments and higher rise apartment blocks. The only way is up in more ways than one, according to David McWilliams, there is an apartment crisis in Ireland and 'the solution to this apartment crisis is an economic one. Ireland needs to build lots of apartments and build up.'[1]

1 David McWilliams, 'Our housing problem is an apartment problem', *The Irish Times*, <https://www.irishtimes.com/opinion/david-mcwilliams-our-housing-problem-is-an-apartment-problem-1.3507287> accessed 8 June 2018.

Eurostat distribution of population by dwelling type[2]:

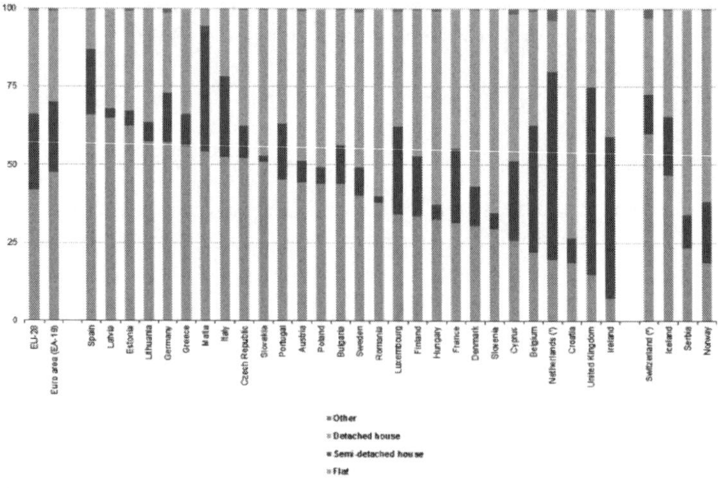

By 2040 it is expected that an additional one million people will live in Ireland and an additional two-thirds of a million people will be working in Ireland. More buildings will be needed to accommodate this rise in population. An ageing population and smaller family sizes will mean we will need an additional half a million homes to accommodate this growth.[3] This will give rise to a huge demand for quality apartment building particularly in urban centres. Regulation of the OMC will be critical to ensuring that the value of a property owner's investment is protected.

The Law Reform Commission's 2006 Consultation Paper discussed in detail the proposals for appointing a regulatory body over OMCs in Ireland. What followed was the Regulation of Property Service Providers which takes care primarily of the service providers in a broad sweep of property services in Ireland. It does not oversee or have any responsibility for the operation of the OMC.

In *Management Fees and Service Charges Levied on Owners of Property in Multi-Unit Dwellings* published in 2006 it was recommended that regulation should 'include regulation of management companies in addition to regulation of Managing Agents and

2 Eurostat, 'Distribution of population by dwelling type, 2015' <http://ec.europa.eu/eurostat/statistics-explained/index.php/File:Distribution_of_population_by_dwelling_type,_2015_(%25_of_population)_YB17.png#file> accessed 7 June 2018.

3 Government of Ireland, *Project Ireland 2040, Building Ireland's Future*, 3, <www.gov.ie/2040>.

consumer information'.[4] Similarly, in 2006, the Law Reform Commission Consultation Paper on Multi-Unit Developments set out in detail the need for regulation of the OMC noting that the idea of having a single specialised regulator for the sector was particularly compelling. The following is an extract from the report which is as relevant today as it was in 2006:

> **'Overview of the Functions Proposed for the Regulatory Body**
> Given that the recommendations with regard to the function of the proposed Regulatory Body are dispersed throughout this Paper, the Commission considers that it is appropriate to summarise these recommendations, which it now does. The functions outlined in this Paper for the proposed Regulatory Body as provisionally recommended by the Commission broadly fall into two main categories; policy and regulation for the multi-unit development sector.
>
> ***(1) Regulatory Body-Policy***
> The Commission's proposals with regard to vesting of responsibility for regulation of the sector in a Regulatory Body envisage that the Body will be at least partially responsible for the development and implementation of policy in for multi-unit developments. Here is a summary of the Body's proposed "policy" function:
>
> - The Regulatory Body will have input into creation of guidelines for developers outlining the suitable time to establish a management company for a development and the duties to be fulfilled by a developer while in control of such a company;
> - The Body will be involved in developing protocols to be followed by both planning authorities and developers during the taking-in charge process;
> - The Regulatory Body will have to undertake an urgent study into the status of sinking/reserve funds in the sector at the moment and address the issues arising where developments have not yet established such funds;

4 DKM Consultants Ltd in Association with Kevin O'Higgins Solicitors, *Management Fees and Service Charges levied on Owners of Property in Multi-Unit Dwellings, Final Report for the National Consumer Agency*, October 2006, ii.

- It will have responsibility for setting standards for the 'reasonable' and 'appropriate' calculation of service charges, and will also have to keep under review the sanctions to be imposed on those who fail to pay their service charges
- With regard to management companies, the Body will play a major role in deciding the proper name to be used by management companies determining who should be given voting rights; development of an alternative sanction to the strike-off provision, and development of standard provisions for management companies' memorandums and articles of association. Such issues arising in relation to the development of policy which has an impact on company law for management companies will be considered in conjunction with the Companies Registration Office.
- The Regulatory Body will review, in consultation with other state agencies, a full scheme of management company Directors' rights and obligations
- The Regulatory Body will advise on and monitor the drafting and implementation of all regulations introduced to regulate the Multi-Unit Development sector.

Once a number of these policy functions are initially achieved, the regulatory role will then be simply to act in a monitoring capacity to ensure that policies do not become outdated, and to review and strategically reform the applicable regulations should this occur.

(2) Regulation – general

The proposals of the Commission with regard to regulation of multi-unit developments can be summarised as follows:

- Every multi-unit development should be registered with the regulatory body. Where developers decide to retain units in the developments which they have constructed, the regulatory body must also be informed of this.
- The regulatory body will be responsible for the monitoring and supervision of management companies.

- To facilitate this, all management companies will be required to file annual reports to the body.
- The body will keep a database of the membership of all management companies.
- The regulatory body will advise companies about which is the most appropriate company type for them to adopt.
- The body will advise management companies on the proper steps to take when they are made aware that such companies face strike-off.
- The body will advise and assist management companies on compliance with the Companies Acts generally
- All of the regulatory and supervisory powers outlined above will also apply to smaller developments.

In so far as possible, the Commission believes that any proposals for regulation should not inadvertently lead to some groups of stakeholders being unnecessarily subject to regulation from a number of different State bodies. Furthermore, in some instances, the role of the proposed body will be confined to simply ensuring that the role of an existing regulator within a given part of the sector (for example, local authorities) is consistent with the wider demands that are required in the sector as a whole.

(3) Regulation Accountability of the sector

- The regulatory body will monitor use of enforcement powers of local authorities in ensuring that developers properly complete developments;
- Developers will be accountable to the Regulatory Body where they are in breach of their statutory obligations. Sanctions for such breaches may include the body instituting criminal proceedings against such developers
- The regulatory body will be able to investigate and, if necessary, take appropriate action where it receives a complaint or discovers that service charges or reserve/sinking fund contributions are excessive;
- It will undertake random audits on the accounts of management companies to ensure that good

practice is followed in the calculation of such charges;

- The body will investigate mismanagement of management companies following complaint from any interested party or as part of its monitoring and supervision mandate. It will be empowered to take appropriate steps where the complaints are substantiated;
- The regulatory body will have power to investigate complaints against any part of the multi-unit development sector and will be able to take appropriate steps where necessary to resolve any disputes;
- The regulatory body will be able to apply to the Circuit Court for a remedial order where problems arise with multi-unit developments.'[5]

The publication of *Management Fees and Service Charges levied on Owners of Property in Multi-Unit Dwellings, Final Report for the National Consumer Agency*[6] identified a gap where the role of the new regulator (the Property Services Regulatory Authority), was to regulate property service providers only and not OMCs. This is a failing because the opportunity was there to incorporate both under the one agency whereas now there is a requirement for another regulator for OMCs. In this vein, the PSRA are raising concerns about the lack of sufficient sinking-funds set aside in OMCs but they do not have any authority in this. In addition to this, the existence of a professional body for property management agents similar to that of the Association of Residential Managing Agents in England is something that is lacking in the Irish system to promote high standards and professionalism in the industry, although it forms part of the Property Services Regulatory Authority's 2017–2020 Strategic Plan.

Many of the problems and complaints which have been reported by property owners to the Property Services Regulatory Authority are about managing agents, but when investigated these complaints are found in fact to arise from the conduct of the members and directors of OMCs around the country and are not as a result of how the managing agent carries out their duties for

---

5 The Law Reform Commission, *Consultation Paper on Multi-Unit Developments* (LRC CP 42—2006) p 120.

6 DKM Consultants Ltd in Association with Kevin O'Higgins Solicitors, *Management Fees and Service Charges levied on Owners of Property in Multi-Unit Dwellings, Final Report for the National Consumer Agency*, October 2006.

the OMC. Registration of OMCs at the Companies Registration Office is not enough to allow for robust regulation of the sector, this is why there needs to be a regulatory body for OMCs.

Regulation of the OMC, in contrast to that of regulation of property service providers, is concerned with the governance and operations of the OMC itself and unlike the Regulation of Property Service Providers, it does not yet exist in Ireland. The likely precursor to such regulation is the creation of a register to determine how many OMCs exist in Ireland today and a method by which each newly incorporated OMC can be entered onto the register. In addition to this, the operational performance of OMCs is an important part of understanding the sector prior to Regulation of the OMC.

In July 2017, Clúid Housing in collaboration with the Housing Agency sought tenders through a public procurement competition for the provision of research in this area. At the time, the scope of the research was to be defined in Lot A which would contain the quantitative element and Lot B the qualitative element of the research. It was expected that Lot A would result in the publication of an up-to-date directory of all OMC's operating in Ireland, this would be a measure of the market. This list would include the name of the OMC, company registration number, address, company contact details, date of incorporation of the company and a sample analysis of OMC company accounts and directors reports. However, this directory was not created and the report cites conflicting data as one of the reasons as to why it is difficult to determine the size of the OMC sector in Ireland.[7]

The qualitative part of the research was to examine and assess the performance of OMC's in Ireland and make recommendations for any necessary changes. June 2019 saw the publication of *'Owners' Management Companies, Sustainable apartment living for Ireland'* authored by Paul Mooney. The key recommendation in this report is that the Government establish a regulator for OMC's on a statutory basis. The report sets out the functions of the proposed regulator as follows:

- To offer guidance on all aspects of the operations of OMC's;
- To maintain a register of OMC's and process annual

[7] Paul Mooney, *Owners' Management Companies, Sustainable Apartment Living for Ireland*, The Housing Agency, Clúid Housing, June 2019, p 25.

returns to incorporate additional return requirements, thereby ensuring compliance within the sector by OMC's;
- To collect data through the annual returns process in respect of expenditure trends, the size of the sector and monitor variances in service charge levels and collection;
- To provide a dispute resolution process through an online tribunal system;
- To impose sanctions on OMC's for non-compliance;
- To appoint independent directors as a sanction on OMC's or at their request;
- To provide mandatory training to OMC directors;
- To provide individual guidance and advice to OMC members and directors;
- To carry out research in the interests of OMC's and unit owners;
- To provide an inspection regime for new apartment developments to ensure compliance with building regulations and fire safety;
- To provide emergency assistance where an OMC fails in its duties or abilities.[8]

The OMC sector is faced with many problems which affect those who own and live in properties in multi-unit developments and it is the considerable size of the sector and the scale of the property investments at stake for the consumers involved that justifies the call for regulation of the OMC.

The issue of the collection of the annual service charge is one that permeates through each and every fibre and affects every action that an OMC is involved in on a daily basis. The complete operation and survival of the OMC hinges upon this one common dominator which all owners are collectively responsible for. The risk to the financial health of an OMC from the non-payment or even slow payment of the annual service charge can be a cause of debilitation to the effective operation of the OMC. Research on this issue indicates that some OMCs have debtor balances outstanding for five years or more.[9] In some cases, service charge debt can exceed 100 percent of the annual budget required to run

---

[8] Paul Mooney, *Owners' Management Companies, Sustainable Apartment Living for Ireland*, The Housing Agency, Clúid Housing, June 2019, p 76.

[9] Adele McKeown, *Service Charge Collection in Multi-Unit Developments* (Dublin Institute of Technology, 2016), 43.

the OMC. Without regulation and new rules surrounding debt collection for OMCs the status quo has the potential to extinguish the value of the consumers' investment. There is a general consensus among commentators in the sector that a formal and statutory regulatory regime with new rules on the collection of service charges is a crucial element to the future success of the sector as the current debt collection procedure through the courts is ineffective for the collection of annual service charges. This was noted as far back as the Law Reform Commission's Consultation Report on Multi-Unit Developments issued in 2006. This report refers to the issues surrounding the setting of the annual service charge, apportionment of the service charge and transparency, all of which were addressed in the Multi-Unit Developments Act 2011, however, the fixing of rules around the collection of the annual service charge were not addressed at the time. This is a core issue which must be addressed within the context of regulation of the OMC. In most cases, the managing agent is charged with the task of collecting the annual service charge and while the implementation and enforcement of a robust company policy on the collection of service charges is useful, it normally falls to the legal system to pursue outstanding service charges. It is because of the ineffectiveness of the legal system in this regard, that regulation is required to provide for specific statutory rules and sanctions relating to the non-payment of a service charge debt which can be used as an instrument to the benefit of the OMC.

The sinking-fund contribution in a multi-unit development, like the annual service charge, is collected each year by the OMC and is required for the purposes of discharging expenditure reasonably incurred on refurbishment, improvement and maintenance of a non-recurring nature. The same problems exist with the collection of the sinking-fund payments each year as exist with the annual service charge in that the non- and slow payment is problematic for the operation of the OMC. Although the Multi-Unit Developments Act 2011 addressed the issue of sinking-fund provision at s 19(5) as follows:

> 'the amount of contribution to be paid as respects a unit by each unit owner of such a unit to the sinking-fund in respect of a particular year shall be the amount of €200.00 or such other amount as may be agreed by a meeting of the members as the contribution in respect of the year concerned… ',

this provision falls short of placing an obligation on OMC

members and directors to set aside a sufficient sinking-fund payment each year. The problem here can be best described as a 'turkeys don't vote for Christmas' scenario. At the Annual General Meeting of the company there is a proposal for setting aside a sinking-fund payment. It is a regular occurrence where members and directors seek to set aside the least possible amount so as to lower their own burden of payments to their OMC in that year. For some owners, their interest is to pay the lowest possible charges in the short-term as they plan to sell their property in the short term, the lack of long term sinking-fund provision will not be an issue for them to deal with. The lack of regulation on how these decisions are made leaves it open for members and directors to act in their own interests in these circumstances rather than the long-term interests of the OMC.

Sinking fund provision should be professionally determined and regulation surrounding the governance of sinking-fund provision would ensure long term sustainability of multi-unit developments and without it there exists the real risk that multi-unit developments will fall into disrepair and have a negative impact on communities throughout Ireland in the future. As the multi-unit development sector grows, this issue will become more problematic if it is left unaddressed and is referred to by the Apartment Owners' Network as a 'ticking time bomb in the sector'.[10]

Service charges which have been set by developers at the initial stages of the development are often miscalculated in that they do not provide accurately for the long-term upkeep and maintenance of the development. When the developer is at construction stage and looking at promoting and selling each of the apartments in the development, their interest may lie in keeping the annual service charge per unit as low as possible in order to attract buyers of the apartments. It has transpired that this grossly inaccurately low service charge projection is problematic in the longer term when property owners find themselves in a situation where the annual service charge is increasing dramatically each year as the buildings get older and more and more repairs and maintenance are required. These property owners may have purchased their property based on how much they could afford to pay for

---

[10] Apartment Owners' Network, 'Written Statement to Joint Oireachtas Committee on Housing, Planning & Local Government, Issues Impacting Apartment and Multi-Unit Developments', 19 April 2018. <https://apartmentownersnetwork.files.wordpress.com/2018/04/aon-jochplg-statement-2018-04-19.pdf>.

their annual service charge each year and in a situation where this dramatically increases, then owners may find themselves in a situation where they can no longer afford to live in that development. Regulation surrounding the setting of the annual service charge is important to ensure that an accurate service charge is professionally determined at the outset to avoid duping of potential owners.

As part of regulating this, it is recommended that a suitably qualified architect or quantity surveyor must be appointed at the initial stages of development to accurately calculate the real annual service charge which will cover all running costs of the development each year to ensure that there are no surprises down the line with large expenditure requirements. Coupled with this, there is a requirement for the regulation of the building life cycle report. This report has been set out by the Department of Housing in their document, *Design Standards for New Apartments – Guidelines for Planning Authorities*.[11] Local Authorities are now required to include planning conditions that a building life cycle report must be provided by the developer at the initial stages of the development. Chapter 6.13 states as follows:

> ' … planning applications for apartment developments shall include a building lifecycle report which in turn includes an assessment of long term running and maintenance costs as they would apply on a per residential unit basis at the time of application, as well as demonstrating what measures have been specifically considered by the proposer to effectively manage and reduce costs for the benefit of residents.'

The governance, operation and control of any OMC is the responsibility of the directors of the OMC. These directors are unpaid volunteers that give their time without any financial remuneration. The Property Services Regulatory Authority states that it is an offence for anyone to provide a property management service for remuneration of any kind unless they have a license to do so.[12] This rule in effect, sets out that directors cannot be paid and that they must act voluntarily. The OMC sector is therefore almost completely run by a group of civic-minded volunteer

---

11 Department of Housing, Planning and Local Government, *Sustainable Urban Housing: Design Standards for New Apartments, Guidelines for Planning Authorities*, March 2018.

12 PSRA, *Guide to Becoming a Licensed Property Services Provider*, Chapter 3, 3.1, 9.

directors who may not necessarily possess sufficient knowledge or skills for the job. This position is misaligned with the essence of what the Property Services Regulatory Authority exists for which is that of maintaining a professional standard within the sector and protecting the consumer. Given the numbers of unprofessional, volunteer directors who hold full control of all aspects of OMCs including the legal, administrative, financial and practical aspects, it is clear that regulation of the OMC to include director training is urgently required in order to protect consumers and property owners. There is a widespread failure by OMC directors to comply with the basics of company law such as the mishandling of board affairs at AGMs and poor management practices. This includes abuse of positions, conflicts of interest, non-compliance with the Multi-Unit Developments Act and poor quality relationships with managing agents and other property owners.

Every director has a duty to their company to act with reasonable care and skill and to act in the best interests of the company at all times. There is no regulation as such in place to ensure that this is the case on a day-to-day and practical level in an OMC. Decisions may be made by way of a vote at the AGM and given the competing interests in an OMC it is easy to see where a conflict may arise. Such an example may be a situation where there is an OMC comprising 30 apartments in a building and the roof of the building is leaking and needs to be replaced. This work will have been planned in advance and the Directors of the OMC will ultimately decide on the various elements of the contract for the job. Of the 30 apartments, 10 apartments are on the top floor. A decision has to be made as to whether or not the OMC will replace the roof to the existing standard, whereby there was no insulation or whether they will insulate the roof when the work is being carried out. The cost to insulate is €60,000 and the cost to replace the roof to the same specification is €30,000. If the two directors in this company both own apartments on the ground-floor then there is no material benefit to them of having the roof insulated. They would be reducing their liability by €1,000 if they vote not to insulate the roof. They may argue that more owners would be disadvantaged by insulating than would be by not insulating, but insulating the roof is a better job for the building overall. The question of how to square this circle is one that requires some consideration. If the OMC was regulated, then the regulator can issue guidance on such conflicting matters as they arise.

The requirement for director training in OMCs has been legislated for in other jurisdictions such as the Condominium Authority of

Ontario. From 1 November 2017, the Condominium Act 1998 ('the Act') requires that all condominium board directors complete designated training courses within a certain timeframe. The Condominium Authority of Ontario is responsible for designating the training courses that directors must complete. The training is available to everyone, free of charge, and covers topics including director responsibilities and obligations. The training consists of six parts with each part addressing an important area of knowledge for board directors. There are a series of e-modules or courses in each part that cover specific topics. In total, there are 21 short e-modules that can be completed in any order and at any pace, as long as they are all completed within the six-month period following the director's appointment, election or re-election. Collectively, these online modules are the designated training courses. Directors must complete their training within six months of being elected, re-elected or appointed and failure to do so will result in their directorship to immediately cease. The modules range in length from approximately 10 to 20 minutes at audio speed. The entire training program will take between three to six hours to complete, depending on whether you listen to the audio recording or read the transcript. The user can control the speed and complete the program at a faster or slower pace. Upon completion of the course, directors are required to provide a copy of their certificate to their condo board within 15 days of completing their training.[13] Regulation of the OMC should provide for such training for OMC directors in Ireland.

Shortcomings of the Multi-Unit Development Act have become more apparent in the years since its enactment. The main shortcomings include the aforementioned lack of guidance on the sinking-fund levels that should be set aside each year and the effective legislative means by which the annual service charge can be collected. Most importantly the lack of enforcement of the Act means that its existence is immaterial in many cases. For a person to seek a remedy under this Act they must incur expensive Circuit Court costs and this is not a viable solution for most property owners and/or home owners in OMCs. Where disputes arise within an OMC, property owners are limited in where they can go to address it. In a case where directors act improperly in fulfilling their duties, members must address these concerns through company law. This remedy is lengthy, expensive and onerous. For this reason, owners are more likely

---

13 Condominium Authority of Ontario <www.condoauthorityontario.ca/en-US/training/>, accessed 7 June 2018.

not to go down this route thereby allowing for the continuance of this type of bad management. The main problem with the Multi-Unit Developments Act is that it does not contain provisions to regulate the effective operation of the OMC by volunteer directors and it is in this regard that some of the holes in the Act may be plugged by the introduction of regulation of the OMC whereby the sector would then have more robust controls. The main function of regulation of the OMC is to control and regulate the operation of every OMC in Ireland and to ensure that there is a standard created that all OMCs must meet. Enforcement of the Multi-Unit Development Act and sanctions for breach should also become part of the Regulators role of the OMC.

The Multi-Unit Developments Act 2011 falls under the remit of the Department of Justice and Equality as it was initiated through the work of the Law Reform Commission and many of the Act's provisions refer to matters of property title. As the sector has developed and grown there is a consensus among commentators that this sector should fall under the Department of Housing, Planning and Local Government and not that of Justice and Equality.[14] The growth of the sector and the increasing number of OMCs in Ireland together with the reforms in the sector that are required indicate that the more appropriate government department would be the Department of Housing, Planning and Local Government. There are precedents of such changes in government department remits in the past. This issue was considered by the Law Reform Commission in their Consultation Paper in 2006 and although they concluded at the time that the Department of Justice and Equality was the most appropriate Government department and given the challenges that the sector faces and the important role that the Department of Housing, Planning and Local Government plays in the sector, it may be worth re-considering this. The Department of Housing, Planning and Local Government is the government department responsible for planning, development, and housing and it has responsibility for many of the issues that abound the multi-unit development sector. It has a role in directing planning authorities to collect information about enforcement, planning issues and to inform the Minister so that policy can be formulated. It is partly responsible for general planning policy for multi-unit developments and also

---

14 Apartment Owners' Network, 'Written Statement to Joint Oireachtas Committee on Housing, Planning & Local Government, Issues Impacting Apartment and Multi-Unit Developments', 19 April 2018. https://apartmentownersnetwork.files.wordpress.com/2018/04/aon-jochplg-statement-2018-04-19.pdf.

deals with more specific policy such as the taking-in-charge of roadways within housing estates in an OMC. The Department also has a Minister of State with special responsibility for housing and urban development.

Given some of the inadequacies in the Multi-Unit Developments Act an overhaul is required and coupled with the need for implementation of regulation of the OMC, issues such as enforcement, building defects, service charge debt recovery, and potential OMC insolvency it follows that the appropriate government department presiding over the governance of these issues should be that of the Housing, Planning and Local Government.

The Multi-Unit Developments Act 2011 provides for dispute resolution at s 24. However, this mechanism to deal with many disputes which arise on a daily basis does not serve most of the smaller disputes which arise and have the potential to escalate. In order to rely on the provisions of the Act, property owners would have to incur considerable legal costs and the process is a lengthy and expensive one. Disputes within multi-unit developments arise on a daily basis and they can be between tenants, owners, managing agents, contractors. They can range from financial disputes, breaches of house rules, Airbnb, animals, odours, etc. The handling of some of these issues could be dealt with by a regulator by the implementation of self-help resources including an issues and solutions forum to help the parties to resolve issues that arise before they escalate and where it is possible to do so as an alternative to the ultimate legal route that they would otherwise have to take. A fast, fair and cost-effective dispute resolution would be a crucial element to improving the operations of an OMC.

3. Funding for regulation

If one of the main areas of concern for OMCs is that of potential insolvency and service charge debt recovery, then the question arises as to who would fund this proposed new regulator. The introduction of regulation to any sector can be seen by many as another layer of bureaucracy, more red tape, etc. However, the benefits would outweigh the costs.

The Condominium Authority of Ontario (CAO) is the regulatory body governing the multi-unit development sector for Ontario,

Canada. They have set fees that all condominium corporations are required to pay to the Authority. The fee has been calculated based on the equivalent of $1 per voting unit per month. In Ireland this would be the equivalent of each OMC paying a fee to the OMC Regulator. In theory if an OMC has 50 apartments and similarly €1 per apartment per month, then this would be €12 per apartment per year which would go towards having the sector properly policed with the required level of enforcement. This fee would be payable by the OMC to the regulator and it would not be payable by an individual unit owner to the regulator. According to the CAO the fee will support the CAO in providing information and self-help resources about condominium living, mandatory online training for condo directors, tools and guides for resolving common condo issues, access to the Condominium Authority Tribunal, a new online dispute resolution forum with exclusive jurisdiction to handle certain condo-related disputes.

The developing law in the OMC sector includes The Property Services (Regulation) (Amendment) (Management Company Regulation) Bill 2018. This Bill seeks to set up an Ombudsman for OMCs, a body which will help with training for Directors of OMCs and assist in dispute resolution. It is proposed that this Ombudsman will be based within the Property Services Regulation Authority.

The Multi-Unit Developments (Amendment) (Sinking Fund) Bill 2018, is a Bill entitled an Act to amend the Multi-Unit Developments Act 2011 to transfer responsibilities to the Minister for Housing Planning and Local Government from the Department of Justice and Equality. This bill also seeks to establish a sinking fund in year one of a development's transfer of ownership and to provide for other matters.

The Management Fees (Local Property Tax) Relief Bill 2018 is a Bill entitled an Act to amend the Finance (Local Property Tax) Act 2012 to make provision for a partial exemption of property tax payable by a property owner whose property is located in an OMC.

Appendices

The following is a list of materials and links that the reader might find useful for further information or reference in conjunction with the book.

1. Management Company Policy for the Collection of Service Charges

2. Sample Annual Service Charge Budgets

3. MUD Act Pre-Contract Enquiries – Requisitions

Appendix 1

Sample Owners' Management CLG

Management Company Policy for the Collection of Service Charges

Policy discussed and approved at Annual General Meeting held on Tuesday, 1st January 2019 at The Lake Hotel, Dublin.

1. Initial "Request for Payment" sent out to all owners after Annual General Meeting where the budget and service charge amount are agreed.

   Payment options offered:
   - Standing Order payments – Standing Order payments to be made for 10 months or less and must ensure that FULL amount is paid in advance of the date of the next AGM. Apt/Unit/House number and/or owner's name must reference the Standing Order payment.
   - Cheque payment – cheques to be posted to the Managing Agents Office and made payable to ***"Sample Owners' Management CLG".***
   - Online transfer – Bank details will be available on "Request for Payment" sent to Owners. Apt/Unit/House number and/or owner's name must reference the payment.
   - Cash may be paid directly into the company bank account using the account details as set out on the "Request for Payment". Cash may also be paid at the office of the Managing Agent. It is not recommend to send cash payments through the post.

2. "Request for Payment-Reminder" will be sent out to all property owners 1 month after the initial "Request for Payment" which will state that if FULL payment is not received or a payment plan is not in place within one month a levy of €200.00 will be applied to the account.

3. After the month has passed a letter will be sent to advise that the aforementioned levy has been applied and Owners will also be notified that their account will be passed to company

Solicitors for collection where outstanding service charges will be pursued legally and all legal costs associated with the collection of this debt will be borne by the property Owner and applied to their account unless a payment plan is in place to pay off FULL amount or FULL payment is received within 10 days from the date of the said letter.

4. After 10 days, if there has been no notification that a payment plan is in place or FULL payment has not been received, company Solicitors are appointed to the debt whereby the Managing Agent will instruct them to issue legal proceedings to recover the debt.

PROPOSED BY: **SECONDED BY:** **DATE:**

Appendix 2

Sample Annual Service Charge Budgets

Sample Apportionment of Service Charges

Unit	Sq. M	Refuse 2018-2019	Service Charge 2018-2019	Total Due 2018-2019
Apt. No. 1	53.4	€83.33	€868.32	€951.65
Apt. No. 2	54.2	€83.33	€881.33	€964.66
Apt. No. 3	39.4	€83.33	€640.67	€724.00
Apt. No. 4	57.7	€83.33	€938.24	€1,021.57
Apt. No. 5	54.2	€83.33	€881.33	€964.66
Apt. No. 6	81.1	€83.33	€1,318.75	€1,402.08
Apt. No. 7	57.7	€83.33	€938.24	€1,021.57
Apt. No. 8	65	€83.33	€1,056.95	€1,140.28
Apt. No. 9	61.5	€83.33	€1,000.04	€1,083.37
Apt. No. 10	65.3	€83.33	€1,061.83	€1,145.16
Apt. No. 11	61.5	€83.33	€1,000.04	€1,083.37
Apt. No. 12	46	€83.33	€747.99	€831.32
Apt. No. 13	52	€83.33	€845.56	€928.89
Apt. No. 14	71.7	€83.33	€1,165.90	€1,249.23
Apt. No. 15	72.3	€83.33	€1,175.65	€1,258.98
Apt. No. 16	72.6	€83.33	€1,180.53	€1,263.86
Apt. No. 17	48.5	€83.33	€788.65	€871.98
Apt. No. 18	58.5	€83.33	€951.25	€1,034.58
Apt. No. 19	53.3	€83.33	€866.70	€950.03
Apt. No. 20	58.7	€83.33	€954.51	€1,037.84
Apt. No. 21	53.4	€83.33	€868.32	€951.65
Apt. No. 22	51.5	€83.33	€837.43	€920.76
Apt. No. 23	47.4	€83.33	€770.76	€854.09
Apt. No. 24	70.8	€83.33	€1,151.26	€1,234.59
Apt. No. 25	52.2	€83.33	€848.81	€932.14
Apt. No. 26	51.3	€83.33	€834.18	€917.51
Apt. No. 27	70.8	€83.33	€1,151.26	€1,234.59
Apt. No. 28	51.4	€83.33	€835.80	€919.13
Apt. No. 29	51.3	€83.33	€834.18	€917.51
Apt. No. 30	72.3	€83.33	€1,175.65	€1,258.98
Comm Unit No. 1	169		€2,748.06	€2,748.06
Comm Unit No. 2	76		€1,235.82	€1,235.82
TOTALS	**2002**	**€2,499.90**	**€32,554.00**	**€35,053.90**

Sample Annual Service Charge Budget for a Housing Estate of 45 Houses

SAMPLE 3 - Budget

Sample Annual Service Charge Budget for a Housing Estate of 45 houses

AGREED ANNUAL SERVICE CHARGE BUDGET

Budget agreed at Annual General Meeting held on Tuesday, the 1st of January 2019 at 6.30pm at Sample Hotel, Dublin.

For the period: 1st of April 2019 to 31st of March 2020

ITEM	COST
Accountant's Fees	€635.00
Managing Agent's Fees	€4,854.00
Grass Cutting and Grounds Maintenance	€5,160.00
Sinking Fund	€2,000.00
Sundry	€1,000.00
AGREED TOTAL	**€13,649.00**

Agreed Service Charge Per Unit: **€303.31**

PROPOSED BY: **SECONDED BY:** **DATE:**

Sample Annual Service Charge Budget for a Housing Estate of 45 Houses

SAMPLE 4 - Budget

Sample Annual Service Charge Budget for a Housing Estate of 32 houses

AGREED ANNUAL SERVICE CHARGE BUDGET

Budget agreed at Annual General Meeting held on Tuesday, the 1st of January 2019 at 6.30pm at Sample Hotel, Dublin.

For the period: 1st of April 2019 to 31st of March 2020

ITEM	**COST**
Insurance	€636.00
Repairs and Maintenance- Sewage Pumps	€625.00
Accountant's Fees	€635.00
Managing Agent's Fees	€4,410.00
Grass Cutting and Grounds Maintenance	€5,000.00
Pest Control	€510.00
Repairs and Maintenance-External	€500.00
Bank Charges	€100.00
Sundry	€300.00
Agreed Budget	**€12,716.00**

Agreed Service Charge Per House	€397.38
Agreed Sinking Fund Levy Per House	€75.00
Agreed Total Service Charge	**€472.38**

PROPOSED BY: **SECONDED BY:** **DATE:**

Appendix 3

MUD Act Pre-Contract Enquiries – Requisitions[1]

REQUISITIONS ON TITLE	REPLIES
36. NEW OR SECOND-HAND PROPERTY IN A MANAGED DEVELOPMENT TO WHICH THE MULTI-UNIT DEVELOPMENTS ACT 2011 ("the MUDs Act") APPLIES	
Reply to 1.–18. and either 19.–23. or 24.–26. below	
All units in a multi-unit development	
1. Furnish evidence by way of Companies Office search that the owners management company ("the OMC") is registered in the Companies Office.	36.1.
2. a. Confirm if the OMC has received any notice threatening a strike-off or liquidation.	36.2.a.
b. If any such notice has been served, furnish details.	36.2.b.
3. Furnish certified copy certificate of incorporation and memorandum and articles of association of the OMC or constitution of the OMC if incorporated on or after 1 June 2015.	36.3.
4. Furnish either:	
a. Copy folio and file plan showing the OMC as registered owner of the common areas and of the reversions in the residential units, or	36.4.a.
b. Copy deed of assurance of the common areas and of the reversions in the residential units to the OMC.	36.4.b.
5. a. If no contract for the sale of a residential unit in the multi-unit development was entered into prior to 24 January 2011, confirm that the voting rights of the members and the name of the OMC are in compliance with Section 14 of the MUDs Act.	36.5.a.
b. If any such contract was entered into prior to the 24 January 2011, confirm that the voting rights of members comply with Section 15 of the MUDs Act.	36.5.b.
6. Confirm:	
a. That one OMC is or will be responsible for the management of the external and/or internal common areas of the entire multi-unit development and all the services relating thereto.	36.6.a.
b. That the only shareholders/members in the OMC are the unit owners.	36.6.b.
c. How the service charge is apportioned between the unit owners.	36.6.c.
d. There has been no breach of Section 16 of the MUDs Act.	36.6.d.
7. Who is presently managing the multi-unit development.	36.7.
8. If a firm of managing agents has been engaged state:	
a. The name of the firm.	36.8.a.
b. The terms of their engagement including (in particular) the amount of their charges.	36.8.b.

1 Available from Law Society of Ireland: *https://www.lawsociety.ie/globalassets/documents/committees/conveyancing/precedents/2019/2019-requisitions-on-title.pdf* <last accessed 2 September 2019>.

REQUISITIONS ON TITLE	REPLIES
c. Whether they are employed by the developer or the OMC.	36.8.c.
9. Furnish the name of the solicitor or firm of solicitors representing the OMC.	36.9.
10. a. Are there house rules of the OMC other than as set out in the memorandum and articles of association / constitution or in the lease.	36.10.a.
b. If so, furnish details of these rules and confirm that they were made in accordance with Section 23(4) of the MUDs Act.	36.10.b.
11. a. Has the OMC put a sinking fund into effect in accordance with Section 19 of the MUDs Act.	36.11.a.
b. If so, what is the present level of the fund and where and in whose name is it held.	36.11.b.
c. What is the amount of contribution required under Section 19 (5) of the MUDs Act.	36.11.c.
12. a. What is the amount of the service charge currently payable.	36.12.a.
b. Furnish details of the scheme in respect of annual service charges as required under Section 18 (1) of the MUDs Act.	36.12.b.
c. Furnish a copy of the estimate for the current service charge year as required under Section 18 of the MUDs Act.	36.12.c.
d. Confirm that the estimate was considered and approved as required under Section 18(2) of the MUDs Act.	36.12.d.
e. Furnish a copy of the last annual report as required under Section 17 of the MUDs Act and confirm that all requirements in relation to the annual meeting have been complied with by the OMC.	36.12.e.
f. Furnish the accounts of the OMC for the previous financial year.	36.12.f.
13. Is the Vendor or the OMC aware of any possible claim against the funds of the OMC. If so, furnish details.	36.13.
14. Is the Vendor or the OMC aware of any proposal by the OMC to carry out any repair work or incur other expenditure which would substantially affect the service charge payable at present. If so, furnish details.	36.14.
15. Has any application to court been made or is pending or has been threatened by any person under Section 24 of the MUDs Act in relation to the OMC or the multi-unit development. If so, furnish details.	36.15.
16. Has the OMC entered into any contracts which would contravene Section 32 of the MUDs Act. If so, furnish details.	36.16.
17. a. Furnish a certified copy of the current block insurance policy together with evidence that it is in force.	36.17.a.
b. Prior to closing furnish a letter of interest noting the name of the Purchaser's mortgagee (if applicable).	36.17.b.

REQUISITIONS ON TITLE	REPLIES
c. Whether they are employed by the developer or the OMC.	36.8.c.
9. Furnish the name of the solicitor or firm of solicitors representing the OMC.	36.9.
10. a. Are there house rules of the OMC other than as set out in the memorandum and articles of association / constitution or in the lease.	36.10.a.
b. If so, furnish details of these rules and confirm that they were made in accordance with Section 23(4) of the MUDs Act.	36.10.b.
11. a. Has the OMC put a sinking fund into effect in accordance with Section 19 of the MUDs Act.	36.11.a.
b. If so, what is the present level of the fund and where and in whose name is it held.	36.11.b.
c. What is the amount of contribution required under Section 19 (5) of the MUDs Act.	36.11.c.
12. a. What is the amount of the service charge currently payable.	36.12.a.
b. Furnish details of the scheme in respect of annual service charges as required under Section 18 (1) of the MUDs Act.	36.12.b.
c. Furnish a copy of the estimate for the current service charge year as required under Section 18 of the MUDs Act.	36.12.c.
d. Confirm that the estimate was considered and approved as required under Section 18(2) of the MUDs Act.	36.12.d.
e. Furnish a copy of the last annual report as required under Section 17 of the MUDs Act and confirm that all requirements in relation to the annual meeting have been complied with by the OMC.	36.12.e.
f. Furnish the accounts of the OMC for the previous financial year.	36.12.f.
13. Is the Vendor or the OMC aware of any possible claim against the funds of the OMC. If so, furnish details.	36.13.
14. Is the Vendor or the OMC aware of any proposal by the OMC to carry out any repair work or incur other expenditure which would substantially affect the service charge payable at present. If so, furnish details.	36.14.
15. Has any application to court been made or is pending or has been threatened by any person under Section 24 of the MUDs Act in relation to the OMC or the multi-unit development. If so, furnish details.	36.15.
16. Has the OMC entered into any contracts which would contravene Section 32 of the MUDs Act. If so, furnish details.	36.16.
17. a. Furnish a certified copy of the current block insurance policy together with evidence that it is in force.	36.17.a.
b. Prior to closing furnish a letter of interest noting the name of the Purchaser's mortgagee (if applicable).	36.17.b.

REQUISITIONS ON TITLE	REPLIES
18. Furnish on closing;	
a. Copy letter sent to the OMC confirming the change in ownership and giving the name and address of the Purchaser.	36.18.a.
b. Written confirmation from the OMC that the service charge has been paid up to date.	36.18.b.
Multi-unit development in which a residential unit was not sold prior to 1 April 2011	
19. Confirm that the OMC complies with Section 3 (5) of the MUDs Act.	36.19.
20. Furnish:	
a. A copy of the certificate required under Section 3(1)(c) of the MUDs Act.	36.20.a.
b. A copy of the contract referred to in Section 3(1)(d) of the MUDs Act.	36.20.b.
c. Confirmation that the OMC had legal representation and was not represented by the same solicitor or firm of solicitors as the developer or owner of the common areas as required under Section 3(6) of the MUDs Act.	36.20.c.
d. The name of the solicitor or firm of solicitors representing the OMC.	36.20.d.
21. If the development stage has ended, furnish a copy of the statutory declaration required under Section 11 of the MUDs Act.	36.21.
22. a. Has any request been made under Section 12 of the MUDs Act.	36.22.a.
b. If so, furnish details and a copy of the statutory declaration required.	36.22.b.
23. If the development stage of the multi-unit development has ended, furnish written confirmation from the OMC that the documents specified in Schedule 3 of the MUDs Act have been furnished to it.	36.23.
Multi-unit development in which a residential unit was sold prior to 1 April 2011	
24. If the development stage has ended, furnish a copy of the statutory declaration required under Section 11 of the MUDs Act.	36.24.
25. a. Has any request been made under Section 12 of the MUDs Act.	36.25.a.
b. If so, furnish details and a copy of the statutory declaration required.	36.25.b.
26. If the development stage of the multi-unit development has ended, furnish written confirmation from the OMC that the documents specified in Schedule 3 of the MUDs Act have been furnished to it.	36.26.

Useful Resources

The following is a list of materials and links that the reader might find useful for further information or reference in conjunction with the book.

- Multi-Unit Developments Act 2011 – this can be found on the following link: http://www.irishstatutebook.ie/eli/2011/act/2/enacted/en/html

- *Heidelstone Company Limited and Courtview Management Limited* – this can be found at – [2006] IEHC 408 http://www.bailii.org/ie/cases/IEHC/2006/H408.html

- Company Constitution information see http://www.akproperty.ie/case-studies.html

- Management Company Lease Agreement including covenants by the Owner and the Management Company see http://www.akproperty.ie/case-studies.html

- Property Services Agreement see http://www.akproperty.ie/case-studies.html

- Sample Notice of Termination RTB (14 notices) see https://onestopshop.rtb.ie/ending-a-tenancy/sample-notices-of-termination/

- Sample Statutory Declaration RTBhttps://onestopshop.rtb.ie/ending-a-tenancy/sample-notices-of-termination/

Index

Adjudication of disputes 182, 183, 184–5
Airbnb
insurance and 163–5
Alternative dispute resolution *see* **Dispute resolution**
Animals
house rules 40, 107
Annual accounts
audit 107
copies of 29
generally 27, 29–30
Annual general meeting (AGM)
attendance levels 46, 47, 49–50
business of 111
directors 29
generally 10, 15, 27, 29–30
minutes of 111
MUD Act 2011 77, 79, 110, 112
notice of 110–11
ordinary resolution 111
quorum 111
resignation of board 29, 45
retirement of directors 45
special resolution 39, 110, 111–12
venues 110
Annual return
electronic filing 146
failure to file 14, 27, 115, 120, 132
filing 27, 146
first annual return 27
penalty for late filing 146
Annual service charge
advance payments 80–1
apportionment 46, 209
budget 22, 23, 32, 58, 59
sample budgets 209–11
calculation 2, 22–3, 24, 26, 32, 57–9, 198–9
by independent quantity surveyor 22, 26, 67, 199
company policy 58–9
debt recovery process *see* **Debt recovery process**
first annual service charge 22, 23, 67
fixing 23
Annual service charge—*contd.*
generally 2, 12–13
insurance policies 152
low recovery rate 58
managing agent and 15
MUD Act 2011 and 44, 77–81
non-payment 7, 11, 13, 14, 25, 36, 132
payment of 26
per-day-rate 23
sample company policy 207–8
Statute of Limitations 78
unsold units 14, 23, 26, 80
Anti-social behaviour 174, 176, 186–7
Apartment blocks
automatic incorporation of OMC 21
first skim of plaster 36, 37
maintenance/repairs 29, 36, 39
Apartment living in Ireland 16, 167
Apartment Owners' Network
generally 86, 109, 149
on sinking funds 22, 53–4, 55–6, 68, 79–80
on tax law 108
on training of officers 117
Auctioneer's licence 92
Australia 56

Blackstone, Sir William 1
Building contract 28–9
Building investment fund *see* **Sinking fund**
Building lifecycle report 68, 199

Canada
Condominium Authority of Ontario 200–1, 203–4
service charges 62
sinking funds 56
Capital project management
case study 70–1
Car parking *see* **Parking**
Celtic Tiger era 48, 126
Chartered surveyor's report 31
Clark, Robert 157

Clúid Housing 16, 195
Co-ownership agreements 9, 103
Collapse of property market 14
Collective responsibility 10–11, 14, 35, 36, 65, 126
Commission on the Private Rented Residential Sector 168–9, 183
Companies Office
amendment of company constitution 39
powers of 8
Companies Registration Office (CRO) 17, 27, 50, 103, 119–21
Company constitution
amendment of 39
generally 28, 38–9
lease agreement and 39
maintenance/repair work 39
see also **Memorandum and articles of association**
Company law
AGM *see* **Annual general meeting**
company limited by guarantee 8, 105–7
company name 42
company secretary 117–19
criminal liability 114, 121–2
definition of company 103–4
designated activity company 8, 105
designated activity company limited by guarantee 105
directors *see* **Directors**
failure to file annual return 14, 27, 115, 120, 132
generally 103–4
governance *see* **Governance of companies**
members' register 35, 42–4
penalties for failure to comply with 42, 121–3
private company limited by shares 105
registered office 42
separate legal personality 19–20
types of company 8, 104–9
Company law code 8–9, 36, 39, 106
Company Law Review Group 119
Company limited by guarantee (CLG) 8, 105–7
Company name
legal requirements 42
Company register
restoration of company to 85–6, 123, 145–9
Company secretary
duties 118–19
eligibility for office 117–18
generally 117–19
negligence 118
Company strike-off
consequences of 122–3, 133
failure to file annual return 14, 27, 115, 120, 132
generally 14, 131–3
Heidlestone
case summary 135–43
generally 133–4
numbers of 131
restoration to register 85–6, 123, 145–9
transfer of common areas where developer not trading 144–5
Compensation Fund *see* **Property Services Regulatory Authority**
Condominium Authority of Ontario 200–1, 203–4
Construction work
house rules 40, 41
Continuous Professional Development (CPD) 101
Corporate manslaughter 114–15
Courtney, Thomas B 109, 119
Criminal liability 114–15
Culture within an OMC 46–50

D licence 49
Deasy's Act 168, 171–2
see also **Landlord and tenant**
Debt recovery
Circuit Court 60
District Court 60–1
enforcement measures 61–5
enforcement of terms of lease 63–5
excludable debt 68–9, 78
forfeiture provision 63
generally 196–7
High Court 60
international element 65–6
MUD Act 2011 78–9
Personal Insolvency Agreement 68–9, 78
process 59–68
statement of claim 60–1
Statute of Limitations 78
writing down of debt 79
Designated activity company
limited by guarantee (DAC limited by guarantee) 105

Designated activity company—*contd.*
limited by shares (DAC limited by shares) 8, 105
Directors
AGM 29
corporate manslaughter 114–15
criminal liability 114–15
D licence 49
disqualification 122, 133
duties/responsibilities 8, 44–5, 86, 112–17, 199–200
failure to file annual return 14, 27, 115, 120, 132
fiduciary duties 113
generally 21, 29, 36, 44–5
insolvent companies 122
insurance 45, 47, 114, 156
liability claims 87, 114
meetings 112
MUD Act 2011 45, 82–3
negligence claims 87, 114–15
nomination forms 49
proposed training for 86, 117, 200–1
retirement of 45
rotation of 45
skills 115–16
as unpaid volunteers 8, 29, 44, 199
urgent cash calls 45
Dispute resolution
adjudication 182, 183, 184–5
generally 203
landlord and tenant 183–4
process 184–5
third party disputes 185–7
lease agreement 83–5
mediation 84–5, 182, 183–4
Disqualification 122, 133
Documentation
on completion of development 87
transfer documents 76–7

England and Wales
generally 15, 16, 194
sinking funds 56, 57
Europe
condominiums legislation 15–16
Extraordinary general meeting (EGM) 43–4, 110

Financial crisis 2008 14, 126, 127
Fire safety
generally 31, 48
house rules 41
maintenance of equipment 115

Fitzgerald, Ann 6

Governance of companies
AGM *see* **Annual general meeting**
company law 109–12
directors meetings 112
MUD Act 2011 10, 81–2
voting rights 10, 43–4, 81–2, 86, 112
see also **company law**

Hanlon, Evelyn
Successful Apartment Living 90, 103
Heller, Agnes 46
Holmes, Oliver Wendell 1
Home Renovation Incentive scheme 69, 108
House rules 39–42, 83, 107
Housing Agency 16, 195
Housing asset values 11
Housing co-operatives 9, 103
Housing estates
building contract 28–9
common areas 13, 20–1
generally 13, 20
maintenance/repairs 36
Rules of the Estate 42
Hutchinson, Brian 84–5

Incorporation of OMC 10, 21
Insolvency
directors 122
Personal Insolvency Agreement 68–9
property development company 29
Insurance
Airbnb and 163–5
all risks cover 151
average clause 155
avoiding pitfalls 162–3
building insurance 152
business interruption cover 153
case studies 165–6
claims process 156–62
contents insurance 154
definitions of cover 152
directors and officers 45, 47, 114, 156
employers liability cover 153
excess 151, 155, 156, 159, 160
generally 23, 151–3
indemnity 152–3
insurable interest 152
insurable/uninsurable perils 153–6
lifts 155–6

Insurance—*contd.*
loss assessor 159–60
personal injury claims 164–5
premiums 153
public liability cover 153
retention 162
scope of cover 154–5
settlement 161–2
structural defects 154
third party damage 158
underinsurance clause 155
warranties 163

Keane, Ronan 8, 105

Land and Conveyancing Law Reform Act 2013 1
Land Registry 38
Landlord and tenant
Deasy's Act 168, 171–2
deposits 173
dispute resolution 183–4
process 184–5
third party disputes 185–7
generally 167–70
insurance 173
landlord obligations 171–4
maintenance/repair work 172–3
National Register of tenancies 182–3
notice of termination 177–8, 179
notice periods 180–1
Part 4 tenancy 177–9
termination 177–8, 179
rent pressure zones 178, 183
Residential Tenancies Act 2004 170–81
exceptions 170–1
RTB *see* **Residential Tenancies Board**
tenants' obligations 174–6
Law Reform Commission
advance payment of service charges 80
companies 106, 109
company law code 106
Consultation Paper 2006 6, 11, 17, 103, 106, 190, 191–4, 197, 202
contribution to OMC development 7–18
corporate manslaughter 114
directors 116–17
housing co-operatives 9
MUD Act 2011 and 86–8

Law Reform Commission—*contd.*
Report on Multi-Unit Developments 1–2, 6, 7–18, 54, 91, 106
sinking funds 54, 55, 56–7
Lease agreement
amendment of 41–2
company constitution and 39
covenants 37–8
dispute resolution 83–5
enforcement of 83–4
enlargement of lease 42
generally 37–8
house rules 39–42
listed house rules 41
maintenance/repair work 39
mediation 84
Letters of engagement 101–2
Licensing of property service providers 92–3
Lifts
safety inspection 155–6
Limited liability 8, 10, 19, 106
Local authority
building lifecycle reports 68, 199
funding crisis in OMC 53–4
generally 16
inconsistencies 13–14
planning permission 12, 68, 199
role of 2, 20–1
Longboat Quay, Dublin 54

McWilliams, David 189
Maintenance/repair work
company constitution 39
costs 29
generally 6, 7, 8, 9, 30–1
landlord's obligation 172–3
lease agreement 39
MUD Act 2011 85
Managing agent
appointment of 25
appointment as receiver 128–30
developer acting as 25
generally 42
independent/professional 46
management company distinguished 14
potential for abuse of role 15
prospective owners and 32
role of 14–15, 21–2, 46
Mediation 84–5, 182, 183–4
see also **dispute resolution**
Meetings
AGM *see* **Annual general meeting**
directors meetings 112

Meetings—*contd.*
extraordinary general meeting 39, 41, 43–4, 110
general meetings 112
special resolution 39, 46, 110, 111–12
voting rights 10, 43–4, 81–2, 86, 112
Members' register
contact details 43–4
contents 43
generally 35, 42–4
place of 42
registered office 42
right of inspection 42, 43
Memorandum and articles of association
company limited by guarantee 106
directors' compliance with 50
generally 28, 135, 138, 140
replaced by company constitution 38, 119
voting rights 10, 81, 86, 112
see also **Company constitution**
Mooney, Paul 195
MUD Act Pre-Contract Enquiries 88, 213–16
Multi-Unit Development Act 2011
AGMs 77, 79, 110, 112
annual service charges 44, 77–81
areas for reform 83–5
debt recovery 78–9
directors 45, 82–3
documentation
on completion of development 87
transfer documents 76–7
effect of 15
generally 1, 16, 73–5, 87–8
governance 10, 81–2
house rules 39–40, 83
implications of 21
Law Reform Commission recommendations and 86–8
mediation 84–5
numbers of 17–18
obligation to transfer common areas 75–7
transfer documents 76–7
Pre-Contract Enquiries 88, 213–16
repairs 85
restoration to Company Register 85–6
retrospective application 74–5
sinking funds 51–3, 54–5, 77–81
Multi-Unit Development Act 2011—*contd.*
voting rights 10, 81–2
Multi-unit developments
common elements 5–6
definition 73
description of 6–7

Name *see* **Company name**
National Consumer Agency
complaints to 14, 74, 90
establishment of 6
'Management Companies and You' 6
publications 6
National Property Services Regulatory Authority
establishment of 15
function of 15
National Register of tenancies 182–3
Negligence
company secretary 118
directors 87, 114–15
Noise
house rules 40
Number of OMCs 16–17

Obstructions
house rules 40
Office of the Director of Corporate Enforcement (ODCE)
complaints to 74
on directors' resignations 50
enforcement powers 8
generally 28, 121–3
on members' registers 43–4
publications 74
role of 8
Ombudsman
proposed appointment of 83
Owners' duties/responsibilities 30, 35–7

Parking
house rules 40
issues 30
Part 4 tenancy 177–9
termination 177–8, 179
Personal Insolvency Agreement 68–9, 78
Pets
house rules 40, 107
Planning permission
building lifecycle report 68, 199
conditions 12, 13, 20
failure to comply 20

Pre-contract enquiries 88, 213–16
Priory Hall, Dublin 48, 54
Private company limited by shares (ltd company) 105
Private property rights 1
Private Residential Tenancies Board (PRTB) 169–70
Property developers
legal obligations 20
role of 19–21
separate legal personality 19–20
Property development company
establishing 19
insolvency 29
role of 20
separate legal personality 19–20
Property, right to 1
Property service providers
licensing 92–4
qualifications 94
skill shortage 93–4
unlicensed 96, 102, 199
Property Services Regulatory Authority
code of standards 100–1
Compensation Fund 95–6
2017 Report 95
claims 95–6
false claims 96
payments to 99
purpose of 95
complaints to 97–9
Continuous Professional Development (CPD) 101
establishment of 89
fines 99
generally 17, 89–91
letter of engagement 101–2
licensing function 92–4
powers of 97–9
role and responsibilities 91–4
sanctions 99
service charges recovery and 58
strategic plan to 2020 98, 100–1, 194
Prospective owners
considerations for 28–33
Public limited company (plc) 104–6

Receivership
appointment of receivers 125–7
benefits of 128–30
generally 125
Regan, Dean 147
Register *see* **Members' register**
Registered office 42
Registry of Deeds 38
Regulation of OMCs
accountability of sector 193–4
funding for 203–4
generally 86–7, 189–203
Law Reform Commission Consultation Paper 191–4
proposed Regulatory Body 191–3
Rent pressure zones 178, 183
Repairs *see* **Maintenance/repair work**
Requisition of Title 88
Residential Tenancies Board (RTB)
generally 169–70, 181–2
National Register 182–3
Private (PRTB) 169–70
reference of dispute to 174
Resident's associations 32
Restoration of company to Company Register 85–6, 145–9
Right to property 1
Role of OMCs 5–7
Rules of the Estate 42

Security
house rules 40
measures 31
Service charge *see* **Annual service charge**
Simmons, Edward C 1
Singapore 56
Sinking fund
calculation of levy 22, 26
by independent quantity surveyor 22, 26, 67
case study on capital project management 70–1
debt recovery process *see* **Debt recovery process**
deficit in 53–4
discretionary nature of 54, 55
generally 2, 17, 31, 51–7, 197–8
held in liquid form 53
inadequate/absent 53–6
increasing 112
insufficient funds 45
mandatory approach 56, 57
MUD Act 2011 51–3, 54–5, 77–81
non-recurring expenditure 53
other jurisdictions 56–7
provision for 30
rules 51–3, 77–8
separate bank account 52, 53, 80
Society of Chartered Surveyors of Ireland report 53
urgent cash calls 45

South Africa 56
Special resolution 39, 46, 110, 111–12
Stages of development 21–8
developer-only 21–6
development-and-owners 26–7
owners-only 27–8
Stakeholder Forum on Multi-Unit Developments 6
Statute of Limitations 78
Strike-off *see* **Company strike-off**

Taxation 69–70
Home Renovation Incentive scheme 108
PAYE 108
VAT *see* **Value added tax**
Tenants *see* **Landlord and tenant**
Third party disputes 185–7
Transfer of common areas
completion of 77
developer not trading, where 144–5
Transfer of common areas—*contd.*
generally 2
obligation to transfer 75–7
timing of 27
transfer documents 76–7

United States 15
University College of Estate Management (UCEM) 94
Urgent cash calls 45

Value added tax (VAT) 69–70
capital expenditure projects 108–9
turnover and 107–8
Volunteer-director model 8, 17, 29
Voting rights 10, 43–4, 81–2, 86, 112

Washing
house rules 40
Wylie, JCW 168

Zeebrugge ferry disaster 115